# PROGRAM MODELS FOR MAINSTREAMING

*Integrating Students with Moderate to Severe Disabilities*

Douglas Biklen
Kristine E. Davis
Valerie Fenwick
Christy Ground
Marianne K. Hesseltine
Ellen J. Knight
James A. Knoll
Nancy Lamb-Zodrow
Michael MacDonald
Eileen F. McCarthy
Luanna H. Meyer
Sandra Mlinarcik
Judy K. Montgomery
Marilyn Patterson
Michael Shoultz
Linda Siegelman
Jo Thomason
Stillman Wood
Beth Yeager

# PROGRAM MODELS FOR MAINSTREAMING

## Integrating Students with Moderate to Severe Disabilities

Edited by

**Michael S. Berres, PhD**
Bellingham School District
Bellingham, Washington

**Peter Knoblock, PhD**
Syracuse University
Syracuse, New York

AN ASPEN PUBLICATION®
Aspen Publishers, Inc.
Rockville, Maryland
Royal Tunbridge Wells
1987

GOVERNORS STATE UNIVERSITY
UNIVERSITY PARK
IL 60466

Library of Congress Cataloging-in-Publication Data

Program models for mainstreaming.

Includes bibliographies and index.
1. Handicapped children—Education—United States.
2. Mainstreaming in education—United States.
3. Mainstreaming in education—United States—Case
studies. I. Berres, Michael S. II. Knoblock, Peter.

LC4031.P77   1986      371.9'046   86-32257
ISBN: 0-87189-622-2

Editorial Services: Lisa J. McCullough

Library of Congress Catalog Card Number: 86-32257
ISBN: 9-87189-622-2

*Printed in the United States of America*

1   2   3   4   5

*Dedicated to the work and memory
of Steven Apter and Burton Blatt*

# Table of Contents

# Preface

In 1969, Peter Knoblock opened a school in Syracuse, New York. The school was called Jowonio: The Learning Place. It started as a cooperative venture between parents and teachers to provide an alternative education for elementary students. In its early years, children came to the school because their public schools could no longer tolerate them or because they could no longer tolerate their public schools. As Jowonio evolved, its teaching staff discovered other students who had been excluded from public schools or whose educational needs were not being served by their current programs. Dedicated to the philosophy that all children—regardless of the severity of their special learning needs—could profit from carefully planned integrated teaching, Jowonio began to include students labeled *seriously emotionally disturbed, severely speech impaired,* and *autistic.* Today, Jowonio is a highly successful primary school that integrates regular education ("typical") children and special needs children in the same classrooms on a full-day basis.

It was the direct experience of Jowonio, as well as observation of and discussions about other programs providing effective integrated learning experiences for students with moderate or severe special education needs, that led us to edit this book. While catchwords such as *mainstreaming, least restrictive environment,* and *most appropriate* are merely used in debate in many parts of the country, the editors note that an increasing number of school systems are moving forward in developing integrated services like those at Jowonio. Rather than edit a book, then, on theory and research, we put together a volume on how educators in the field are working to implement the integration of moderately and severely disabled children within their own school systems.

This book starts with an assumption different from that of many other books on special education. The assumption is that the success or failure of integrating moderately and severely disabled children largely depends upon the attitudes and problem-solving skills of the educators. We believe that these attitudes are as important—if not more important—than are the skills of the students. Thus, we believe that all children with disabilities can be educated on regular education campuses. The assumption of traditional special education practices seems to be that moderately or severely disabled students must prove they are ready to be integrated by attaining a certain level of skill.

On the one hand, then, this is an optimistic book. We believe that the field of special education clearly possesses the pedagogical strategies to allow for the integration of all students. There are dedicated and trained professionals who can now provide, given an adequate level of support, quality educational programs for virtually any type of special need. We are witnessing an increasing number of educators willing to institute such programs. On the other hand, this is a cautious or pessimistic book, because we take the major impediment to integrated education to be a general failure to perceive the dignity of children with disabilities and the extent of their rights. And it is hardly a secret that attitudinal resistance to change is exceedingly difficult to overcome.

We attempt to alter the sometimes regressive attitudes still held about special needs children by presenting a number of credible examples of school districts that have undertaken the complicated task of providing integrated educational experiences for all of their students. The school districts described in this book face the usual constraints of any school district. They face budget constraints. They have teachers and administrators who feel overburdened. They must divide their precious resources among many student interest groups, children with disabilities being but one.

At the same time, they are districts—or at least there are individuals within those districts—that have made the commitment to do whatever is necessary to bring about integrated education. Some of the people and the strategies for change described in this book are extremely rational and proactive. We have also included many examples of how program managers have been able to utilize "accidental" or less-worked-out strategies to effect positive change in their systems. In essence, we have tried to provide a variety of stories of change that the reader will find credible. The reader may even see a striking resemblance between the situations we describe and the situation in his or her own school system.

The first section is composed of three chapters that provide the philosophical basis for the book and a fourth chapter describing a systematic, participatory model for implementing change in school systems. In chapter 1, we describe the historical trends within special education and our society that led to the development of the concept of integration for moderately and severely involved students. The question is then posed how two students with very similar special learning needs—both demonstrating moderately involved, autistic-like behavior—who attend school in different parts of the country can receive a dramatically different type of education. One student is served in a self-contained classroom without contact with regular education peers, while the other is served in an integrated classroom environment.

The difference in the service models—for these two very similar students—is explained by the way that these students' educators define such critical concepts as *least restrictive environment* and *integration*. The reader is then provided with our definitions of these terms—definitions which take into account not only the quantity of integrated or mainstreamed time, but also the quality and planned purpose of that time. Finally, we detail the extent of integrated program efforts now functioning in this country and suggest a number of barriers that have hindered the expansion of this type of service model.

In chapter 2, Douglas Biklen of Syracuse University uses the term *behavioral or programmatic twin* to describe a principle that is concisely stated thus: "If it can be done there, it can be done here." This notion of the behavioral or programmatic twin is important because, according to our observation of innovation in the field, practitioners are at least as likely to make changes for this rationale as they are from a basis of quantitative academic research. Before a program manager is willing to subject a program to the stress caused by a change, the manager needs to believe that the change is feasible and that it will result in long-term advantages outweighing the attendant discomfort. Validation of the benefits is easier if one can see a working example of the change than if one has to rely upon that ever-present, vaguely defined creature known as "the research."

James Knoll and Luanna Meyer, also from Syracuse University, describe in chapter 3 principles and practices of effective integrated education. They describe how the recent emphasis on educational excellence should result in excellence for all children in a district—including those with severe disabilities. They offer a compelling argument, based on recent research, that the integration of students with severe disabilities into regular education settings not only is compatible with educational excellence, but actually helps to achieve it. A variety of activities—including research, planning, and staff development—are then listed as critical components of any change towards integration. The outcome of these efforts should be an "integrated community in the schools" of the same nature that we desire for the larger society.

Ending the first section, Nancy Lamb-Zodrow of the University of Washington details a planning process which can aid a district beginning the change towards integrated education. It is a five part process and it can be continually repeated until a district reaches its own criteria for effective integrated education. Rather than involving only the administration, the proposed model is a participatory one and would include all impacted constituent groups in the planning and implementation of change.

The second section of the book is composed of nine chapters, each describing integration efforts in school systems throughout the country. Though our philosophical position as editors is to support noncategorical programs, each chapter generally pertains to students with one particular type of disability. Allowing focus on one type of disability made it easier for the contributors to illustrate specific change processes and strategies. Each chapter is also structured to give the reader an understanding of the following: i) the social and political forces that led to the changed service model; ii) the training provided to regular and special education students, teachers, administrators, and the community; iii) curricular, physical plant, and staffing issues; and iv) future trends based on current assessments of each program's status and problems.

The chapters offer examples of how change might occur—not how it must occur. Several of the chapters are about districts with long histories of innovative practice in integration. The reader is provided with accounts not only of easily achieved victories, but also of hard-won victories and defeats. Accounts of all three types have value to those who are charged with looking at the effectiveness of service within their own systems.

The first two chapters of the second section are about large districts and place a particular emphasis on students with moderate, severe, and profound developmental disabilities. Eileen McCarthy and Michael Shoultz, both of the University of Wisconsin at Madison, describe the changes that have evolved in the Madison Metropolitan School District since the late 1960s. Madison has been a pioneering district in the providing of services to severely involved students. The authors describe how services have changed (e.g. the actual closing of a school) as the research supporting different instructional models has changed.

Jo Thomason of the Albuquerque Public Schools describes in chapter 6 the Albuquerque district's multiyear effort to develop its *Side-by-Side* model of integrating students with moderate and severe developmental disabilities into regular education settings. Like Madison's, the Albuquerque model began to be implemented in the early 1970s—prior to the passage of PL 94-142 (the Education for all Handicapped Children Act) in 1975, which mandated special education services for children with handicapping conditions. Thomason eloquently describes a number of effective innovations that have led to the stabilization of this program. Both districts are similar in that the changes involved large groups of special needs students on a district-wide basis and both have sufficiently long histories that some of their best in-novations resulted from an analysis of earlier errors or problems.

The next two chapters address the integration of students with sensory impairments. They also address the problems that small school districts face when attempting to provide quality integrated programs for children with low-incidence needs. In a small or rural district, program development for a very small number of students often has the same importance that program development for a hundred students has in a Madison or an Albuquerque. Kris Davis, Ellen Knight, and Marilyn Patterson describe their efforts over a five year period to provide an integrated educational experience for a single boy. It took great patience and commitment before the three were able to collaboratively structure what they judged to be a quality integrated ex-perience for this blind student in the Medford School District in Oregon.

Davis, Knight, and Patterson used an intermediate educational agency to provide technical assistance and consultation to the Medford school system. Marianne Hesseltine of Syracuse University describes the use of a similar agency to develop integrated services for a small number of children with hearing impairments in a rural part of upstate New York. Both chapters pro-vide exact details of the financial, personnel, and philosophical tensions that are manifested in small districts during change processes.

In chapter 9, Judy Montgomery describes the development and current operation of the Plavan School—a remarkable school established in 1973 in the Fountain Valley School District in California. The Plavan School was es-tablished to provide integrated education to regular education students and those with physical impairments. Montgomery describes not only the more obvious issues of integration, such as school accessibility, but also some of the less obvious ones, such as the importance of the entire school community's usage of nonstigmatizing language when talking about students with physical impairments.

We have included one chapter about children with behavioral disabilities. Although these children are often conceptually grouped with students hav-ing "mild handicaps" (e.g., learning disabilities), school systems frequently have a particularly difficult time providing service in integrated settings to children with behavioral needs. Chapter 10 describes a program of the Olym-pia School District in Washington State for serving elementary children with behavioral disabilities. Stillman Wood, Michael MacDonald, and Linda Siegelman detail Project MERGE's efforts to provide effective programming to these elementary students. One benefit resulting from this project has been the dramatic increase in teacher skills and interest in teaching students with diverse special needs. A second benefit has been the significant decrease in the number of students that the district now declares eligible for special education services for being behaviorally disabled. The district provides service in a preventative manner so as to eliminate the later need for behaviorally oriented special education programming for many children.

The book's next two chapters describe the provision of services to moderately and severely involved preschool children. Christy Ground and Beth Yeager detail their efforts to have the Santa Barbara County Schools and the Santa Barbara City School District collaborate in providing integrated services to young children with a variety of disabilities. Ground and Yeager highlight the turning of unplanned circumstances in these school systems into part of a larger design for change. While those of us who work in public schools would like change to always be purposeful, we know that that just isn't the case. Given this, it is probably wise to maintain the creative flexibility of Ground and Yeager, who were able to turn "accident into design."

We have included a second chapter on preschool integration efforts, because many of the districts that provide integrated preschool programming do so through interagency relationships with public or private agencies for the provision of regular education preschool students. The chapter by Sandra Mlinarcik describes joint efforts by Jefferson County Schools in Kentucky and Seven Counties Services (a non-profit human services agency). Mlinarcik's article shows the importance of basing interagency relationships on careful planning and groundwork.

The final program chapter, by Valerie Fenwick of the Syracuse City School District, describes that district's program for integrating students with autistic behavior into regular education classrooms. Integration is defined by the author as serving special needs students in the same classroom with their regular education peers on a full-time basis. This model is an example of a program where the change started for a specific group of children—in this case, primary aged students who had "graduated" from Knoblock's Jowonio—and then spread to older groups of students with autistic behavior.

In the final chapter, we summarize both the differences and similarities of the district programs. We note the differences in the size of the districts, their funding sources, their initial philosophies about integration, their distance from large urban centers, and other such factors. But far more importantly, we describe the common characteristics. We note the commitment and dedication of staff who maintain their belief in integration—even when faced with major obstacles. We describe staff who refuse to settle for programs they know will not in the long run be the most beneficial for the students they serve. And we also note the benefits for the various groups—students, teachers, administrators, parents, and the greater community—of integrated programs for children. This book is a testament to the commitment, endurance, and creativity of those people who have strived to create opportunities for children with disabilities to be educated in truly the most appropriate settings.

*Michael S. Berres*
*Peter Knoblock*

# Chapter 1

# Introduction and Perspective

*Michael S. Berres* and *Peter Knoblock*

In 1975, Congress passed the Education for All Handicapped Children Act (PL 94-142). This law is a milestone in the recent struggle to provide education to moderately and severely handicapped children in the least restrictive environment (LRE). It was the culmination of ten years prior work by parents, advocates, legislators, and progressive educators, and it evolved logically from a larger social context in which many powerless and disenfranchised groups were asserting their right to participate in our society.

While the mainstreaming of children with special education needs has generated great lay and professional interest since 1975, actual practice in the spirit of PL 94-142 has lagged behind theory with regard to many groups of handicapped children. Anecdotal accounts, academic research (Biklen, 1985; Stainback and Stainback, 1985), and state and federal monitoring reports (U.S. Department of Education, 1985) convincingly show that the vast majority of school programs for moderately and severely handicapped children (e.g., children who are autistic, developmentally disabled, visually and hearing-impaired, orthopedically impaired, health-impaired, severely speech-impaired, severely emotionally or behaviorally disabled) place these children apart from their regular class peers in separate classrooms, buildings, facilities, and nonresidential school districts. The general belief in the field is that while most students with mild handicaps (e.g., learning disabilities, mild developmental disabilities) can be mainstreamed, the more involved children are best served in segregated programs. This practice stems from an adherence by districts to a narrow interpretation of PL 94-142.

This book reports ways that some school districts have chosen to act in accordance with both the letter and the spirit of the law. To those who believe that the regular neighborhood school is the best educational setting for all children, whether or not they are viewed or labeled as handicapped, the trend towards inclusion has been painfully slow in development. To those uncer-

1

tain about or fearful of allowing children with disabilities to be educated along with nondisabled peers, the march towards inclusion may seem to be proceeding far too quickly. One thing, though, is certain. The question of how and where to most appropriately serve moderately and severely handicapped children is increasingly of concern to educators.


## THE ORIGINS OF THE MANDATE

Least restrictive environment is addressed by PL 94-142 in the following way:

> . . . to the maximum extent possible, handicapped children, including children in public or private institutions or other care facilities, are educated with children who are not handicapped, and that special classes, separate schooling, or other removal of handicapped children from the regular educational environment occurs only when the nature or severity of the handicap is such that education in regular classes with the use of supplementary aids and services cannot be achieved satisfactorily, . . . (20 U.S.C. 1412 [5] [B])

This philosophy—along with the philosophies stated in each of the state's policies established since 1975 to implement LRE at the local district level— is strikingly different from the traditional philosophy concerning treatment and education of disabled children. Using rationalizations derived from craniologists and other early psychologists and social scientists, society excluded children with disabilities from public schools, separated them from family and friends, institutionalized and sterilized them, and frequently made them victims of unsafe medical experimentation (Wolfensberger, 1975; Gould, 1981).

It was not until the mid-1950s that the legality of providing segregated learning environments for children was challenged. In 1954, the United States Supreme Court declared in Brown v. Board of Education that educational segregation based upon race was unconstitutional. To those concerned with the rights of disabled children, the Court's extending the equal protection clause of the Fourteenth Amendment to the Constitution to children of all races was a very positive omen.

A series of major court decisions in the 1970s pushed this extension of the Fourteenth Amendment's protection to disabled children. In 1971, for example, the Pennsylvania Association for Retarded Children successfully sued the Commonwealth of Pennsylvania for failure to provide access to a free public education for all children with developmental disabilities. One part of the district court's decree was that Pennsylvania should educate the plaintiff's children in programs most like those provided to non-disabled children. One year later, in Mills v. Board of Education (1972), U.S. District Court Judge Joseph Waddy ruled in favor of the parents and guardians of seven District of Columbia students who the plaintiffs claimed were denied a publicly supported education. In his decree, Waddy stated that all children—regardless of the nature of their handicap—were entitled to an appropriate, publicly funded education. It is important to note that Waddy prohibited the District of Columbia from failing to educate its handicapped students on the basis of financial hardship. The implication was that if a school district was experiencing financial constraints, then all student groups should be affected equally, not just students with disabilities. These two decisions were only the opening victories in a series of court decisions which proclaimed the right of children to be educated in the least restrictive environment.

The growing legal challenge to segregated and often inhumane treatment of children with disabilities was concurrently supported by a number of special education and developmental disabilities advocates who challenged the established practices within their own fields. Two Scandinavian theorists, Bank-Mikkelsen and Bengt Nirje, posited the concept of *normalization,* that is, that people with developmental disabilities ought to be accorded the same type of life experiences accorded to people without disabilities. Other advocates, such as Wolf Wolfensberger and Burton Blatt at Syracuse University, gave the growing normalization debate an American flavor. From the concept of normalization grew a variety of political, social, and educational innovations. The deinstitutionalization movement, for example, used tactics ranging from exposé to providing expert testimony to Congress on the degradation and the ineffectiveness of institutionalizing children. The logical extension of concepts such as normalization and practices such as deinstitutionalization to the public schools meant an ever-increasing effort to mainstream or serve children in the least restrictive setting possible.

A critical force behind most efforts to create integrated educational programs has been made up of the parents and guardians of children with special needs. While professional and legislative advocates approached the issue of integration from a theoretical or political perspective, parents confronted the issue from a very personal one. Many parents who eventually became advocates initially feared integrated and mainstreamed programs for their children. They recognized the harshness and often the cruelty of the "normalized" world. Despite all the criticisms that could be made against segregated programming, it at least provided some safety from that cruelty.

Throughout the 1960s and 1970s, though, growing numbers of parents came to join professional advocates in seeking changes. They formed support groups, studied laws, learned the painstaking patience required to lobby legislators, raised money, requested due process hearings, filed lawsuits, and formed organizations with increasing political clout. It was—and still is—the power of such organizations that often precipitates progressive change in educational systems.

Summarizing, then, there were a variety of forces that led to a dramatic change in the way that our culture has come to think about educating moderately and severely handicapped children. Those forces included legal challenges, changes in the views of leading professionals, growing sophistication of parent advocates, and growing acceptance in the general public of the right of people with disabilities to share in the basic benefits of citizenship accorded to all.

## TWO CASE STUDIES

One might assume—given changes in the last two decades—that all moderately and severely handicapped children are educated in the least restrictive setting possible. Let us look briefly at two case studies of children with similar educational needs. These studies highlight the ways in which the mandates have been implemented.

Joshua is an 8-year-old boy living in a western city of 100,000. He has been described by the special education professionals in his school district as exhibiting autistic-like behavior. This behavior includes some self-stimulation with objects that spin, frequent use of echolalic speech patterns, an aloofness from peer interactions, and a fear of change in his daily routines. Joshua enjoys, among other things, arts and crafts, group musical activities, cooking, and looking at picture books.

Much knowledge of Joshua's present skills and deficits comes from assessment and observation while he was in a previous educational program. That program was an integrated service model in which children with various disabilities were served in the same classrooms as nondisabled children. Upon moving with his family to the present city, Joshua was placed in a self-contained classroom for "emotionally disturbed" children.

Joshua's present teaching staff is concerned because of the discrepancy between his current day-to-day behavior and the behavior reported by his former teachers. In fact, his present teaching staff has come to doubt many of the strengths reported by his former district. Joshua, when stressed, is significantly less interactive and more aggressive towards other children than reported. Joshua's new principal has recommended that he be placed on a half-day schedule and that a hallway closet be cleaned out and used as a timeout room in a newly developed behavior management program.

Joshua's behavior at home has become more sullen and withdrawn. He participates less frequently in those activities, such as cooking and arts and crafts, that he used to enjoy. His parents have become angry at the school system. They have criticized his placement in a self-contained classroom for handicapped children, the use of the timeout room, and the proposal for a shortened school day. The principal now views the parents as "malcontents" who are "meddling in things that they don't understand." Although the parents and the school staff still have periodic conferences, it is probable that the parents will file a due process hearing shortly against the district for violation of Joshua's right to a free appropriate public education.

Staci is a 9-year-old girl living in an eastern city of 180,000. For the last two years, Staci has been served in an integrated second grade/third grade split classroom. The classroom is composed of twenty-two regular education students and two students, besides Staci, with special needs: John, who has a learning disability, and Sarah, who has spina bifada. Staci is eligible for special education services under a state designation of *autism*. The staff was composed of a teacher and a half-time aide prior to the placement of Sarah and Staci in the room. There is now an additional half-time aide allocated to provide the necessary support to these students. Staci goes to a resource program for about 45 minutes a day for additional assistance in reading.

As in Joshua's case, Staci has been described by professionals as exhibiting autistic-like behavior. This behavior includes self-stimulatory mannerisms such as rocking her body and grinding her teeth, an occasional tendency to treat classmates as if they are inanimate objects to be observed rather than interacted with, and a sudden tighting of her entire body when the noise level of the classroom increases. Staci has learned to initiate verbal interaction with other children and adults to get many of her basic needs met. She reads on a mid-first-grade level and can do some of the mathematics problems that the other children in her class can. Because she has basic verbal skills and understands verbal cues, she is able to participate in group activities in her classroom.

Staci's teacher has developed a simple behavior management procedure to deal with her distractibility. The procedure is for either the teacher or one of Staci's classmates (who have been trained in the procedure) to provide the least intrusive motor or verbal cue needed to redirect Staci into appropriate classroom behavior. Upon being given the cue, Staci then states where she is going to go. This system works approximately 90% of the times when Staci needs direction. For the other times, it is necessary to engage Staci in a short relaxation strategy before redirecting her, so as to eliminate the stress causing the distractibility. Staci's behavior has changed dramatically in the two years that she has been in the integrated classroom in which she is now served. Upon entering the class, she needed relaxation techniques plus physical redirection done by the teacher for approximately 80% of her off-task, inappropriate behavior.

Staci's parents are extremely pleased with her progress in the integrated program. It took them several years to fully comprehend the nature of Staci's special needs. When she was five years old, one team of professionals at a well-known children's hospital recommended to her parents that they consider institutionalizing her. When she was six years old, the family moved to the present city because of a change in her father's position. They were surprised when local school staff suggested that the most appropriate placement for Staci would be in her neighborhood school. They were even more surprised—and somewhat fearful—when it was suggested that Staci might be placed in a regular classroom. The new district had tried a regular class placement with supplemental help on two previous occasions with children whose needs were similar to Staci's—and both children had made reasonable progress. It is important to note that while Staci's parents and her teachers have not agreed on all of her programming needs, they have agreed most of the time; they also have been able to establish a friendly, cooperative relationship in which each party views the other as a valued collaborator.

Joshua and Staci provide many educators with a difficult dilemma. For all intents and purposes, the two children have quite similar educational needs. Both have been described by a variety of educational and medical professionals as exhibiting autistic-like behavior. While neither shows the severest forms of that behavior, such as mutism or the self-injurious acts that sometimes accompany this still-mystifying condition, both exhibit behavior which clearly set them apart from their regular education peers.

The differences in the educational programming for Joshua and Staci are more than geographic. Joshua is served in a self-contained program with five other boys. All have been labeled by their district as emotionally disturbed. Joshua's day—soon to be shortened to three hours—is geared heavily toward strict behavior modification aimed at teaching the students appropriate social interaction. Staci is served in a regular elementary school classroom with twenty-four other students. With the exception of some extra assistance from an aide, Staci's educational program is quite similar to those of the other students in her classroom. In addition to the partially modified academic goals, Staci's teacher has also established goals for social interaction and classroom routine. Staci's learning is not only provided by the teacher and aide, but also by her peers, who have learned how to model behavior and teach her socially important ways of interacting.

In both schools, educators state that they are providing quality educational programs to these two children. It is said by both sets of educators that each student is being served in the most appropriate, least restrictive setting. Both students are served by school districts which have been regularly monitored by their respective state education departments for compliance with state and federal laws—and both districts have passed this compliance monitoring. Both Joshua's and Staci's schools are staffed by educators who firmly believe that they provide the best possible education given current financial, legal, and other regulatory constraints.

In talking with educators in both settings, it is also clear that they have difficulty understanding the other's definitions of *appropriate* and *least restrictive environment*. Joshua's educational staff believes that the mainstreaming of moderately involved children, particularly those with unusual autistic-like behavior, exceeds the least restrictive environment mandates of the law. They see it as disruptive to the educational programming of their regular education students. They also see it as a cruel hoax to both the child and the parents by placing the child in a environment where he or she cannot, by traditional standards, possibly succeed.

The staff at Staci's school believe that the goal of education for any child, regardless of disabilities, ought to be the gaining of competence to deal with the surrounding society. They believe that a regular classroom in a neighborhood school is the best training ground. They also believe that it is possible, with only minor modifications, to accomodate most children with special needs. They see it as a cruel hoax to try and prepare a student to become a useful citizen by placing that student in a setting in which he or she cannot practice interacting with other children.

In discussing both programs with each set of educators, two distinct reasons for the differences between programs were given. The educators working with Staci generally attribute program differences to the perspectives of the educators, whereas those working with Joshua generally attribute program differences to the discrepant abilities of the two children. Staci's educators talk about their district's evolution toward more inclusive and less restrictive classroom options. They note—with some surprise—how much their perspectives have changed over the years with regard to the amount and quality of integrated programming that they believe should be provided to moderately and severely disabled children. Their surprise comes from their awareness that they now, as a matter of district policy and practice, routinely integrate children in regular school settings whom they would never even have considered as candidates for such integration a few years previously. These educators clearly believe that the main factor leading to their integrated model has been the evolution of their perspectives rather than any significant change in student capabilities.

Those educators working with Joshua see the different programs as logical extensions of the differences in capability between students such as Joshua and Staci. Although they question the overall placement of Staci in a regular classroom, they are willing to rationalize it because of what they view as her significantly higher skill levels. They believe that the severity of Joshua's deficits necessitates a separate class placement. They appreciate the concept of "least-restrictive placement" but believe that the "reality" of a Joshua or other similarly functioning students requires a more restrictive placement. They believe that Joshua is truly a different type of student than Staci.

One set of educators sees Staci and Joshua as quite similar in their needs. They believe that these two students can benefit from educational programs that provide them physical, social, and instructional proximity to their regular education peers. Not only do they believe that Staci and Joshua are similar in need, however; they also believe that the similarities between Staci and her regular education peers are more important to focus on when designing her educational interventions than the differences between Staci and these children. The other set of educators focuses on the differences between Joshua and his regular education peers—and even on the perceived differences between Joshua and Staci—as a rationalization for separate programming. His educational program focuses on controlling the differences; her program focuses on enhancing the similarities.

Again, one is faced with two schools serving students with similar needs, where both sets of educators believe that their practice is supported by state and federal law. While it is true that both programs meet the letter of the law, it is debatable whether both are in accord with the spirit of the law. Most school districts presently serve children like Joshua and Staci within the confines of the law. A much smaller number of districts attempt to provide programming that speaks to the fullest intent and spirit of PL 94-142.

## THE PHENOMENOLOGY OF SPECIAL EDUCATION SERVICES

Because the state and federal laws addressing such issues as least restrictive programming, mainstreaming, and integration are vague, the actual degree to which the concepts are implemented is often determined at the local level. State education departments, in monitoring local district practices, often merely try to ensure minimal compliance with the law. This means that the main regulatory force behind the mandates—the state education departments—generally accept a district's status as long as it assures minimal compliance with the requirements of PL 94-142. While this practice is not unreasonable, given that many districts have still not achieved even minimal compliance, it hardly acts as an incentive for districts to exceed minimal standards.

In addition to the lack of regulatory incentive for exceeding minimal compliance, there is also a problem in the way that special education is funded. Special education programs are, in effect, rewarded for finding students in need of special assistance. Some have termed it a "bounty system," since every student who is captured generates additional dollars for a district above and beyond the dollars generated for a regular education student. In effect, the more students identified needing special education services, the more dollars flow to both state and local education systems.

Beyond this, there is little quality control of the service formats to which the dollars flow. As long as a student is properly identified according to the state regulations, dollars follow the student. It does not matter whether the student is being served in a separate facility or if the student is being served in a mainstreamed classroom through a special education consulting teacher model.

A third factor causing the wide range among programs serving special needs students is that most local programs are managed by administrators who were not trained in the specifics of special education. While urban school districts often have directors who have had training in the field, most nonurban programs are managed by part-time directors with a variety of other responsibilities. It is unreasonable to expect them to champion service models to which they have not been exposed or that they perceive will cause stress to the very districts to which they have multiple responsibilities.

Given such factors as minimal compliance standards, financial disincentives, and a lack of training in special education among program managers, it is understandable that these program managers come to define complex concepts such as *least restrictive environment* on the basis of their own experience and that how one district defines a mandate will be very different from how another district defines the same mandate. That is why two students with similar educational needs, such as Joshua and Staci, can end up in extremely different programs. The managers who define the way in which a system operates have different life experiences from each other. These differences lead them to define their job mandates in different ways. It is not a case of one type of program being "right" and another type of program being "wrong." Rather, it is a situation where the life experiences of many program managers preclude them from doing more than minimally complying with their mandates.

A growing body of literature, particularly from social scientists and educators using qualitative research methods, strongly supports the premise that special education program development is often based upon the limited phenomenological views of the program builders (Biklen, 1985; Stainback and Stainback, 1985). While we would hope that important decisions about children are made using data-based decision points, it is simply unrealistic to believe that program managers can put aside their personal biases and beliefs.

Differences in beliefs account for much of the discord when advocates of less restrictive program formats try to persuade more traditional managers of the benefits of integrated education. This discord is even more evident when the discussion is about children with moderate and severe disabilities. Just as some educators view PL 94–142 as creating and justifying a cascade system which includes segregated program options, other educators now see that law as a force working against the creation or maintenance of segregated programs.

## CURRENT VIEWS OF THE INTEGRATION MANDATE

The everyday implementation of mainstreaming takes many forms, but all program developers rely on the least restrictive environment clause contained in Public Law 94–142. The clause, cited earlier in this chapter, includes the phrase "to the maximum extent possible" and goes on to advocate the placement of students with their nondisabled peers. The programs described in this book are based on the view that it is always possible, and desirable, to educate students with moderate and severe disabilities in classrooms and programs with their nondisabled peers. Program administrators and teachers have turned the federal mandate into a call for schools to structure opportunities for learning and social interaction for all students, regardless of their disability.

Providing equal educational opportunity was the original intent of P.L. 94–142, and the authors in this book have described instructional and organizational designs that maximize students' learning once given this opportunity. It is, in fact, a child's right under the law to receive an education in the least restrictive environment. Once this is understood and accepted, it becomes necessary to focus on the how-to-do-it of mainstreaming. Sets of practices that foster competency and independence are required, including physical and social/instructional integration.

### Physical Integration

The placement of students with moderate and severe disability into regular school buildings while maintaining them in segregated classrooms is one example of physical integration. Such placement does not preclude integration with nondisabled peers, but it does mean that strenuous efforts will need to be made to bring students together to counter the effects of homogenous groupings.

The issue is reminiscent of the early school programs developed by voluntary associations in the community like the Association for Retarded Citizens. Many of the early day programs for children become day treatment programs for young adults; the students became older and the public schools were slow to mainstream them. Gradually those community agencies offered a range of services—educational, vocational, and recreational. However, persons with disabilities remained segregated from their nondisabled peers, despite the fact that they remained in their communities. Today, there are classrooms for students with moderate and severe disabilities located within school buildings, but again students in these classes may remain isolated from other students and teachers. The *contact hypothesis* assumes that it is beneficial for all students to be in close proximity to one another, yet a growing number of researchers and practitioners are concluding that physical integration may be necessary, but not sufficient, for the fulfillment of short-term and long-term needs of students with disabilities.

The case studies of Joshua and Staci described earlier suggest the need for going beyond physical integration. Joshua, placed in a self-contained classroom with five other students with disabilities, was not provided with opportunities to apply the social skills he learned previously in an integrated program. Instead, his behavior was considered deviant compared to other students' behavior. Staci, on the other hand, was placed in a regular classroom, and a behavior mangement plan that took into account her challenging behavior and included interaction with nondisabled peers was developed. The approach used with Staci is an example of social and instructional integration.

## Social and Instructional Integration

Social and instructional integration is characteristic of each program described in this book. The programs did not always begin by fully integrating their students, but they are now examples of more or less complete integration. One of the barriers to achieving this level of integration is the practice of placing services on a continuum, from most restrictive to least restrictive, and requiring a student to function in one program on that continuum before moving the student to another program. Unfortunately, when that decision-making model is used, some students never progress beyond the initial placement, because of their perceived lack of readiness. Advocates of complete mainstreaming do not believe it is valid to restrict a student's placement in a mainstream setting because he or she did not function "satisfactorily" in a more restrictive environment. Gresham (1982), on the other hand, states:

> The extent of a handicapped child's level of social skills should guide placement committee decisions on whether or not mainstreamed placement for that child is indicated at that time. If the

child's level of social skill does not suggest that he or she would function successfully in a mainstreamed setting, then he or she should be placed in a more structured setting until the required social skill level has been obtained. (p. 430)

An equally strong case can be made for teaching students the necessary social skills in classrooms with their nondisabled peers. Instruction in more natural environments can provide opportunities for disabled students to observe appropriate social interactions and then to practice their newly acquired skills.

School programs that emphasize social and instructional integration teach skills in natural environments in which students have the opportunity to practice their skills when they are needed. If the objective is to teach appropriate behavior in social situations, then it is necessary to teach those skills in the presence of others. If the goal is to teach transportation skills, then it is desirable, for example, to ride city buses instead of practicing with cardboard buses in the classroom!

School programs adhering to complete mainstreaming are purposely designed to include students with diverse learning and social needs. Typically they include opportunities for social interaction with peers in individual and group siutations; individualized learning plans that emphasize the interrelationship of a student's cognitive, social, and physical skills and needs; parent involvement in the designing and implementation of programs; and the teaching of functional academic and social skills to promote student competency and independence. How close are we to achieving this level of integration? The information in the next section points to mixed results in our move toward integrating all students.

## CURRENT STATUS OF INTEGRATED PROGRAMS

Each year the United States Office of Special Education and Rehabilitative Services issues a report to Congress on the implementation of the Education of the Handicapped Act. In its current report (U.S. Department of Education, 1985) the following statement is made:

During school year 1982–83, the majority of handicapped students continued to be served in regular education buildings. As in school year 1981–82, 68 percent of all handicapped children received most of their education in regular classes. An additional 25 percent received services in separate classes within a regular education building. Taken together, these settings accounted for 93 percent of the handicapped students who received special education and related services in environments that included nonhandicapped peers. Only 7 percent of all handicapped children were educated in separate schools or other environments, such as hospitals or homebound instruction. (p. 36)

Unfortunately, the children excluded from opportunities to learn in more integrated classes are those students with moderate and severe disabilities. In the same government report, the numbers of children served in four educational environments (regular classes, separate classes, separate school, and other environments) are displayed in tables for each state. In New York State, for example, 42% of all students between the ages of 3 and 21 with handicapping conditions were served in regular classes during the 1982–83 school year. And in that same year, 41% were in separate classes and 15% in separate schools. An examination of which students are placed in each environment reveals a less positive picture. For example, only 4% of those students classified as multihandicapped received their education in regular classes; 27% were in separate classes and 67% in separate schools. This pattern of placing students with moderate and severe disabilities in more restricted settings is repeated in the majority of states. On the other hand, those students with mild disabilities, such as learning disabilities and speech impairment, are more frequently placed in regular classes.

Program managers may face the dilemma of working in a state that does not support their efforts to integrate more severely disabled students because of ideological or financial barriers. Biklen (1985) addresses this issue of variability between states when he writes:

... the variation from jurisdiction (i.e. state or territory) to jurisdiction is nothing less than extraordinary. In mental retardation services, for example, the leading segregationist jurisdictions are Delaware and the District of Columbia (37% each), Maryland (40%), Louisiana (23%), New York (30%), Nevada (29%), New Jersey (23%), and Texas (20%). ( p. 14)

Needless to say, there are states that have made much more of a commitment to integration (Nebraska does not segregate any of its students with retardation), and the pattern within states and individual school districts may vary considerably. Nevertheless, it is important for all of us, and particularly for those who develop programs within school districts, to understand the barriers standing in the way of more complete integration.

## THE REAL WORLD OF PUBLIC SCHOOLS

Those of us involved in the development of integrated school programs must compete for recognition and resources. Many technological barriers to progress for students with moderate and severe disabilities have been overcome. It is now possible to teach all students, regardless of their disability, the skills necessary to help them function more independently. And the programs described in this book attest to the variety of school organizational and curriculum adaptations that can be made. On the other hand, ideological and economic barriers remain as obstacles to the continued development of integrated programs.

### Ideological Barriers

There are many professionals in public schools, both in regular and special education, who do not believe that students with moderate and severe disabilities are best served in integrated classrooms. Their reasons vary, ranging from the view that the required degree of intensive instruction cannot be delivered in an integrated class to the view that the learning potential of these students is limited, much more limited than it is thought to be by the authors in this book. Recently, a public school representative visited an integrated preschool for the purpose of evaluating the options for a child returning to his home school district. In conspiratorial tones, the visitor turned to the child's teacher and said, "As teacher to teacher, you don't really believe that a child can be integrated into a regular classroom, do you?" As we know, ideologies and attitudes change slowly, but they do change. Many of us now engage in professional behaviors we never thought possible, thus reflecting changes in attitudes as well as behaviors. By respecting each other's positions and showing, as we do in this book, that integration can take many forms, it may be possible to encourage larger numbers of public school personnel to mainstream their more involved students.

### Economic Barriers

The problem of competition for scarce economic resources within the public schools may be as difficult to overcome as the ideological barriers. The administrative efficiency of special class programs, for example, has been touted as one of the arguments for maintaining students in segregated teaching models. There are integrated programs, however, that can be pointed to in response to this argument. The argument is addressed by demonstrating that related services can be organized to respond to students in integrated classes; that qualified teachers and other personnel can be trained and recruited for these classes; that any specialized curriculum can be adapted for use in regular classes with disabled students; and that special equipment can also be used in integrated classes.

Despite these arguments against the administrative efficiency of special classes, it is still important to demonstrate the cost efficiency of integrated programs along with their instructional benefits. The programs described in this book indeed reflect the realities of cost conscious school districts. They reduced transportation costs by constructing school buildings or providing school programs closer to students' homes. They designed team teaching situations allowing regular and special education teachers to work together. They utilized resource personnel creatively to allow them to work within classrooms so more students and staff members could benefit from their skills. They found additional human resources in parents, volunteers, and university students, all of whom helped staff classrooms. And the list goes on. No one has yet made the argument that mainstreaming is less expensive in the short-run, but as a form of prevention of more serious disability it is clearly cost effective. It prepares young students to function competently in school and in communities, thus avoiding having to place them in more restrictive community and institutional programs later on. While it is important to recognize the potent nature of certain barriers to the implementation of integrated programs, it is equally important to acknowledge the progress being made to address these concerns.

## THE GOOD NEWS

We conclude this chapter with a description of new and exciting published initiatives for moderately and severely disabled students.

1. School districts are renewing a commitment to teacher training and in-service preparation of teaching assistants. The unavailability of trained personnel for integrated classrooms has motivated districts to look inside their sytems for individuals who are suited for this work and who believe in the importance of diversity within classrooms. Once these persons have been identified, a variety of training opportunities can be made available. A Syracuse City School District program, described in this book, pairs regular education teachers with those trained in special education in a team teaching situation. In effect, elementary education teachers are given opportunities for developing skills in behavior management, writing behavioral objectives, preparing written individualized education plans, and communicating with parents. These skills are learned by observing the behaviors of the special education teacher, by getting continual feedback in the course of the school day, by attending team-planning meetings at which students are discussed

and instructional decisions are made, and by going with the special education teacher on home visits. The special education teacher also benefits from this form of inservice training by learning more about the regular fourth grade curriculum, for example. In addition, efforts are underway to provide inservice training opportunities for classroom assistants in integrated classrooms, which depend upon the availability of skilled support personnel to work with individual students and with small groups. Teacher-to-teacher training opportunities are gaining in importance as we recognize that questions of "how to do it" can be addressed by thoughtful practitioners.

2. University preparation programs are responding to the public schools' growing training commitment by placing practice students and student teachers in integrated classrooms. Early experiences in integrated classes provide trainees with opportunities to clarify their views about mainstreaming and sharpen their instructional skills as they learn to plan lessons for disabled and nondisabled students alike. Ultimately, such programs will help supply the needs of public schools for trained teachers for mainstreamed classrooms.

3. These new teachers will most likely come to their new mainstreamed classrooms with training in the use of technology for instructional purposes. This technology is facilitating the integration of students with moderate and severe disabilities by enabling teachers to adapt instruction and materials to individual learning needs.

4. The increased use of technology and optimism about the learning potential of more disabled students have helped create new learning opportunities for them. This expansion of learning opportunities makes it vital to support teachers as they struggle to help disabled students acquire, maintain, and generalize their skills. Student behavior changes and academic growth may be slow, and support can include finding ways to measure incremental progress, thus providing moral reinforcement. Support also can include ongoing feedback to teachers by supervisors and outside support personnel, who can provide fresh insights.

5. Students with complex disabilities need systematic teaching. In response to that need, more teachers are developing a larger repetoire of skills and approaches. Certainly, some may come to a mainstreamed classroom with those skills, but it is more likely, as pointed out above, that teachers will learn much by what they do daily in the classroom. The danger here is that a teacher may not be able to originate ideas for every situation. Nonjudgmental supervision and support can serve as a stimulus to hardworking teachers to come up with new ideas. University preparation programs and school district inservice education should avoid inculcating teachers with one technology or approach.

6. As a way to respond to diverse student needs, school districts are systematically utilizing school resource personnel. An increasing number of mainstreamed programs are finding ways to use occupational, physical, and language therapists, as well as other resource personnel, in their classrooms. By reducing the use of "pull out" models, in which students are frequently taken from class to work with resource personnel, the opportunities for teachers and other students to learn the skills possessed by such personnel are increased. For example, if we want to create a communication environment within the classroom for a student with autism, there may be advantages to having the language therapist work within the room and model appropriate language stimulation and intervention approaches for the teacher and other students.

7. Increasingly, schools are emphasizing the importance of taking a broader perspective. For teachers, their effectiveness in designing meaningful programs for their students is enhanced by learning more about what it is that other professionals and parents have to offer them. For administrators, their helpfulness as a support or resource person is maximized by learning as much as possible about the integrated classrooms in their building. Children, too, are benefited by broadening their perspectives. Increasingly, schools are moving away from merely setting aside one week for handicapped awareness, instead devoting continuous attention to celebrating differences of many kinds within a school. Racial differences, varied cultural heritages and life experiences, and so on, can be highlighted and appreciated by all students and adults in a school. In many subtle ways students learn to understand one another if teachers treat all children fairly when disputes arise, foster cooperation rather than competition, teach children to resolve their own conflicts, and demonstrate to them that adults, too, can appreciate one another despite differences. People can learn from their differences and the mainstreaming controversy is part of the larger question of who should be part of the human community. We take the position that all children are deserving of full membership in our schools and communities.

REFERENCES

Biklen, D. (1985). *Achieving the complete school: Strategies for effective mainstreaming.* New York: Teachers College Press.

Biklen, D. (in press). The myth of clinical judgment. *Journal of Social Issues.*

Gould, S. (1981). *The mismeasure of man.* New York: W.W. Norton and Company.

Gresham, F. M. (1982). Misguided mainstreaming: The case for social skills training with handicapped children. *Exceptional Children, 48,* 422–433.

Stainback, S., & Stainback, W. (1985). *Integration of students with severe handicaps into regular schools.* Reston, VA: Council for Exceptional Children.

United States Department of Education. (1985). *Seventh Annual Report to Congress on the Implementation of the Education of the Handicapped Act.* Washington, DC.

Wolfensberger, W. (1975). *The origin and nature of our institutional models.* Syracuse, NY: Human Policy Press.

Chapter 2

# In Pursuit of Integration

*Douglas Biklen*

One way to study and understand a field such as special education of severe disabilities is through a careful examination of a clinical event or issue. How is the event or issue framed? Who takes "sides" and how do these play out? What does the debate tell us about the field, its past and its future? And what does the debate tell us about the larger social context (e.g., education in general or attitudes about disabilities)?

At the risk of being what some might consider sensationalistic, this chapter explores the question of integrated programming through the lens of a major national controversy, namely the use of noxious aversives (read *punitive treatment*) on people labeled *autistic* and *retarded*. By examining this particular controversy, we come to understand the critical link between integration and the future of quality services and quality lives for people with disabilities, their families, and society in general.

## JAILERS OR EDUCATORS?

On July 23, 1985, Vincent Milletich, a nineteen-year-old young man who was classified as having autism, died while receiving aversive conditioning at a group home in which he resided. The home was run by the Behavioral Research Institute (BRI), a Rhode Island–based treatment center that operates programs in Rhode Island and Massachusetts and serves people with severe disabilities from several states. According to news accounts of the death, Vincent Milletich had a seizure while undergoing "a treatment called 'white noise visual screen' where a helmet is placed on the patient's head, his face is covered by a mask and he is forced to listen to static through earphones" (Impemba and Carroll, 1985).

BRI has a reputation for taking in people with severe disabilities who have exhibited abusive and self-abusive behavior. But its treatments are con-

19

troversial. Two months after Milletich's death, the Office for Children (OFC) of Massachusetts issued a report of its investigation into the death and BRI procedures in general. The OFC is the state agency that had licensed BRI to operate the group home in Seekonk, Massachusetts. In issuing the report, the OFC also issued an "emergency suspension of BRI's license to operate."

An OFC (1985) press release summarized some of the controversial BRI practices:

> One student was placed on a 30 day loss of privilege program when he attempted to run away. He was denied any social interaction with staff or other residents; his beard was shaved; he was required to wear a helmet . . . ; he had to eat cold meals within a 15 minute span; he slept without a mattress; and although his clothes were cleaned, he wore the same clothes for 30 days. . . .

> The student was placed in ankle cuffs with an 11 inch chain which he wore throughout the day and night. It was removed only during his shower time. . . .

> BRI's records indicate that behavioral rehearsal lessons, which involve *prompting* a student's inappropriate behavior followed by punishment for the prompted behavior, were used on 23 students over a period of time. (In other words, the staff incited bizarre behavior in order to "extinguish" it.) . . .

> On three successive days in July, (another) student received over 1500 repeated corporal aversives the first day, he received 37 finger pinches to the thigh, 62 finger pinches to the buttocks, 12 finger pinches to the foot, 68 finger pinches to the hand, 37 spanks to the thigh, and 49 vapor sprays to the face between 10:30 p.m. and 2:00 a.m. for aggressive acts and head to objects. . . .

> During 1984, BRI began to implement an Automatic Vapor Spray procedure (AVS), which places a client in leg and wrist restraints while standing barefoot on an uncomfortable rubber mat. While restrained to the AVS, the clients most often receive ammonia vapor in each nostril and a bucket of chilled water is dumped on him or her. During August of '85, 11 students received AVS for inappropriate behavior. . . .

> (An observer noted) students in AVS received no breaks, regardless

of the total time spent by the student in the AVS, and observed that some students were in AVS for up to two hours. . . .

(BRI also denied students their regular allotment of food giving them) water, dessicated liver powder and sustagen at 9 p.m. only. The amount of the supplement given to each student was measured in correlation to the amount of solid food not earned. . . .

(This food denial program posed serious health threats) which included, but were not limited to hypoglycemia, *increased probability of seizures* and/or weakness, *that a seizure prone individual should not fast for 8-10 hours,* and that giving the supplement in one sitting could produce vomiting, diarrhea, or constipation.

These disclosures generated stiff criticisms from professional leaders and organizations on the use of aversive conditioning. On October 20, 1985, the Massachusetts Chapter of the National Society for Autistic Children (1985) released a policy statement saying it was "adamantly opposed to the use of cruel and unusual measures . . . in . . . treating people with autism." A month earlier, Bob Bowles (1985), then president of the National Society for Children and Adults with Autism, stated that "it is time to declare war against the barbaric, inhumane tactics which are being practiced in some facilities in this country on autistic people under the guise of training." Then on November 23, at its annual convention, the Association for Retarded Citizens/United States (1985) passed a resolution on the use of aversives in which the association unleashed a string of invectives, calling them ineffective, illegal, unethical, and inimical to dignity. In obvious reference to the BRI controversy, the resolution called for " a halt to those aversive practices that 1) deprive food, 2) inflict pain, and 3) use chemical restraint in lieu of programming." Similarly, the Association for Persons with Severe Handicaps (1986) chose its national convention as a forum in which to speak out against the BRI-style aversives and to draw attention to an earlier association (1981) resolution on the subject, which opposed "intrusive interventions (another term for aversives) on moral, legal, and scientific grounds."

But BRI was not without its defenders, both inside and outside the organization. Numerous parents whose youngsters had attended BRI programs came forward to defend the treatments, arguing their effectiveness. One couple, for example, was cited as crediting the treatments with achieving a turnaround for their son. A news account reported:

until . . . accepted at BRI . . . at the age of 12, there were times when he broke kitchen and bathroom padlocks to swallow lye, bleach, perfume and shampoo. Now, after seven years at the school, . . . P. J. has learned to eat only the contents of a cup or dish and no longer breaks furniture, bangs his head on the walls or bites his hands until the skin is raw. (Dietz, 1985)

Similarly, another parent was reported as saying BRI saved his son from the untenable dilemma of self-abuse or a listless stupor induced by the psychotropic drugs needed to control his behavior. "If you are asking me if I would rather see my son get some pinches and cold showers, or in that condition banging his head against a wall, you can guess my answer" (Dietz, 1985, October 4).

In an editorial on the BRI controversy, the Boston Globe seemed persuaded by these parents and other BRI advocates when it concluded that indeed some autistic children have such severe disabilities that they "cannot respond to the conventional therapy of kindness and rewards."

Mathew Israel, director of BRI, likens his punitive strategies to the surgeon's scalpel. He suggested in an NBC Nightly News report that aversive treatments are importantly different from assault and battery, since they are carried out in a treatment setting and in a controlled fashion for the purpose of effecting improved behavior. That is essentially the same view professed by Israel's mentor, B. F. Skinner, widely recognized as a leader in the behavioral psychology movement. In a news account published at the time of the BRI controversy, Skinner was quoted as saying:

> I don't like the use of punishment. I am opposed to it. But there are people who are out of reach of positive reinforcement. . . .
>
> Israel's methods are not comparable to torture. Whether he needs so many aversives, I'm not prepared to say. It's a question of intent. I have talked with some who claim that person-to-person contact can bring out autistic people. I have not seen this. The alternatives in our times are heavy drugs and straightjackets. (Dietz, 1985, October 17)

Who are we to believe? Are the Office for Children and the national associations correct in opposing the use of aversive treatments? Or are there some children, as Skinner suggests, beyond the reach of positive reinforcement? Are there some youngsters who are prone to self-abuse and for whom no amount of conventional education and programming can prove successful? Are there some for whom drugs, straightjackets, and physical punishment are the only salvation from devastating self-injury? Or is punitive treatment, no matter what the context, abusive? These were questions that Vincent Milletich's death unleashed.

When the Association for Persons with Severe Handicaps held a press briefing on the issue of aversives, reporters asked the staunchly anti-aversives experts some pointed questions. "Are you willing to go to BRI, to show the staff there how to work with these clients in a non-aversive way?" "Where are there alternative programs?" "Where should these children be sent?" "Who will take them?" With the possible exception of the last one, these were the wrong questions to ask. The implication of the reporters' queries was that the problems of BRI were caused by the children that BRI attempted to serve, suggesting these youngsters abuse themselves because of their severe disabilities.

One can hardly dispute the presence of severe disabilities in these young people or the very real self-abusive behavior they manifest. But the problem of their severe behavior, as any sincere behaviorist would have to agree, is not simply their responsibility or of their making. As educators we are compelled to ask whether these youngsters could respond in dramatically different ways to different environments and to different treatments? In other words, are there problems caused by how public education and society at large have traditionally responded to people with severe disabilities (e.g., people with autism, multiple disabilities) and to their families that may explain the disastrous and depressing reality of BRI? One problem was that no one would take these students in. Public education, the social institution to which every student has a right of access, had rejected them. The assumption on which this chapter is based and which will be elaborated upon in the subsequent pages is that, to be treated well, it was necessary first that these youngsters be seen as everyone else's peers. And that plainly was not the case.

To return to the specific question of whether punishment is necessary, the answer is simply no. As challenging a problem as some youngsters are to their parents and schools, the field now has incontrovertible evidence of effective alternatives to punishment. That evidence exists in (i) the new research on curricula for students with severe disabilities; (ii) demonstrations by numerous school districts, small as well as large, that they can effectively and positively serve all students, however disabled, in their communities; and (iii) the reports of families that have successfully raised their children without punitive methods. Not surprisingly, the experiences of parents who have been successful in meeting the challenge of their sons' and daughters' extremely difficult behavior reveal all of the same principles that have been documented in successful school programs and in the new curricula. Taken together, these developments can be used to make a case that the failure of BRI style punishment is indeed a failure of education and in large measure a direct product of wrong-minded notions about people with autism or other severe disabilities. As we will see, the central question raised by the literature on successful programs—the programs documented in this book—is how society can continue to tolerate the tragedy implicit in the wholesale use of aversives or other dehumanizing treatments when alternatives not only exist but have been proven successful. This question is connected with what I call the *behavioral or programmatic twin argument,* which provides the focus for the latter part of this chapter.

In many ways, parent experiences have been catalytic in the development of successful school practices and curricula. For this reason, it is instructive to consider the reflections and recommendations of parents who have found these positive approaches. In the following section, one parent (Sue) explains her son Ben's behavior and the ways in which her family and his school have learned to understand him, respect and love him, and respond to him.

## A MOTHER'S STORY

"Given the opportunity, he will smash his head, he will pull his hair out, he will bite himself, he will cut himself. Given the opportunity, he loves to take knives and draw straight lines on himself with a knife until he bleeds. He has the potential to be as self-abusive as the kids I have seen on the (BRI) tapes, but there is a difference." The difference is that "we don't give him that opportunity."

After a few minutes with Sue, or her husband Bob, and their three children, even the casual observer could not help noticing their sensitivity to each other. Ben's parents can tell his moods by his behavior. They can often tell the cause of his feelings at a given moment or predict how he will feel a few moments afterwards. Also, the family members share a fundamental acceptance and understanding of each other that includes Ben as fully as each of the other family members.

Sue believes that acting out relates directly to Ben's difficulties in communicating. Ben is 15 years old and has a hard time communicating with the people around him, even with his family. Sue tells us that non-communicative individuals like Ben "simply don't have a way of letting people know what is going on [inside them]. That's what we work on with Ben.

"I know that if he says to me 'I'm sick' that means he is going to vomit. But if he has a cold or runny nose and I say, 'Do you feel sick?' he'll say no, because he is not going to vomit. The word *sick* is associated only with vomit. And if I say, 'You hurt here in your face because you have a runny nose,' that will also not work. He reserves *hurt* for bleeding. So I have to find a word that will describe what it is like to have a cold. But the word *cold* won't work, because to Ben *cold* is the temperature outside. If I cannot come up with the right word, that can make him frustrated. You have to find something that will describe to him how he feels and then he can communicate back to me, 'Yes that is how I feel and now I feel better because I have a word for it.' I don't know if that is true with other kids, but for him that is really important.

"It might take him a week to get something out. We may have to keep saying sentences to him. Sometimes we will just say, 'Boy, you really feel angry because ———— ,' and hope that he can fill in the blank. If he can't, our questioning can make him even more upset.

"He will go and pick up the receiver and say to the receiver, 'Sherry, come home now.' When there is no response, he might start hurting himself. He will take his fists and start hitting his head like it is his fault. Imagine his frustration. He did what he was supposed to do, he said what he was supposed to (i.e., he communicated his feelings), and it still didn't work. We could just let him do that and sit there and scream and cry and smack himself; he will do that if given the chance. Instead we say, 'We understand how you feel angry and that's alright'; then we try to channel Ben's feelings. So we say, 'Sherry's not going to be coming home immediately but she *will* be coming home.' We put a picture of Sherry on the calendar over the day when she will be home."

But life with Ben is not all a game of twenty questions, or even of strategizing to redirect Ben's frustrations. Sue sees other factors as equally crucial to Ben's development (and therefore to proving that no one *needs* punitive or aversive conditioning). Among the key elements is the integration of all students, those with disabilities and those without. She sees integration as providing positive role models. Segregation, on the other hand, keeps students entrapped within a deficit model. "If everybody else in the room is also banging their head on the table and pulling their hair, then [to Ben] that must be the accepted norm." In integrated schools and classrooms of the sort Ben attends, Sue sees peers exerting positive influences on Ben. (Ben attends a regular elementary school and is in a class for 35 youngsters, six of whom have autism or severe retardation; there are two teachers, one regular and one special, and three teacher aides.) Sue recalls, "I have heard kids in my son's class say to him, 'Ben, that looks dumb,' when he is doing something that looks silly. Now he may repeat the comment, 'That looks dumb,' but he is also more likely to stop." Sue believes that all students, no matter how disabled, should experience such integration as early as possible, in preschool if possible.

A second key element is interest level or excitement. Ben is far less likely to exhibit frustration through violence when he is involved, stimulated, and challenged. In other words, students who exhibit challenging behavior (i.e., destructive, self-abusive, or abusive to others) are people who have not themselves been challenged. As Sue suggests, Ben responds to stimulation, to new opportunities, and to people who help him develop. At his school, Ben has been given jobs in addition to a more academic regimen for learning such things as communication and money management. He works at collecting used soda cans, at placing them in the correct bags to be returned for deposits, and at keeping the soda machine filled. He also works in the school office, doing things like collating, stapling, mimeographing or duplicating papers. These activities all contribute to Ben's development and to his growing independence. Other challenges include teaching Ben to walk unaided from his school bus to his homeroom class and from there to other classes, and helping Ben attend to tasks for longer periods of time—in this regard, a teacher's aide discovered that he attends better when he can stand up while doing a task.

The third key element that Sue cites for youngsters like Ben is what she calls "believing." You have to believe in Ben as a human being, she tells us. She has often heard people say to her, "Oh, you must be so patient. I don't know how you do it." But "it is not a matter of being patient," she insists, "it is a matter of *believing* in human beings, believing that they are capable of doing things. It means looking past the label, past retardation or autism, and seeing a capable person. Patience? That is just garbage. To be very honest, I think [people's saying that you need patience] is a way of making an excuse for themselves to explain why they are not going to interact with a person who has a handicap."

But "believing" also seems to mean more than just having a positive attitude toward the potential of people with severe disabilities. To Sue, believing means being willing to ask questions about why a person may hurt him or herself. It means not taking it personally when a person with a severe handicap acts out. As Sue explains it, people who lack experience with those who have severe disabilities may be afraid, but they shouldn't be. For example, she says, "Regular teachers are often still intimidated by kids who are self-abusive, [particularly if] . . . they do not know how to respond. And if a student pinches them or hurts them or another student, they might take it personally. But they really shouldn't. I don't think it is personal. I think that person [teacher or student] just happens to be there, . . . the wrong person at the wrong time."

Also, believing means taking an interest in students like Ben. Sue can rattle off a series of incidents—she adds them up as evidence in her arsenal of arguments for the advantages of integrated schooling—in which the people around Ben took an interest in him, like the student who stopped outside the school one day and said, "Hi, Ben, do you remember me? You remember me.

Ben, look at me, remember me from Thornden Park. Remember Thornden."
When Ben responded after all this prompting with the word, "swimming,"
the student beamed, "That's right, at Thornden!"

And finally, believing means knowing that change is possible for Ben. It
takes a commitment, and a willingness to take risks, or, in Sue's words, to
make mistakes and flounder. It means looking into Ben's future, predicting
his needs in becoming as independent and integrated as possible, and carefully sequencing useful instruction to help him achieve these goals. Ultimately, the challenge that Ben poses is to his educators' creativity. "You
see," Sue reminds us, "it is easier to be a jailer than it is to be an educator. It is
easier to confine and isolate and to say, 'Stop doing these things' than it is to
say 'How can I help you change.'" Believing "requires you to really think
things through."

## THE CONCEPT OF BEHAVIORAL AND
## PROGRAMMATIC TWINS

The obvious questions posed by Ben's development and the skill and caring of his family are: If such progress has been possible for Ben, why can it
not occur for other young people who have similarly challenging behaviors?
If a school program can be provided to Ben, can programs not be made available in local communities to others who share Ben's needs? What are the important characteristics of such exemplary programs? If Sue and other family
members can demonstrate such caring, determination, and skill, can other
families and professionals not learn from their example?

The existence of one positive example such as Ben's cannot *prove* there will
be similar outcomes for other individuals or families. But neither would
failure to achieve similar results with similarly disabled students disprove the
potential of the methods that worked so well for Ben. The point is that while
we cannot prove the effectiveness of these strategies in all situations for all
youngsters, there certainly are reasons for optimism. One of these is the
remarkable consistency in principles that are reflected in the experiences of
families such as Ben's, in findings in the research literature, and in the characteristics of model programs. Each source of information suggests that what
has been possible for Ben may very well be possible for all youngsters, no
matter how disabled.

First, let us examine the research literature. Then, we will look at the
characteristic principles of model programs (i.e., those that serve all students, integrate disabled and nondisabled students, and engender student
progress).

## EDUCATIONAL RESEARCH: A GUIDE TO PRACTICE

We began this chapter with a discussion of what is possible for meeting the needs of students who engage in self-abuse or abuse others. Now, as we look to the literature on "best practices" in education for students with disabilities, we must become clearer about the kind of students we are referring to. In part we must do this because the literature on people who have engaged in self-abuse is limited and too often focuses on "behavior management" or "behavior control" rather than more broadly on education and development. Further, even a brief perusal of the severe disability literature reveals that educational research for this more broadly defined area includes students with severe behavioral needs as well as those without them.

One of the persistent problems with the literature on integrated education is due to a seeming confusion among researchers over what is a research question and what is more appropriately regarded as a values question. Before examining the research literature on integrated education, let us first note that what society does (e.g., to integrate or segregate) is of course a values question. No matter what we learn from the research, society may choose to integrate or segregate people with disabilities. Indeed, the presumption of American education, as guided by the constitutional principle of equality, is that all students are entitled to the same quality of education. Thus, in the absence of compelling evidence that segregated schooling produces superior educational results (i.e., enough to cause us to forego the value of integration), we hold no brief for segregation.

As Assistant Secretary for Special Education and Rehabilitation, Madeleine Will termed school integration the "fundamental issue confronting parents and professionals" (Will, 1985). She identified two principles as key to the concept of *least restrictive environment* (LRE). First, LRE "requires an educationally compelling justification for any proposed 'separate schooling' of handicapped children" (p. 1). Second, even where some segregation may be necessary, there must still be as much student-to-student contact and integration as possible. "Separation or segregation is permissible only when education itself cannot be successful without it, and even then, that separation or segregation must be limited by a concept of maximum appropriate integration" (p. 1; see also Gilhool and Stutman, 1978).

Fortunately, support for integration does not rest exclusively on the absence of data supporting segregation. Indeed, integration offers clear advantages.

Integrated education helps minimize the difficulty that people with severe retardation (including students with severe autism) have in generalizing from one situation to another. In other words, if students can learn communication, social interaction, and other similar skills by a combination of structured learning, trials in typical situations, and interaction with peers and other nondisabled people, they are more likely to be able to use these same skills in other typical situations. One advantage of integration is that it offers nondisabled peers on whom disabled students can model their own behavior. Furthermore, it provides natural situations and natural cues, and it communicates the all-important message, "You are part of the community." In fact, these advantages have proven so effective that many educators now favor using curricula that maximize the numbers and types of interactions that students have in natural situations (e.g., in shopping centers, at integrated work sites, on public transportation, in social and recreational programming) in order to ensure that students will be able to generalize skills learned in their formal education and apply them to life in the community after they leave school (Brown et al., 1979; Brown, Nietupski, and Hamre-Nietupski, 1976; Certo, Haring, and York, 1984; Knoblock, 1982; Knoblock and Lehr, 1986; Meyer and Kishi, 1985; Stainback and Stainback, 1985).

The community-based functional approach stands in marked contrast to more laboratory-like behavioral curricula that predominated in the early years of educational programming for students with severe disabilities. Recently, researchers and curriculum leaders have suggested that more natural, less highly structured behavioral teaching techniques are equally effective for instruction and help minimize the difficulties of generalizing a skill from one setting to another (Halle, 1982; Brown et al., 1983; Liberty, Haring, and Martin, 1981; and Coon, Vogelsberg, and William, 1981).

Not surprisingly, nearly all of the recent research on program strategies or educational approaches for people with severe disabilities in one way or another relates to integration. Through integration comes growing acceptance of students with disabilities by their nondisabled peers (Towfighty-Hooshyar and Zingle, 1984). And, when schools structure interaction of disabled and nondisabled students, the effects are even more encouraging than those that come from mere physical proximity. That is, students relate to each other more and exhibit greater tolerance and acceptance (Voeltz, 1982; Knoblock, 1982; and Biklen, 1985). If proximity and interaction continue for an appreciable time, these effects increase (Voeltz, 1982). Interestingly, the increase in interaction that comes with planned, systematic integration also seems to have an effect on student performance. Brinker and Thorpe (1984) found that when the interaction of disabled and nondisabled students increases, so too does the achievement of educational goals on students individualized education plans (IEPs). Moreover, research on the postschool experiences of students suggests that those who have been involved in community-based schooling and integrated education are far more likely to find and hold jobs when they leave school (Brown et al., in press; and Wilcox and Bellamy, 1982). This is as true for students with severe disabilities as it is for those with moderate disabilities.

Each of these findings in educational research has its analogue in studies of community-living programs. For example, it is well documented that community-living programs which *emphasize* interaction (e.g., in schooling, recreation, work, and social activities) *yield* interaction (Hull and Thompson, 1980). Those programs or settings based on an ethic of normalization, with systematic strategies to involve people with severe retardation in helping to maintain and participate in their own home, tend to facilitate the development of skills and increase independence (Seltzer, 1981). When provided with a modicum of support, even those people who have behavioral difficulties are successful in remaining in the community (Schalock, Harper, and Genung, 1981). And finally, community living has been demonstrated to benefit everyone, however severely disabled. In fact the benefits of community integration appear to be greatest for those with the most severe disabilities (Hemming, Lavender, and Pill, 1981; Raynes, 1980; Conroy, Efthimiou, and Lemanowicz, 1982; and Keith and Ferdinand, 1984); this may reflect the fact that people with the most severe disabilities were historically those most victimized by institutionalization (Blatt and Kaplan, 1966).

Aside from variations in student achievement and resident behavior between integrated and segregated settings, there are remarkable differences in social experiences as well. Congregating people with severe disabilities creates extraordinary problems, including modeling of bizarre behavior, absence of positive models, increased difficulty with control, dehumanization, and lowered expectations by staff for the people served. The most extensive data on congregate settings has been collected in large residential institutions (e.g., Biklen, 1973, 1979; Goffman, 1961; Giles, 1971; Taylor, 1978; Vail, 1967; Blatt and Kaplan, 1966; Blatt, 1970, 1973; Blatt, Ozolins, and McNally, 1980; Holland, 1971). This literature paints a picture of a situation diametrically opposite to that achievable through integration and normalization. It is therefore not surprising that those who have systematically studied institutional congregation are virtually unanimous in their plea for institutional alternatives, indeed, for integration. In his last major treatise on institutions, for example, Blatt (Blatt et al., 1980) wrote:

We must evacuate the institutions for the mentally retarded. . . .

The quicker we accomplish that goal the quicker we will be able to repair the damage done to generations of innocent inmates. . . .

To live with our retarded children, our handicapped friends, our aging parents does place burdens on us. What we must learn from the nightmare of institutions is that these are burdens which cannot be avoided or delegated: to have a decent society we must behave as decent individuals. . . .

Thus we demand that every institution for the mentally retarded in the United States be closed. We insist that a society which claims to be civilized can find the proper ways and means to include the people who have been institutional inmates in decent community environments.

Similar pleas for integration have come in recent years from people with disabilities. In 1970, for example, a group of people with retardation spoke eloquently of their "demands," including opportunities to work, to live in apartments, to go on vacations with nondisabled people, and not constantly to be grouped with other disabled persons (in Blatt, 1973). The autobiographical accounts edited by Bogdan and Taylor (1976; 1982) and an extensive self-advocacy literature (e.g., Williams and Shoultz, 1984; Browning, Thorn, and Rhoades, 1984; and People First of Washington, 1985) also reveal a consistently powerful thrust for integration. While the research literature lacks the drama that attends the personal testimony of parents like Sue, it does reveal a remarkably consistent message concerning the successful strategies by which to promote educational and community integration.

## MODEL PRINCIPLES

Since its inception in the 19th century, formal "special education" has generated at least two important questions. Should we try to educate all children? (That is, is every child educable?) And, if every child is educable, where shall we provide the instruction? People who operate school programs—or for that matter community service programs in apartments, group homes and other independent living quarters, vocational programs and transportation systems—continue to return to these key questions.

On the matter of educability, most educators now share the presumption that all persons are educable. They recognize that there really is no alternative, for to presume that some could not benefit from an education would consign those so labeled to custodialism. Yet an educator simply cannot predict the degree to which individuals may benefit from educational intervention. To presume universal educability and institute programs for all ensures no educable person will mistakenly and unjustly be denied an education. On the other question, the *where* question, controversy still reigns, despite the fact that the positive evidence seems to support only one side of the dispute.

I recall a conversation that Burton Blatt had with the director of a community program. The program director was justifiably proud that his agency had successfully returned every institutionalized person from his county to community programs. People were being served in a special agency-run school, in sheltered workshops, in group homes, or in their natural homes. Nevertheless, Blatt took issue with the director, arguing that returning people to the community was not sufficient if there was not also integration. Blatt believed that community programs could never be termed "exemplary" or regarded as the antithesis of institutions as long as they perpetuated segregation. He found the separate school, however small and regionally located or "community-based," to reflect the same principles that perpetuated the large segregated, congregate institutions.

School districts, individual schools, and community programs that have made the education and servicing of all people, however disabled, their mission, show accord with the belief in integration that Blatt espoused. School leaders in the model programs presented in this book, together with leaders of job placement programs, dispersed apartment programs, and other model integrated community programs, share a common view at odds with the notion that to provide an education or run a program necessarily satisfies one's professional obligation. Their assumption is that they must not only educate and develop skills, but also ensure equal opportunity to the benefits of their programs, educational and other. And of course it does not escape them that separate programming, however intense or technically proficient, perpetuates what in Brown v. Board of Education was termed "separate and inherently unequal."

With integration, *public* education will have earned its name. We will no longer need to refer to it as integrated or as mainstreamed. Rather it will be simply public education—serving all of the public, including those with severe disabilities. Already, in the models that are described in this text, we can see the signs of a new commitment to pluralism. Imagine educational integration where administrators speak of students by their names and not by their categories. Imagine teachers who struggle as intensely to create curricula that will help nonverbal students communicate as other teachers do to instruct their pupils in a complex algebraic principle. And imagine schools that take parents seriously, where administrators and teachers learn from parent experiences, where disability issues are not special issues, add-ons, or afterthoughts, but where the needs of students with disabilities are important to everyone. In other words, when integration is fully implemented, school districts will express a tenacious sense of ownership for the programs that serve disabled and nondisabled youngsters alike. We will see integrated programming regarded as fundamental and non-negotiable, not as something temporary, not as an experiment or demonstration, and not as a gift by the benevolent to those "less fortunate."

There are essentially three types of school integration. One type emphasizes differentness, and there is little more than physical proximity. Special classes are in a wing or section, sometimes even a basement area or a separate building on a public school campus. Students in special education classes may follow a different schedule, come to school on special buses, eat lunch in their rooms or together in a section of the cafeteria. Special teachers might not attend the same faculty meetings. Students with disabilities might not participate in extracurricular events, or they might have special events of their own, for example, special olympics. Parents of students with disabilities may have their own association and feel unwelcome in the Parent Teacher Association. Principals may "house" a program but not feel a sense of ownership of it. Special education students may be walked in a line from one activity to another, while other students move more freely. In other words, being physically located in a school does not guarantee a sense of being a full member of the school, of being able to say "this is my school." Students with disabilities hear the message, "You're different; you are not one of us." This type of integration has been called *islands in the mainstream* (Biklen, 1985).

Some schools *experiment* with integration, usually on an informal basis—one youngster at a time or with a single teacher reaching out to build relations with other teachers. A resource teacher may become the soccer coach. A teacher of severely disabled students may teach nondisabled students to use sign language. But such minimal experimental efforts typically exist at odds with the ethos of separateness that otherwise pervades the school. The teachers who reach out are considered extraordinary. Those disabled students who find a more truly integrated role in the school through participation in the world of nondisabled students are considered exceptional—we might hear, "She's amazing; look what she has accomplished. I don't know if I could ever do that." But even such expressions of awe confirm the message that "they're really different; they're not like us." This type of integration has been called the *teacher deals approach.*

The last type takes integration as a central goal to be struggled toward without compromise. Typical characteristics of the consciously integrated school include such features as the following: (i) downplaying and even removal of overt labels of students with disabilities, (ii) common scheduling for all students, (iii) modified curricula for students with disabilities, (iv) a problem-solving attitude on the part of the staff, (v) integrated faculty meetings, (vi) leadership on integration by the principal, and (vii) resistance against treating special programs as add-ons. Integration is regarded as crucial to the mission of quality schooling in general. Such integration has been called *unconditional integration*.

Good unconditional integrated programs rest on the same principles typically associated with effective schooling:

- Students learn more effectively when their teachers enjoy a measure of creative license to develop and adapt curricula and when their teachers present materials systematically.
- Teachers and students tend to feel more committed to and more productive in a program that engenders common expectations, goals, and rewards. (Since special education programs have typically neglected to identify and measure student achievement, the introduction of specific goals and strategies for measuring them reflects a newfound commitment to quality instruction.)
- Students perform better in schools where they feel valued, challenged, and supported.
- Schools that foster a cooperative learning environment produce improved achievement among less capable as well as more capable students. (Consider, for example, the effects of cooperative learning experiments with disabled and nondisabled students [Slavin, Madden, and Leavey, 1984].)
- Educational groupings that include students of varying abilities prove more successful than those that segment and segregate. (Consider, for example, the effects of the alternative learning environment methods reported by Wang and Birch [1984], the effects of the integrated autism programs reported by Knoblock [1982], and the effects of integration on individualized education plan goal attainment reported by Brinker and Thorpe [1984].)
- Students with severe disabilities, as all students, learn effectively by modeling the behavior of others, including their teachers and nondisabled peers (Biklen, 1985; Knoblock, 1982).
- Programs oriented toward the future needs of students prove effective. This has always been recognized for nondisabled and mildly disabled students; it also holds true for severely disabled students (Wilcox and Bellamy, 1982; Brown et al., 1983).
- Students are more likely to perform to expected levels if the school program evaluates student progress in relation to the school curricula.
- Parent/teacher communication and participation in the educational process has a positive effect on student performance.

Those who have led in the development of quality integrated programs tend to share a vision of the future. They foresee a better life for people with disabilities. They speak of a world in which a person with a disability need not constantly feel "on stage" (Asch, 1984). They speak of small, home community living options for people who traditionally have been institutionalized (Bruininks and Lakin, 1985; Lakin and Bruininks, 1985; Rothman and Rothman, 1984; Community and Family Living Amendments, 1985). They rail against charity as a dependency-generating, pity-promoting shackle (Massie and Massie, 1973; Biklen, 1983). They would rid the media—films, literature, and journalism—of disability stereotypes (Gartner and Joe, in press; Biklen and Bailey, 1978; Bogdan and Biklen, 1977). They hope for a world devoid of segregated institutions. They envision people with severe disabilities taking their rightful place in the work force. And they view issues such as the right to medical care for newborn severely disabled infants, not as isolated questions of discrimination, but as intimately connected with society's obligation in every other area of opportunity (e.g., education, housing, jobs, and transportation) to guarantee access for people with severe disabilities.

On the one hand, such an expansive vision frees schools from bearing the total responsibility for transforming the social experience of people with disabilities. But it also connects school integration to a larger mission, and therefore to something of unusual importance and worth. The goal is not to reform people with disabilities. The goal is also not merely to introduce educational integration as it if were just another curriculum innovation. Rather, it is to change those aspects of the culture that keep people with disabilities from full inclusion. It calls not only for educational integration, but also for a broader social and cultural integration.

---

REFERENCES

Asch, A. (1984). Personal reflection. *American Psychologist, 39,* 551-552.

Association for Persons with Severe Handicaps. (1981, October). Resolution on intrusive interventions. Seattle, WA: Author.

Association for Persons with Severe Handicaps. (1986, December 5). Notice of press availability. Seattle, WA: Author.

Biklen, D. (1973). Human report, in B. Blatt (Ed.), *Souls in extremis: An anthology on victims and victimizers* (pp. 50-92). Boston: Allyn & Bacon.

Biklen, D. (1979). The case of deinstitutionalization. *Social Policy,* May/June, 48-54.

Biklen, D. (1983). *Community organizing.* Englewood Cliffs, NJ: Prentice-Hall.

Biklen, D. (1985). *Achieving the complete school: Strategies for effective mainstreaming.* New York: Teachers College Press.

Biklen, D., & Bailey, L. (1978). *Rudely Stamp'd.* Washington, DC: University Press of America.

Blatt, B. (1970). *Exodus from pandemonium: Human abuse and the reformation of public policy.* Boston: Allyn & Bacon.

Blatt, B. (1973). *Souls in extremis: An anthology on victims and victimizers.* Boston: Allyn & Bacon.

Blatt, B., & Kaplan, F. (1966). *Christmas in purgatory.* Boston: Allyn & Bacon.

Blatt, B., Ozolins, A., & McNally, J. (1980). *The family papers: A return to purgatory.* New York: Longman.

Bogdan, R., & Biklen, D. (1977, March/April). Handicapism. *Social Policy, 7*(5), 14-19.

Bogdan, R., & Taylor, S. (1976). The judged not the judges: An insider's view of mental retardation. *American Psychologist, 31*(1), 47-52.

Bogdan, R., & Taylor, S. (1982). *Inside out.* Toronto: University of Toronto Press.

Bowles, B. (1985, September 18). Campaign launched against maltreatment of autistic people. *NSAL News,* p. 1.

Brinker, R., & Thorpe, M. (1984). Integration of severely handicapped students and the proportion of IEP objectives achieved. *Exceptional Children, 51*(2), 168-175.

Brown, L., Branston, M.B., Hamre-Nietupski, S., Johnson, F., Wilcox, B., and Gruenewald, L. (1979). A rationale for comprehensive longitudinal interactions between severely handicapped students and nonhandicapped students and other citizens. *AAESPH Review, 4*(1), 3-14.

Brown, L., Ford, A., Nisbet, J., Sweet, M., Donnellan, A., & Gruenewald, L. (1983). Opportunities available when severely handicapped students attend chronological age appropriate regular schools. *Journal of the Association for the Severely Handicapped, 8,* 16-24.

Brown, L., Nietupski, J., & Hamre-Nietupski, S. (1976). Criterion of ultimate functioning. In M. Thomas (Ed.), *Hey! Don't forget about me* (pp. 2-15). Reston, VA: Council for Exceptional Children.

Brown, L., Shiraga, B., Ford, A., Nisbet, J., VanDeventer, P., Sweet, M., York, J., & Loomis, R. (in press). Teaching severely handicapped students to perform meaningful work in non-sheltered vocational environments. In R. Morris & B. Blatt (Eds.), *Special education: Research and trends* (pp. 131-189). New York: Pergamon.

Browning, P., Thorn, E., & Rhoades, C. (1984). A national profile of self-help/self-advocacy groups of people with mental retardation. *Mental Retardation, 22*(5), 226-230.

Bruininks, R. H., & Lakin, K. C. (Eds.). (1985). *Living and Learning in the Least Restrictive Environment.* Baltimore: Brookes.

Certo, N., Haring, N., & York, R. (Eds.). (1984). *Public school integration of severely handicapped students: Rational issues and progressive alternatives.* Baltimore: Brookes.

Community and Family Living Amendments of 1985, Senate Bill 2053.

Conroy, J., Efthimiou, J., & Lemanowicz, J. (1982). A matched comparison of the developmental growth of institutionalized and deinstitutionalized mentally retarded clients. *American Journal of Mental Deficiency, 86,* 581-587.

Coon, M., Vogelsberg, R., & William, W. (1981). Effects of classroom public transportation instruction on generalization to the natural environment. *The Journal of the Association for the Severely Handicapped, 6*(2), 46-53.

DeGrandpre, B. (1974). *The culture of a state school ward.* Doctoral dissertation, Syracuse University, New York (1974), University Microfilm No. 74-17570.

Dietz, J. (1985, October 4). Parents sue over closing of facility for the autistic. *Boston Globe.*

Dietz, J. (1985, October 13). Parents defend program for autistic son. *Boston Globe.*

Dietz, J. (1985, October 17). Psychologist B. F. Skinner comes to defense of autistic center leader. *Boston Globe.*

Ford, A., & Mirenda, P. (1984). Community instruction: A natural cues and correction decision model. *The Journal of the Association for Persons with Severe Handicaps,* 9(2), 79-87.

Gartner, A., & Joe, T. (in press). *Images of the Disabled.* New York: Praeger.

Giles, A. (1971). Language simulation in state institutions. In B. Blatt & F. Garfunkel (Eds.), *Massachusetts study of educational opportunities for handicapped and disadvantaged children* (pp. 151-178). Boston: Commonwealth of Massachusetts.

Gilhool, T. K., & Stutman, E. A. (1978). Integration of severely handicapped students: Toward criteria for implementing and enforcing the integration imperative of P. L. 94-142 and Section 504. In *Developing criteria for the evaluation of the least restrictive environment provision.* Washington, D.C.: Department of Health, Education, and Welfare, Bureau of Education for the Handicapped.

Goffman, E. (1961). *Asylums.* Garden City, NJ: Anchor/Doubleday.

Halle, J. (1982). Teaching functional language to the handicapped: An integrative model of natural environment teaching techniques. *The Journal of the Association for the Severely Handicapped,* 7(4), 29-37.

Hemming, H., Lavender, T., & Pill, R. (1981). Quality of life of mentally retarded adults transferred from large institutions to small units. *American Journal of Mental Deficiency, 86,* 157-169.

Holland, H. (1971). The social experiences of newly committed retarded children. In B. Blatt & F. Garfunkel (Eds.), *Massachusetts study of educational opportunities for handicapped and disadvantaged children* (pp. 101-150). Boston: Commonwealth of Massachusetts.

Hull, J. T., & Thompson, J. C. (1980). Predicting adaptive functioning of mentally retarded persons in community settings. *American Journal of Mental Deficiency, 85,* 253-261.

Impemba, J., & Carroll, M. (1985, July 26). 'Disturbed' teen dies during mind-bend therapy. *The Boston Herald,* p. 4.

Keith, K. D., & Ferdinand, L. R. (1984). Changes in levels of mental retardation: A comparison of institutional and community populations. *Journal of the Association for Persons with Severe Handicaps,* 9(1), 26-30.

Knoblock, P. (1982). *Teaching and mainstreaming autistic children.* Denver: Love Publishing Company.

Knoblock, P., & Lehr, R. (1986). A model for mainstreaming autistic children. In E. Schopler & G. Mesibor (Eds.), *Social behavior in autism* (pp. 285-303). New York: Plenum.

Lakin, K. C., & Bruininks, R. H. (Eds.). (1985). *Strategies for achieving community integration of developmentally disabled citizens.* Baltimore: Brookes.

Liberty, K., Haring, N., & Martin, M. (1981). Teaching new skills to the severely handicapped. *The Journal of the Association for the Severely Handicapped,* 6(1), 5-13.

Massie, R., & Massie, S. (1973). *Journey.* New York: Alfred A. Knopf.

Meyer, L.H., & Kishi, G.S. (1985). School Integration Strategies. In K.C. Lakin & R.H. Bruininks (Eds.), *Strategies for achieving community integration of developmentally disabled citizens* (pp. 231-252). Baltimore: Brookes.

National Society for Autistic Children, Massachusetts Chapter. (1985, October 20). Policy Statement. Boston: Author.

Office for Children. (1985, September 26). Press release on OFC emergency suspension of BRI's license to operate. Boston: Author.

PARC v. Pennsylvania, 334 F. Supp. 1257 (E. D. Pa. 1971), amended settlement approved. 343 F. Supp. 279 (1972).

People First of Washington. (1985). *Speaking up and speaking out*. (Report on the Self-Advocacy Leadership Conference, July 23-29, 1984.) Tacoma, WA: Author.

Provence, S., & Lipton, R. (1962). *Infants in institutions*. New York: International Universities Press.

Raynes, N.V. (1980). The less you've got the less you get: Functional grouping, a cause for concern. *Mental Retardation, 18,* 217-220.

Rothman, D.J., & Rothman, S.M. (1984). *The Willowbrook wars*. New York: Harper & Row.

Sailor, W., & Guess, D. (1983). *Severely handicapped students: An instructional design*. Boston: Houghton Mifflin.

Sailor, W., Wilcox, B., & Brown, L. (Eds.). (1980). *Instructional design for the severely handicapped*. Baltimore: Brookes.

Schalock, R.L., Harper, R.S., & Genung, T. (1981). Community integration of mentally retarded adults: Community placement and program success. *American Journal of Mental Deficiency, 85,* 478-488.

Seltzer, M.M. (1984). Correlates of community opposition to community residences for mentally retarded persons. *American Journal of Mental Deficiency, 89,* 1-8.

Seltzer, G.B. (1981). Community residential adjustment: The relationship among environment, performance, and satisfaction. *American Journal of Mental Deficiency, 85,* 624-630.

Slavin, R., Madden, N., & Leavey, M. (1984). Effects of cooperative learning and individualized instruction on mainstreamed students. *Exceptional Children, 50,* 434-443.

Stainback, S., & Stainback, W. (1985). *Integration of students with severe handicaps into regular schools*. Reston, VA: Council for Exceptional Children.

Stainback, W., Stainback, S., Rosche, D., & Anderson, R. (1981). Three methods for encouraging interactions between severely retarded and non-handicapped students. *Education and Training of the Mentally Retarded, 16,* 188-192.

Taylor, S. (1978). *The custodians: Attendants and their work at state institutions for the mentally retarded*. Ann Arbor, MI: University Microfilms.

Towfighty-Hooshyar, N., & Zingle, H. (1984). Regular-class students' attitudes toward integrated multiply handicapped peers. *American Journal of Mental Deficiency, 88,* 630-637.

Vail, D. (1966). *Dehumanization and the institutional career*. Springfield, IL: Charles C. Thomas.

Vincent, L., & Broome, K. (1977). A public school service delivery model for handicapped children between birth and five years of age. In E. Sontag, J. Smith, & N. Certo (Eds.), *Educational programming for the severely and profoundly handicapped* (pp. 177-185). Reston, VA: Council for Exceptional Children.

Voeltz, L. (1982). Effects of structured interactions with severely handicapped peers on children's attitudes. *American Journal of Mental Deficiency, 86,* 180-190.

Wang, M., & Birch, J. (1984). Comparison of a full-time mainstreaming program and a resource room approach. *Exceptional Children, 51*(1), 33-40.

Wilcox, B., & Bellamy, G.T. (1982). *Design of high school programs for severely handicapped students*. Baltimore: Brookes.

Will, M. (1985, January 8). Speech before a Topical Conference on Least Restrictive Environment, Washington DC.

Williams, P., & Shoultz, B. (1984). *We can speak for ourselves: self-advocacy by mentally handicapped people.* Bloomington, IN: University of Indiana Press.

Chapter 3

# Integrated Schooling and Educational Quality: Principles and Effective Practices

*James A. Knoll* and *Luanna H. Meyer*

The 1980s have been marked by a clarion call for a return to "excellence" in American education. Some commentators take "excellence" to be a slogan for those desiring a return to a narrow definition of and restricted access to educational opportunity (e.g., Howe, 1984; Troy, 1985). Gross and Gross (1985) list 20 "essential documents," usually characterized as blue ribbon reports, which critique public schools for their apparent failure to foster academic excellence and achievement. The opening paragraphs of *A Nation at Risk,* published by the National Commission on Excellence in Education (1983), highlight this concern and decry the fact that schools "are routinely called on to provide solutions to personal, social, and political problems that the home and other institutions either will not or cannot resolve" (p. 6). This point of view is expressed unequivocally by the Heritage Foundation:

> For the last 20 years, the federal mandates have favored "disadvantaged" pupils at the expense of those who have the highest potential to contribute positively to society.... By catering to the demands of special interest groups—racial minorities, the handicapped, women, and non-English-speaking students— America's public schools have successfully competed for government funds, but have done so at the expense of education as a whole. (cited in Pincus, 1985, p. 331)

These sentiments imply that excellence and equality are somehow in conflict with one another. Rather than emphasizing the role of public education in meeting the needs of all of America's children, these critics see the interest of one subgroup of students taking precedence over all others.

41

Cain and his colleagues (Cain et al., 1984) critique what they view as the exclusionary nature of such a definition of excellence:

A normative definition is . . . inequitable for it measures all students against the same standard and does not provide for variation in abilities and aspirations. Such a definition neither encompasses nor acknowledges the diversity of America's students. (p. 487)

These authors offer an alternative definition of excellence, which would celebrate the individual educational accomplishments of each student, and not seek achievement for some at the expense of opportunity for all. Crucial to this vision of excellence is a truly integrated educational system which goes far beyond "mainstreaming" to the formation of all-inclusive learning communities within our schools.

The Education of All Handicapped Children Act of 1975 (PL 94-142) was legislated to insure that the American ideal of equal educational opportunity was a reality for millions of children who had previously been underserved or not served at all by the public school system. Children with various disabilities had presented a significant challenge to the lockstep, age-graded curricula which have dominated America's schools since the 19th century. Consequently, these children either did not attend school at all or were required to attend separate educational programs that kept them apart from their regular education peers. In addition to the intended guarantee of a free and appropriate education, PL 94-142 challenged existing educational systems to design individualized program options which would meet the needs of each student.

This individualization and extension of equal educational opportunities is a significant reform and could benefit all students, both disabled and nondisabled. Rather than viewing the educational rights guaranteed by PL 94-142 as special privileges provided to a particular subgroup of children at the expense of others, we would argue that this legislation increases the integrity of public education in America.

Where public education fails to address the needs of children—whether they are described as being gifted, typical, or disabled—this failure might properly be traced to the erroneous assumption than an invariant, singular curriculum can serve all children. Schools must adapt, expand, and individualize curricula and programs to insure that serious and sincere efforts are made on behalf of each child. Individualization is just as beneficial for those children whom the blue ribbon commissions expect to become tomorrow's leaders as it is for children with disabilities.

This chapter begins with a discussion of the central elements of an effective, fully integrated school, and includes a brief rationale for the integration of students with severe disabilities into their neighborhood public school alongside their nondisabled peers. We shall highlight efforts on behalf of these children for two reasons: (a) the translation of principles into practices can be judged most clearly by society's treatment of those children who have historically been the first excluded and the last included in all aspects of the community, and (b) evidence of both educational and social benefits of the integration of children with severe disabilities strongly supports the contention that excellence and equality are not only compatible but mutually beneficial educational goals for America's schools. The remainder and majority of the chapter will focus upon the description of a wide range of specific strategies that have been effectively utilized in a variety of public school settings and geographical locations to foster integration in educational environments.

## INTEGRATING REGULAR AND SPECIAL EDUCATION

There is a growing awareness that the distinction between regular and special education is an ill-conceived, inefficient, and counter-productive historical anomaly (Biklen, 1985; Peterson, Albert, Foxworth, Cox, and Tilley, 1985; Reynolds and Birch, 1977; Stainback and Stainback, 1984; Will, 1984). Critics argue the present dual system of education entails an unnecessary duplication of services, division of resources (which are selectively made available only to some), dissipation of advocacy potential (as special interest groups develop and compete for limited educational resources), and segregation of students from one another throughout their school years.

This division between special and regular education evolved during the period from 1850 to 1975 in most areas of the country. Compulsory education laws required that all children attend school. So, the educational system attempted to address the needs of most students by developing an efficient approach to group instruction which was based on three assumptions:

1. All students of the same chronological age are ready to be taught the same objectives.
2. All students require the same amount of time (i.e., an academic year) to master the predesignated objectives.
3. All students can master the predesignated objectives for a grade level across all curricular areas during the same year (Stainback, Stainback, Courtnage, and Jaben, 1985, p. 147).

Those pupils whose educational needs did not match this age-graded structure or who otherwise disrupted the regimented flow of instruction were either excluded from school or placed into new ungraded "special" classes and schools (Meyer and Putnam, in press).

The extent of the gulf which developed between these two systems was evidenced by the way the various reports on the state of American education either ignored the existence of special education or treated it as a problematic add-on. Nevertheless, a number of educators have begun to identify those commonalities across the two systems which augur well for a single integrated educational system.

The myth that there are fundamental differences between regular and special education has both perpetuated and been perpetuated by this separation of services. Stainback and Stainback (1984) explicitly identify and refute several components of this myth:

1. There are said to be two distinct group of students: regular students are "normal" and special students deviate from the "norm" with respect to some significant characteristic. In fact, the normal student does not exist; instead, every student is a unique combination of physical, intellectual, psychological, and social characteristics.
2. Special education students are said to require individualized services to meet their educational needs. In fact, individualized instruction could significantly enhance the achievement of all students.
3. There are said to be two (or more) discrete groups of instructional methods, one for regular classes and another for special students. In fact, there are no "special" instructional methods that differ fundamentally from those used with most children.

An increased awareness that a quality education should transcend the artificial boundaries between special and regular education has been associated with a movement to explore material from the effective schools literature for possible application to a merger of special and regular education (Goodman, 1985; Jewell, 1985; Mackenzie, 1983; Peterson et al., 1985; Rutter, Maugham, Mortimore, Ouston, and Smith, 1975; Searl, Ferguson, and Biklen, 1985). This research has been responsible for the delineation of a number of variables which directly and positively affect school achievement. While each list of variables differs slightly, certain dominant themes can be identified:

- Principals in effective schools are instructional leaders, not just administrators and supervisors. They create high expectations for student and teacher achievement, spend time in the classrooms, and demonstrate a knowledge and interest in the activities in the classroom.
- The climate in an effective school is orderly, disciplined, and comfortable; a commitment to excellence is evident.

- Students' goals and objectives are meaningful, clearly written, sequenced, and reviewed and updated periodically based on student progress data which are collected regularly.
- Student achievement is recognized and rewarded frequently.
- Student progress is monitored using a criterion-reference approach: the measures used are directly related to the instructional objectives.
- Within effective classrooms, "downtime" is kept to a minimum. Students spend a high percentage of their time actively engaged in learning tasks.
- Effective teachers spend a high percentage of their time involved in active instruction.
- Effective teachers adapt, modify, and create curricular units for their own class; the units are sequenced and integrated into the long-range educational goals of the school.
- Effective schools tend to have a low teacher/student ratio.
- Administrators, teachers, support personnel, students, and parents in effective schools cooperate and communicate openly.
- Parents support and are actively involved in effective schools.
- The community expresses support for the school program.

The Adaptive Learning Environments Model (ALEM) developed by Wang and her colleagues represents the implementation of these principles of effective schooling along with the provision for the individualized instruction of all students—including those who would otherwise be described as disabled—within regular classrooms (Wang and Birch, 1984b). Their attempt to fully integrate special and regular education is marked by:

> (a) early identification of learning problems through a diagnostic-prescriptive monitoring system integrally related to the program's instructional component; (b) delabeling of mainstreamed "special" students and description of learning needs in instructional rather than categorical terms; (c) individually designed educational plans that accomodate each student's learning strengths and needs; and (d) teaching of self-management skills that enable students to take increased responsibility for their learning. (Wang and Birch, 1984a, p. 33)

In an analysis of the implementation of ALEM in 156 classrooms located in 10 highly diverse school districts, Wang and Birch (1984b) found that the program was able to be instituted effectively in 96.4% of the classrooms.

Students in classrooms with the highest level of ALEM implementation spent more time on tasks and were less likely to be distracted than students in rooms where this model was not fully implemented. In another study, Wang and Birch (1984a) compared classroom process, achievement in basic skills, perceived self-competence, and program cost of 108 randomly assigned regular and "special" students in the ALEM classes with those of 71 students in a traditional mainstream/resource room program. They reported that the students with a disability in the ALEM group exceeded similar students in the resource room group in attaining desirable classroom behavior, improvement in perceived self-competence, and achievement in basic skills. The results for the non-disabled students were similar, and the ALEM program also generated a significant financial saving for the school district. The ALEM results offer strong support for the contention that a reorganization of American education is both possible and beneficial: The program demonstrated not only that children with mild disabilities can be "delabeled" and effectively served along with their regular education peers in regular education classrooms, but that all students can benefit. Finally, this programmatic improvement was also less costly in comparison with more traditional resource room "pullout" models of service delivery for students with mild disabilities.

## INTEGRATING STUDENTS WITH SEVERE DISABILITIES

Johnson and Meyer (1985) have stressed that the integration of children who have severe disabilities into regular neighborhood schools is crucial for the attainment of the following goals:

1. the development of positive attitudes by nonhandicapped persons toward persons with disabilities to prepare for an adult society in which diverse people live and work together (Voeltz, 1980; 1982)
2. the normalization of the social status of persons with disabilities to facilitate their participation in typical environments and situations enjoyed by others who are not handicapped (Voeltz, 1984)
3. the development of a social context to enable nonhandicapped children to master skills needed to interact constructively with persons with disabilities (Strain, Odom, & McConnell, 1984; Voeltz, 1982)
4. the development of friendships and other positive social relationships by persons with severe disabilities (Voeltz, 1984)

Numerous reports are now available which document such positive outcomes can occur as a result of integration and peer interactions between children with severe disabilities and their nondisabled peers (Brady et al., 1984; Brinker, 1985; Donder and Nietupski, 1981; McHale and Simeonsson, 1980; Meyer, et al., in press; Voeltz, 1980, 1982; Voeltz and Brennan, 1984).

Until very recently, interactions between children with severe disabilities and their nonhandicapped peers have been primarily episodic and relatively artificial in nature (Meyer-Voeltz, Johnson, and McQuarter, 1983). Often these two groups of children have not had an opportunity to interact with one another in a "normalized" way in school, in the neighborhood, in community programs, and so forth, simply because they were both physically and socially isolated from one another throughout their school years. Even when children with severe disabilities attend the same school as their nonhandicapped peers at the same age level, they may remain in a self-contained special education classroom all day. They often arrive via separate transportation systems, enter and exit through a special entry chosen because it is "more accessible" than the main entry, do not share recess or extracurricular activities with their nonhandicapped peers, and may even eat lunch in the special education classroom. These unfortunate and unnecessary separations preclude the numerous natural interaction times which occur for most children. As a result, children in these classes may be as socially isolated from their nonhandicapped peers as are children who attend a handicapped-only school.

Programs for children with severe disabilities are often centralized in one school in their district. This means that the special education students may be located in the same building as their peers in regular education, but they are socially isolated because they come from different neighborhoods. Kishi (1985) recently reported the results of a series of interviews she conducted with nondisabled teenagers. These young people had, several years earlier, when they were in elementary school, spent a significant amount of time socially interacting with peers who had severe disabilities. Kishi found that while the nondisabled children had moved on to their neighborhood high schools, the children with severe disabilities had "graduated" to a secondary program which was centralized. As a result, there were no longer any significant daily opportunities for these children to maintain the friendship they had begun years earlier.

Strully and Strully (1985), as parents of a teenager with severe disabilities, describe the three-year friendship that their daughter has enjoyed with a nondisabled peer. They argue that such friendships would not be possible without the daily shared interactions that occur when two children attend school together. They also maintain that the number of skills that their daughter learns will only partially determine whether or not she will be successfully integrated into the adult world when she graduates from school. The ability and willingness of other persons, who are not disabled, to accept and welcome her participation in a variety of roles and environments are essential ingredients if she is to have an opportunity to even use the skills she does learn.

There is a rapidly expanding literature on the consequences of exposing nonhandicapped children to information about and contact with children with severe handicaps. The current trend toward increased contact between nonhandicapped persons and persons with severe disabilities is accompanied by a concern for public opinion and the prevention of any negative effects that might occur if children are not properly prepared for these interactions. As Johnson and Meyer (1985) point out, the literature on the social acceptance of students with mild handicaps can be interpreted either negatively or positively. The key appears to be whether any intervention occurred to assist those students during the process. When neither the handicapped nor the nonhandicapped children are prepared for the interaction, the outcomes are negative and researchers report that children with disabilities are socially excluded. But if there is preparation, the outcomes are positive (Gottlieb, 1978). Donaldson (1980) notes that when children engage in negative behaviors and express negative attitudes toward one another, it probably reflects the fact that society has not successfully prepared them to interact with the diverse people whom they will encounter throughout their lifetimes. Voeltz (1982) presents clear evidence that structured interactions could be designed which do prepare children to interact. Further, she argues, such experiences enhance the ability of persons in general to cope with diversity and individual differences far more effectively than pedagogical activities and written materials could ever do.

## COMMITMENT—THE KEY

Before we proceed to describe strategies to achieve an integrated school, a caveat is in order. Integration is more than a technical accomplishment. There is one consistent message in all of the materials on effective integration practices which we reviewed. In the words of Taylor (1982):

> What distinguishes the programs . . . is a strong belief in the value of educating children with severe disabilities alongside typical peers and preparing them to participate fully in community life. Integration works when people are committed to it. (p. 48)

The importance of personal and philosophical commitment to integration at the administrative level also was emphasized by those involved in Hawaii's decision to implement integrated services statewide (Meyer & Kishi, 1985). And in her study of national practices, Stetson (1984) claimed as well that this commitment—by administrators, teachers, and parents—was a critical component in the design and implementation of effective strategies to accomplish integration.

Leadership is crucial to insure that students with severe disabilities are not only physically present in the public school building, but are socially part of the life of the school along with other children (Biklen, 1985). Building principals, in particular, are responsible for the climate of their schools. Their attitude regarding goals such as integration, equality, and excellence will have a tremendous impact upon the way these ideals are realized. A first step toward integration occurs when the principal sees that he or she provides leadership to all the students in the school, not just the students in regular education. The principal forms the first line of defense against the development of an us-and-them attitude. Just as improved instruction is related to the principal's interest in it, so integration will profit as the principal actively strives to accomplish it. Biklen (1985) suggests that principals pursue personal changes for integration by learning about special education; listening to students with disabilities, their parents, and other people with disabilities; and learning about various integration efforts.

Similarly, the district administrator can facilitate integration by supporting those at the school level who are attempting to integrate, and by anticipating problems or sources of opposition. In their study of Hawaii's integration effort, Meyer and Kishi (1985) found that a proactive integration plan and timetable at the district and state level was identified by all those involved as critical to success. This integration plan included strategies to inform interested constituencies (e.g., parents) about the planned changes, as well as the early establishment of a model but "typical" class in one of the public schools which could serve as a "fishbowl" of excellence. Those who initially opposed such changes as unworkable or who needed reasssurance that it could be done were then able to see a firsthand example. When it was time for their own district or school to integrate, they were able to learn from the administration, staff, parents, and children at the model program. In general, this demonstration of excellence in action helped to assuage the concerns of all those who had no experience of integrated programs.

## Planning

A change in any established system requires careful planning and preparation. But a change like integration of severely disabled students into a previously segregated school system demands more than usual care. This type of major change is not like the introduction of a new curriculum or the opening of a new school. It can be fraught with misconceptions and can excite high emotions and nervous questions on the part of parents and staff. Who are these kids? Don't they need constant medical supervision? Don't they display the kind of behavior that is dangerous to the regular kids? Won't the other kids make fun of them? Will the public school ever be able to provide the level of program that my child had at the private school? And so forth. Careful planning can provide a forum within which to quiet the concerns of all groups touched by an integration effort.

In their descriptions of successful system changes toward integration, Biklen (1985), Meyer and Kishi (1985), and McGregor, Janssen, Larsen, and Tillery (1986) consistently identified several principles of planning to help smooth the transition:

1. Establish an integration task force with specific goals and timetables. The membership should include administrators, principals, regular and special education teachers, the parents of disabled and nondisabled students, and other support personnel.
2. Designate a faculty member, middle level administrator, or consultant with primary responsibilities to coordinate integration efforts.
3. Assess needs. Consideration should be given to the students to be integrated, their support needs, their age, and to the accessibility of school buildings, receptivity of school staff, distribution of classes in the district, and proximity of schools to community resources and the homes of specific students.
4. Establish definite goals. In this way the planning group has an unambiguous understanding of its purpose.
5. Establish in advance a schedule for the implementation of an integration plan, to be communicated clearly to all concerned parties and held to firmly.
6. For an initial site choose a school with a receptive principal and enthusiastic staff who are likely to be comfortable serving as "leaders" for other schools later on.
7. Meet with administrators, teachers, and parents at the site(s) targeted for new integrated programs.
8. Develop a plan for any facilities which will no longer be needed as result of integration efforts.
9. Use a variety of means (e.g., presentations, newsletters, open houses, integration handbooks, local news media, etc.) to maintain open communication with school staff, students, parents, and the community at large regarding integration efforts.

Meyer and Kishi (1985) point out that during the planning phase it is particularly critical to address the fears and concerns of the parents of students who have been receiving service in segregated settings. With good reason, these parents are likely to be initially skeptical that the public school—which has for so long ignored their children—is now truly committed to providing these programs. They will need to be reassured with more than rhetoric. Advocates for integration will need to demonstrate to these parents that:

1. The quality of integrated programs will at least equal what existed in the special schools.
2. The integrated programs have a permanent place in the public school system and are not merely a passing fad.
3. Their children will not be exposed to social rejection, ridicule, and unnecessary risks to safety and health.
4. Everyone in the school will receive preparation for this change.

## Staff Preparation, Involvement, and Training

Stainback and Stainback (1985) highlight the crucial role which regular educators can play in the establishment of integrated schools as they (i) provide nonhandicapped students with opportunities to interact with students who have severe disabilities, (ii) encourage and reinforce interactions between the two groups, and (iii) provide a model for and train nonhandicapped students to deal positively with human differences. Unfortunately, preservice preparation of regular education teachers continues to be deficient in providing sufficient information concerning students with disabilities (Ganschow, Weber, and Davis, 1984). So, if regular educators are to make an active positive contribution to school integration efforts, an effective inservice program is necessary to provide them with basic training and information.

While inservice preparation facilitates the integration of all students with disabilities, Stainback and Stainback (1982b) point out the particular need for a program which specifically focuses on students with severe disabilities. They identify three essential components of such a program:

1. A description of students with severe handicaps that emphasizes their individuality and the nature of their educational needs.
2. A discussion of the moral, philosophical, historical, legal, and empirical rationales for the education of students with severe handicaps in regular schools.

3. A delineation of the role of regular educators in the integration effort.

Several studies have found that this approach to inservice training (Stainback and Stainback, 1982a), together with opportunities to observe and interact with students with severe disabilities (Stainback, Stainback, Strathe, and Dedrick, 1983), has a significant positive impact on the attitude of regular educators.

The program outlined above provides an efficient first step in staff training for integration, but by itself is insufficient. The ALEM program has found that ongoing systematic inservice training is part of effective schools in general and effective integration in particular (Wang, Vaughan, and Dytman, 1985). The essential elements in ALEM's inservice program, which participating teachers identified as crucial to the program's overall effectiveness, include:

1. adapting to the interest and needs of individual staff
2. addressing ongoing needs at regular inservice sessions
3. providing strong administrative support
4. involving all personnel who are either directly or indirectly affected
5. providing individualized needs assessment for each teacher
6. holding individual and small group sessions
7. encouraging active staff participation
8. supplying supervisory feedback based on direct observation

In addition, the literature on effective strategies for fostering integration (e.g., Taylor, 1982; Hamre-Nietupski and Nietupski, 1981) suggest a number of other nontraditional approaches for preparing staff for integration:

1. Before integration, encourage regular educators to visit the special schools and encourage the special educators to visit the regular schools.
2. Arrange an informal faculty "drop-in" in to discuss issues related to integration.
3. Designate one person in each school as the primary contact person for concerns regarding integration.
4. After integration takes place, maintain an open door visitation policy for the classes containing students with severe disabilities.

## CREATING AN INTEGRATED COMMUNITY
## IN THE SCHOOLS

A universal merger of regular and special education within a structure which emphasizes individualized instruction for all students remains a distant goal. Nonetheless, it is possible *today* for administrators and teachers to develop an approach to education within a particular school district or an individual school which will achieve most of what is desirable in such a merger. The research on effective schools provides direction for implementing many substantive reforms and 10 years of experience at integrating severely disabled students in the public schools offer some clear guidelines for completing the transformation.

In reviewing the literature on integration, seven sources stood out as having particularly useful and comprehensive discussions of strategies for effective integration programs. One is based on Hawaii's experience in providing service for all handicapped children in public schools (Meyer and Kishi, 1985). Another source describes Philadelphia's efforts to implement integrated services as the result of litigation (McGregor et al., 1986). A group of interrelated materials describe strategies which have been used in a number of urban and rural school districts in Iowa and Wisconsin (Hamre-Nietupski and Nietupski, 1981; Hamre-Nietupski, Nietupski, Stainback, and Stainback, 1984; Stainback and Stainback, 1985). And, two sources synthesize the findings of two overlapping federally-funded research projects which conducted in-depth examinations of integration efforts in 45 locations around the country (Biklen, 1985; Taylor, 1982). In this section and in Table 3-1 we have adapted and expanded the list of "integration markers" which was developed by Meyer and Kishi (1985) to identify those characteristics which should be present in a truly integrated school. While most of the elements described here were captured in the initial formulation of this list, we have incorporated some additional elements based on these other sources.

A comprehensive listing like Table 3-1 helps to dispel the fallacy that integration is accomplished by merely physically transferring students with severe disabilities into buildings where they are educated in physical proximity to their nondisabled peers. Integration is a complex phenomenon that is accomplished by a concerted effort cutting across the various organizational levels within the school system. In Table 3-1, the integration markers are grouped by the individuals who should have primary responsibility for assuring they are realized. It should be apparent that efforts to achieve integration at higher levels in the organization are necessary preconditions to achieving it at the level where the important integration occurs—in relation-

**Table 3-1** School-Based Integration Markers

| Decision-Making Personnel | Integration Marker | Definition |
|---|---|---|
| District Administration | Neighborhood School Attendance | Students with disabilities attend same school (generally in their neighborhoods) they would attend if nonhandicapped. This involves chronological age appropriate school placements according to the natural proportion (i.e., percentage of children with disabilities is approximately parallel to their percentage of the population as a whole). |
| | Supervisory and Resource Personnel | Special education personnel are supervised by general education building principal, and access to general resource personnel (e.g., librarian, physical education teacher) for instruction and consultation is parallel to that of regular education personnel. |
| | School Calendar | Students with disabilities follow general school calendar for age range, including vacation schedules and school arrival and departure times. |
| | Transportation | General transportation available and accessible to all students, including students with disabilities. |
| Building Principal | Classroom Assignment | Homerooms for all students are integrated, and classroom assignments made according to general school procedures (i.e., students with disabilities receives same homeroom assignment they would have if not handicapped. |
| | Classroom Location and Schedules | Location of resource rooms and any other specialized program option is consistent with general education room location, and students with disabilities follow same general daily class schedule (class times and changes, free or study periods, lunch times, etc.) as their nondisabled peers. |
| | Use of General School Facilities | Students with disabilities share use of general school facilities (including restrooms, cafeteria, library, gym, and so forth) and participate in integrated activities according to natural proportion (i.e., percentage of children with disabilities in any program is approximately parallel to percentage of population). |
| | Attendance in Regular Classes | Students with disabilities participate in class change patterns, including variously grouped regular class placements according to needs and interests, along with their nonhandicapped peers. |
| | Extracurricular Activity | Extracurricular and after-school activities are integrated with itm for |

| | |
|---|---|
| | ...to interests and general program guidelines. |
| Parent Organization | The Parent Teacher Association is supported as a communication/involvement vehicle for all parents. |
| Faculty Interactions and Organization | All school personnel participate equally in and share responsibility for school staff organization patterns (e.g., general faculty meetings, supervision of extracurricular activities and free time, and so forth). |
| Classroom Teacher | |
| Daily and Weekly Class Schedule | Schedule follows normalized pattern typical for same-age peers who are not handicapped, including class changes, and regroupings, free time, lunch, and so forth. |
| Administrative Supervision | Teachers report to building principal and various program chairpersons at the building level according to general school patterns (i.e., not differentiated for regular versus special education). |
| Team Teaching | Special education personnel participate in team teaching arrangements with regular education personnel for instruction of integrated groupings of students with and without disabilities. |
| Normalized Instructional Goals and Intervention Strategies | Skills being taught students with disabilities are functional and age-appropriate, and instructional procedures are consistent with criterion conditions as well as with community standards for regular education students (e.g., guidelines for discipline). |
| Student and Family Interests and Needs | Students and families are encouraged to participate in available generic resources (e.g., extracurricular activities, parent organizations, school open house, and so forth). |
| Peer/Social Interactions | Students with and without disabilities are prepared and encouraged to interact with one another socially and in cooperative work and activity groups during the various "natural" contexts available during the school day and year (e.g., lunch, recess, joint science projects, and so forth). |
| Teacher/Staff Interaction | Teachers interact formally (advice and assistance) and informally (socially, during break times, etc.), with no differentiation evident for special versus regular education. |

*Source:* From L.H. Meyer and G.S. Kishi, "School Integration Strategies," in *Strategies for Achieving Community Integration for Developmentally Disabled Citizens* (pp. 247–248) by K.C. Lakin and R.H. Bruinicks (Eds.), 1985, Baltimore, MD: Paul H. Brookes Publishers. Copyright 1985 by Paul H. Brookes Publishers. Adapted by permission.

ships among individual students. There can be extensive planning for integration; it can have enthusiastic administrative support; a building can be fully accessible; yet, if integration is not addressed in a coherent manner at the level where individual students interact, it will remain an unrealized social ideal. In the final analysis, integration of the educational system is really about learning how our common humanity transcends myriad individual differences. And this objective in the educational plan is achieved only when students get to know each other.

Those schools and districts that have been identified as models of integration all share one basic presupposition: Students with severe disabilities have the same status as other students in the system. Such a system recognizes the need of students with severe disabilities for specialized support, but it does not make these supports and services contingent on setting those students aside for "special" treatment. From an integrated administration perspective, whatever is typical for most students in the school should be typical for students with severe disabilities. This principle has numerous implications for a wide range of administrative issues. Adoption of the principle will undoubtedly change decisions that in the past have too often fostered the segregation of students with disabilities.

The teachers who have been the most successful at achieving integration are those who have made it an accepted part of daily life. Episodic special activities and artificial arrangements should be a thing of the past; the integration of students with severe disabilities must occur at the level of daily routine. When this happens, a subtle but significant message is conveyed to all the students involved: The students with severe disabilities belong here.

Integration is a necessary condition for the functional, community-based curriculum that has become state-of-the-art in the education of students with severe disabilities. It should also cause changes in the regular education curriculum, for students with disabilities must be fully included. Voeltz (1984) describes in detail the various changes that can be incorporated into the regular education curriculum and so develop more positive attitudes and allay old prejudices and stereotypes. For example, many school systems have established a list of social competencies that students are expected to achieve at appropriate times during their school careers. Among them are the ability to interact with peers and others, to accept and deal positively with diversity and individual differences, and to develop a positive self-concept. In Hawaii, material dealing with disabilities and individual differences were incorporated into the curriculum and directly supported the stated regular education goal (Voeltz, 1984). This type of curricular integration helps convey the message that individual differences are respected in our culture and that people with disabilities always have been and will be integral members of our communities.

---

## REFERENCES

Biklen, D. (1985). *Achieving the complete school: Strategies for effective mainstreaming.* New York: Teachers College.

Brady, M.P., Shores, R.E., Gunter, P., McEvoy, M.A., Fox, J.J., & White, C. (1984). Generalization of an adolescent's social interaction behavior via multiple peers in a classroom setting. *Journal of the Association for Persons with Severe Handicaps, 9,* 278-286.

Brinker, R.P. (1985). Interactions between severely mentally retarded students and other students in integrated and segregated public school settings. *American Journal of Mental Deficiency, 89,* 587-594.

Cain, L., Melcher, J., Johns, B., Ashmore, J., Callahan, C., Draper, I., Beveridge, P., & Weintraub, F. (1984). Reply to "A nation at risk." *Exceptional Children, 50,* 484-494.

Donaldson, J. (1980). Changing attitudes toward handicapped persons: A review and analysis of research. *Exceptional Children, 46,* 504-514.

Donder, D., & Nietupski, J. (1981). Nonhandicapped adolescents teaching playground skills to their mentally retarded peers: Toward a less restrictive middle school environment. *Education and Training of the Mentally Retarded, 16,* 270-276.

Ganschow, L., Weber, D.B., & Davis, M. (1984). Preservice teacher preparation for mainstreaming. *Exceptional Children, 51,* 74-76.

Goodman, L. (1985). The effective schools movement and special education. *Teaching Exceptional Children, 17,* 102-105.

Gottlieb, J. (1978) Observing social adaptation in schools. In G.P. Sackett (Ed.), *Observing Behavior, Vol. 1: Theory and application in mental retardation* (pp. 285-309). Baltimore: University Park Press.

Gross, B., & Gross, R. (Eds.). (1985). *The great school debate: Which way for American education?* New York: Simon & Schuster.

Hamre-Nietupski, S., & Nietupski, J. (1981). Integral involvement of severely handicapped students within regular schools. *Journal of the Association for the Severely Handicapped, 6*(2), 30-39.

Hamre-Nietupski, S., Nietupski, J., Stainback, W., & Stainback, S. (1984). Preparing school systems for longitudinal integration efforts. In N. Certo, N. Haring, & R. York (Eds.), *Public school integration of severely handicapped students: Rational issues and progressive alternative* (pp. 107-141). Baltimore: Brookes.

Howe, I. (1984, March 5). Towards an open culture. *The New Republic,* pp. 25-29.

Jewell, J. (1985). One school's search for excellence. *Teaching Exceptional Children, 17,* 140-144.

Johnson, R.E., & Meyer, L. (1985). Program design and research to normalize peer interactions. In M.P. Brady & P.L. Gunter (Eds.), *Integrating moderately and severely handicapped learners: Strategies that work* (pp. 79-101). Springfield, IL: Thomas.

Kishi, G.S. (1985, December). *Long-term effects of a social interaction program between nonhandicapped and severely handicapped children.* Paper presented at the twelfth annual conference of the Association for Persons with Severe Handicaps, Boston.

Mackenzie, D.E. (1983, April). Research for school improvement: An appraisal of some recent trends. *Educational Researcher,* pp. 5-17.

McGregor, G., Janssen, C.M., Larsen, L.A., & Tillery, W.L. (1986). Philadelphia's urban model project: A system-wide effort to integrate students with severe handicaps. *Journal of the Association for Persons with Severe Handicaps, 11,* 61-67.

McHale, S., & Simeonsson, R. (1980). Effects of interaction on nonhandicapped children's attitude toward autistic children. *American Journal of Mental Deficiency, 85,* 18-27.

Meyer, L.H., Fox, A., Schermer, A., Ketelsen, D., Montan, N., Maley, K., & Cole, D. (in press). The effects of teacher intrusion on social play interactions between children with autism and their nonhandicapped peers. *Journal of Autism and Developmental Disorders.*

Meyer, L.H., & Kishi, G.S. (1985). School integration strategies. In K.C. Lakin & R.H. Bruininks (Eds.), *Strategies for achieving community integration for developmentally disabled citizens* (pp. 231-252). Baltimore: Brookes.

Meyer, L.H., & Putnam, J. (in press). Social integration. In V.B. Van Hasslt, P.S. Strain, & M. Hersen (Eds.), *Handbook of developmental and physical disabilities..* New York: Pergamon.

Meyer-Voeltz, L., Johnson, R.E., & McQuarter, R.J. (1983). *The integration of school aged children and youth with severe disabilities: A comprehensive bibliography and selective review of research and program development needs to address discrepancies in state-of-the-art.* Minneapolis, MN: Minnesota Consortium Institute, University of Minnesota.

National Commission on Excellence in Education. (1983). *A nation at risk: The imperative for educational reform.* Washington, DC: U.S. Government Printing Office No. 065-000-00177-2.

Peterson, D., Albert, S.S., Foxworth, A.M., Cox, L.S., & Tilley, B.K. (1985). Effective schools for all students: Current efforts and future directions. *Teaching Exceptional Children, 17,* 106-110.

Pincus, F.L. (1985). From equity to excellence: The rebirth of educational conservatism. In B. Gross & R. Gross (Eds.), *The great school debate: Which way for American education?* (pp. 329-344). New York: Simon & Schuster.

Reynolds, M.C., & Birch, J. (1977). *Teaching exceptional children in all of America's schools.* Reston, VA: Council for Exceptional Children.

Rutter, M., Maugham, B., Mortimore, P., Ouston, J., & Smith, A. (1975). *Fifteen thousand hours: Secondary schools and their effects on children.* New York: Wiley.

Searl, S.J., Ferguson, D.L., & Biklen, D. (1985). The front line . . . teachers. In D. Biklen (Ed.), *Achieving the complete school: Strategies for effective mainstreaming* (pp. 52-103). New York: Teachers College Press.

Stainback, S., & Stainback, W. (1985). *Integration of students with severe handicaps into regular schools.* Reston, MD: Council for Exceptional Children.

Stainback, W., & Stainback, S. (1982a). Nonhandicapped students' perceptions of severely handicapped students. *Education and Training of the Mentally Retarded, 17,* 177-182.

Stainback, W., & Stainback, S. (1982b). Preparing regular class teachers for the integration of severely retarded students. *Education and Training of the Mentally Retarded, 17,* 273-277.

Stainback, W., & Stainback, S. (1984). A rationale for the merger of special and regular education. *Exceptional Children, 51,* 102-111.

Stainback, W., Stainback, S., Courtnage, L., & Jaben, T. (1985). Facilitating mainstreaming by modifying the mainstream. *Exceptional Children, 52,* 144-152.

Stainback, W., Stainback, S., Strathe, M., & Dedrick, C. (1983). Preparing regular classroom teachers for the integration of severely retarded students: An experimental study. *Education and Training of the Mentally Retarded, 18,* 205-209.

Stetson, F. (1984). Critical factors that facilitate integration: A theory of administrative responsibility. In N. Certo, N. Haring, & R. York (Eds.), *Public school integration of severely handicapped students: Rational issues and progressive alternative* (pp. 65-81). Baltimore: Brookes.

Strain, P.S., Odom, S.L., & McConnell, S.R. (1984). Promoting social reciprocity of exceptional children: Identification, target skill selection, and interventions. *Remedial and Special Education, 5,* 21-28.

Strully, J., & Strully, C. (1985). Friendship and our children. *Journal of the Association for Persons with Severe Handicaps, 10,* 224-227.

Taylor, S.J. (1982). From segregation to integration: Strategies for integrating severely handicapped students in normal school and community settings. *Journal of the Association for the Severely Handicapped, 7*(3), 42-49.

Troy, F. (1985). The day the schools died. In B. Gross & R. Gross (Eds.), *The great school debate: Which way for American education?* (pp. 466-470). New York: Simon & Schuster.

Voeltz, L.M. (1980). Children's attitudes toward handicapped peers. *American Journal of Mental Deficiency, 84,* 455-464.

Voeltz, L.M. (1982). Effects of structured interaction with severely handicapped peers on children's attitudes. *American Journal of Mental Deficiency, 86,* 380-390.

Voeltz, L.M. (1984). Program and curriculum innovations to prepare children for integration. In N. Certo, N. Haring, & R. York (Eds.), *Public school integration of severely handicapped students: Rational issues and progressive alternative* (pp. 155-183). Baltimore: Brookes.

Voeltz, L.M., & Brennan, J. (1984). Analysis of interactions between nonhandicapped and severely handicapped peers using multiple measures. In J.M. Berg (Ed.), *Perspectives and progress in mental retardation, Vol. 1: Social, psychological, and educational aspects* (pp. 61-72). Baltimore: University Park Press.

Wang, M.C., & Birch, J.W. (1984a). Comparison of a full-time mainstreaming program and a resource room approach. *Exceptional Children, 51,* 33-40.

Wang, M.C., & Birch, J.W. (1984b). Effective special education in regular classes. *Exceptional Children, 50,* 391-398.

Wang, M.C., Vaughan, E.D., & Dytman, J.A. (1985). Staff development: A key ingredient of effective mainstreaming. *Teaching Exceptional Children, 17,* 112-121.

Will. M. (1984). Let us pause and reflect—but not too long. *Exceptional Children, 51,* 11-16.

# Chapter 4

# Preparing the School Environment for an Integrated Model

*Nancy Lamb-Zodrow*

It is often difficult for educators to accept new practices. The integration of students with moderate to severe handicaps within a school district is a change that is almost certain to cause anxious or resistant behaviors in any building staff. Many educators, for example, will perceive integration as creating additional demands on their already strained workloads. Special education teachers may feel pressured to write elaborate instructions and suggestions for regular education teachers serving integrated students. These teachers may resist releasing students into what they perceive as an unstructured situation, fearing that the students will be lost within a regular classroom of 25-30 students.

Regular education teachers, on the other hand, may feel resentful for having to bear responsibility for this change. These teachers may feel unprepared and untrained for the sudden responsibility of programming for a student with special needs. Administrators may be disappointed with their teaching staff who have not dealt with the change in a more positive and problem-solving manner. Regular education students may feel resentful of the extra attention they believe that the students with special needs are receiving from their teachers. And the students with special needs may feel embarrassed over the extra attention and confused as to exactly what their status is in this complicated classroom experience.

Because educators often perceive integration efforts as stressful and upsetting to their normal routines, change agents need to be aware of the emotional, intellectual, and physical difficulties that people encounter when facing such major changes in their work settings. It is important both to know how people respond to systems change forces and to be able to predict how the educators in a particular system will react to specific efforts in the change process. Although system-wide, long-range benefits will result from the move to integrated programming, many educators will find the initial changes painful. And the change agent, remembering that many outcomes can result from a change process—ranging from the successful implementation of new teaching models to intense resistance to change—should take care to use change strategies that will not be sabotaged due to faulty groundwork and preparation.

This chapter is designed to help you decide if there is a common interest or need within your school system that justifies beginning a change process. A systematic, ongoing approach to change within systems will be presented, one that is participatory in nature, has a problem-solving orientation, and utilizes the services of a consultant or facilitator. The systems change model that will be presented is intended to be used in any organization interested in making changes. This chapter will then help you assess the feasibility of preparing your organization for a change towards a successful integration program model.

This chapter will encourage readers to use a participatory process to assist in changing attitudes and facilitating the smooth transition of students with moderate and severe disabilities into regular education settings. The first step will be to systematically prepare your organization for this change process so as to minimize potential causes of failure. The second step will be to find a skilled facilitator who can orchestrate the change process. And finally, the chapter will discuss the consultant or facilitator skills which will be needed to assist the integrated program at difficult decision-making points.

This is written for those administrators and other program catalysts who seek practical strategies for creating an environment that will lead to the integration of students with moderate and severe disabilities into regular education settings.

## A NOTE ABOUT PARTICIPATION

A guiding premise for this chapter is that building and district staff impacted by the integration efforts will need to be informed of and involved in the entire change process. This is true regardless of the level that an individual holds in a district's hierarchy. While a building or district administrator clearly has more power to support or hinder change, it is the direct service staff—teachers, support service personnel, aides, custodians, and others—who will be immediately responsible for implementing the change. This type of participatory process involves a dispersal of hierarchical control and fosters the abilities of different people to engage in problem-solving efforts. It requires that all constituents who will be affected by the change should have the opportunity to participate in the process—knowing that some groups will be more involved than others depending upon commitments, interests, and talents.

If all constituents support and believe in the direction of the proposed changes, the likelihood of successful implementation is enhanced. The history of educational reform is unfortunately riddled with examples of innovations that did not succeed or were not maintained because of the failure to secure the commitment of those actually charged with implementing the change. A focus placed on integrated education solely by administrators may only serve to reinforce teachers' beliefs, for example, that they exercise little control over their own classrooms and that the administration does not truly understand the needs of its own staff.

We should understand that the goals we have—and expect others to eventually share—may be only some of many educational goals held by the district constituents. Most regular education teachers whom we know, for example, would list the following among their goals:

1. helping students develop a healthy self-concept
2. helping students develop a respect for other students
3. helping students learn to successfully function within the prescribed classroom structure
4. encouraging the natural curiosity of students to learn
5. teaching content material to students in the most effective way possible

It is challenging enough to reach these goals with "well-adjusted" and "motivated" students. Many teachers may feel a sense of potential frustration when expected to extend these same goals to students with special needs. If we are seeking this extension as a goal, then we will need to create a process that allows others to voluntarily place integrated education as a goal on their priority lists. The change agent's goal of integrated education will be strengthened if it is a voluntarily shared rather than an imposed goal.

At the same time, we are aware of situations where the strident support of regressive and ineffectual special education models by direct service staff would make it difficult to use a full-fledged participatory model. There are situations in which it will be necessary to use, at least temporarily, a tradtional decision-making process—from the top down. In these situations, direct service providers are ultimately forced to change their practice—in the hope that they will change their perspective as a result of experiencing the different model. This type of policy decision making should only be done when there is ample evidence that a participatory process will not succeed.

While we understand the necessity for top-down administrative decrees, we believe that such decrees, especially when made frequently, violate the long-term viability of any change. Whether decisions are made in a top-down or participatory process, there will come a time when direct service staff will have to assume full responsibility for a practice. And if they haven't developed a sense of responsibility for the practice, it may be described by the administrators as a "change," but it will actually be carried out within the classroom in such ineffectual ways as to make no difference.

The reader is encouraged to utilize a participatory format in which all constituents feel able to voice their concerns and fears about the proposed change. Administrators and change agents will need to be open and receptive to hearing criticisms of the proposals. Yet it is far better to have these criticisms voiced at the planning phase by people committed to the overall process than to have the criticisms voiced—or acted out in passive-aggressive behaviors—at the implementation phase. It is our belief that when engaging in systems change efforts, the sharing of decision making does not entail administrators give up power or authority. On the contrary, administrators who are able to share decision making gain self-confidence, cooperation, and respect from others, additional knowledge about the needs of the organizations in which they work, and ultimately power from the increased support given to them by other constituents.

## A Systems Change Model

Administrators, teaching staff, parents, and students will all have different issues, needs, and perceptions when looking at a change as global as mainstreaming students with moderate to severe disabilities. When looking at the magnitude of this type of change and at the many school and community personnel it will touch, the need for a systematic change process is vital. Using a systematic change process model assures that the change will be defined, planned, implemented, and monitored in a logical, orderly sequence, thereby assisting in the routinization of the change within the school system.

The change process model we will be discussing was developed at the University of Washington and refined in two school districts in Washington State. The staff in both school districts wished to improve the service delivery to students with severe disabilities and their families. This model is systematic, rational, and has a problem-solving orientation. It also has a participatory emphasis and utilizes the services of a facilitator to assist the organizations's movement through the change process. Additionally, the model incorporates the existing structure and resources of the organization and depends upon broad-based involvement to foster a sense of ownership in the change process.

While there exist many viable working models for change, we discuss this model because of our direct experience with it. Additionally, we realize that while systematic change makes the most sense, change also occurs from other types of planning—sometimes even accidentally or from a partial plan. Being alert to and able to take advantage of unplanned circumstances is a necessary skill.

The systems change model we are presenting is divided into five phases, of which the last four phases can be repeated over and over again. The first phase is Entry.

## Entry

In the entry phase, the initiator of change determines if the organization is indeed open to change. The initiator prepares a needs statement and then identifies the constituent groups that will be impacted by that need. The initiator also assesses the change model and determines its appropriateness, perhaps concluding that another model is preferable.

The initiator will need to do some groundwork prior to going public concerning the intent to institute a change in the service delivery system to students with moderate to severe disabilities. If integrated services to these students is identified as a need, the initiator can assess the extent of the district's resources and the degree of interest among its staff members to support such a change.

Anticipated outcomes from this phase include: a decision of approval and support from the administrative staff to instigate the change process; the establishment of a statement of need; a determination of the feasibility of the change; and an analysis of the system to determine whether it will support the desired changes.

An initiator might want to use the following questions as a guide while moving through the entry phase.

- Do we have a need? In what general area?
- What is the scope of the problem or need?
- Who is affected? Who will benefit from the changes?
- Do we have the necessary approval and willingness?
- Does this model best meet our needs or are there more effective models to meet our needs?
- What structures and resources do we already have in place?
- How can we best prepare the participants for this change?

In some instances, the district will want to find the facilitator during the entry phase to assist in the process. A facilitator will need to assist the initiator in answering the questions on the Feasibility Questionaire (see Exhibit 4-1), to provide encouragement to the initiator, and to attend the initial meeting with constituent representatives and other interested members of the school district staff in order to explain the change process and need perceived by the initiator.

*Example:* In one school, the principal gained informal support from the representatives of constituent groups by disseminating written materials describing potential areas for change and a process for change. He asked that each person determine whether a change effort should be pursued and identify any concerns about such an undertaking.

*Example:* In another organization (a special services program), the program administrator asked each professional discipline to identify a representative to advise him on a potential change effort. He held a meeting during which he discussed some of the needs he perceived in the program and described the change process. These were discussed with the representatives. The representatives took this information back to their colleagues for discussion and approval. (Heggelund et al., 1984).

## Mobilization

During this phase, all participants in the change process gain an understanding of the organization's direction or mission and the areas identified for change. The participants also formulate goals and objectives used to measure progress towards the organization's larger mission. Objectives are prioritized and the participants acquire the needed skills and resources to begin planning for change. An important part of the mobilization phase is the establishment of a steering committee which oversees the activities of the change process.

The mobilization phase is the time to build excitement, to create energy, to build a working philosophy for the integration of students with moderate and severe disabilities into regular education settings. It is the time to create commitment and a feeling of ownership among the participants.

Anticipated outcomes during this phase include (i) team building, (ii) increased interactions among all staff members, (iii) agreement on the roles and responsibilities of all involved in the change process, (iv) development and approval of a mission statement of goals and objectives, (v) establishment of the steering committee, and (vi) establishment of a system of communication for all participants.

The participants may want to use the following questions as a guide during the mobilization phase.

- Where are we and where do we want to go?

- How will we get input from and communicate with all participants?
- How will we determine if our communication system is working?
- Who will make up the steering committee?

Many educators will need to develop new skills and attitudes about students with special needs. Staff development thus is extremely important during the mobilization phase and the facilitator can be of invaluable assistance. The facilitator should help with a needs assessment of staff members, with the creation of a staff development training plan, and with the provision of necessary resources and training for continuing through the change process. Sometimes these staff development needs will be glaring, and at other times very subtle. The facilitator utilizes the participants' present levels of awareness and knowledge in preparing the training activities.

*Example:* One school began to develop its mission statement by asking each staff member and a number of parents to submit sample mission statements for their school. A task force was then formed to write the school's mission statement using the set of ideas generated. This statement was then submitted at a meeting of school staff, parents, and community agency representatives for ratification.

*Example:* Another organization wanted to closely examine the effectiveness of its service delivery to handicapped students by special services personnel. The steering committee included one member from each special services discipline (nurses, occupational and physical therapists, communication disorders specialists, psychologists) as well as an elementary school principal, secondary school principal, the special services director, and the outside facilitator.

## Planning

During this phase, participants develop action plans to accomplish each objective, as well as evaluation plans that will be used to determine success at the completion of the action plans. The steering committee develops a plan to monitor the implementation of all activities during the next two phases. The planning phase is a time to work out the plans for action (who will do what? by when?), as well as the plans for monitoring and testing the processes of the change.

Anticipated outcomes during the planning phase include: (i) problem-solving strategies related to the goals and objectives of change, (ii) continued educational staff development, and (iii) an increased commitment to the plans and changes.

The participants and the steering committee may want to use these questions as a guide during the planning phase.

- How will we get there?
- Who will do what? In what sequence? By when?
- How will we review the changes and the timelines?

The facilitator will be involved with training members of various groups and task forces in group process skills—including conflict resolution and consensus building skills—and problem-solving procedures. The facilitator will also want to help originate the initial task force meeting and develop a system for monitoring its progress thereafter. The facilitator will provide assistance with the development of the action plans and with their ratification in meetings with the entire staff. Lastly, the facilitator will continue to provide support and encouragement to the steering committee at this critical stage.

*Example:* In a special education program, the special services staff wanted to examine their service delivery and find better ways to efficiently serve children with disabilities. Each group of specialists (e.g., psychologists, nurses) constituted separate task forces. They requested that the facilitator assist in problem-solving work sessions to identify what they needed to change and what steps they needed to take in implementing the changes. Each group met for an average of three to four planning sessions of two to four hours each.

## Implementation

During this phase, participants implement the action plans and subsequently monitor the progress and make modifications as needed. We were once told by a systems change participant that this phase could be explained in two words: *Do it.* In many cases, this phase may be the most enjoyable for the participants because they see movement toward their objectives.

During the implementation phase, an accountability and monitoring system should be put in place. This will reinforce participants by letting them see the changes in the educational programming for students with moderate to severe disabilities as they occur.

The participants and the steering committee may want to use these questions as a guide during the implementation phase.

- Are we doing what we said we would do?
- What adjustments are needed in our plans (e.g., more planning, more realistic timelines)?
- How will we plan for and communicate the action plan adjustments?
- How are we supporting those who are doing the work?

During the implementation phase, the skills and duties of the facilitator are once again varied. The facilitator will help plan for and implement the changes, as well as encourage and support the participants during this often lengthy phase. The facilitator will help participants keep informed of the plans and changes that are occurring. The facilitator will also help the steering committee monitor the implementation of the overall action plans and encourage it to remain focused on specific objectives during this phase. Lastly, the facilitator must remain alert to any issues that may undermine the implementation of change.

*Example:* The school nurses in a special education program worked for three years to implement procedural changes in their department. Written descriptions of roles and functions of nursing staff were developed and a procedure for delivery of nursing services was established. They rewarded themselves by throwing an "Aren't Nurses Super?" party for the whole special services support staff. It was a great morale booster for everyone.

*Example:* A steering committee found that after a new assessment format and curriculum was established for a group of severely involved students, it needed to expand committee representation to include a vocational teacher and a parent to ensure appropriate representation from the areas of post-secondary vocational and community placement.

## Review

During this phase, participants determine if the implemented changes had the desired effect. They then decide where to re-enter the mobilization phase to continue the cycle of change. The participants will also need to determine whether the implementation of the action plans was successful and if the techniques and procedures used in the model would be useful for future applications.

This phase is a critical moment of truth in the change process. Did the process work? If so, what is next? If it didn't work, what went wrong and how can it be fixed?

Anticipated outcomes during the review phase include (i) the completion of evaluation plans, (ii) the achievement of desired goals and objectives, (iii) a decision to adjust or restructure the original action plans, (iv) the establishment of a mechanism for periodic review, and (v) a decision to re-enter the change process at some particular point.

The participants, steering committee, and the initiator may want to use these questions as a guide during the review phase.

- Did the planned strategies achieve the desired outcomes?
- What impact has there been on the people involved?

- Are the outcomes fulfilling the mission statement?
- Do we need to alter the mission statement, goals, and objectives?
- Does the steering committee need to be restructured?
- Are people finding out needed information on results in a timely manner?
- What additional resources need to be allocated?

During the review phase of the change model, the facilitator will need to assist the participants with problem-solving techniques, data collection and analysis, decision-making, and evaluation of the change process. At this point, one of the duties of the facilitator is to determine—with others in the process—whether there still remains a need for the facilitator's services or whether the group members are sufficiently trained in the skills of facilitating the process to continue on their own.

## Summary

The following is a brief review of the phases of the systems change model (Heggelund et al., 1984).

*Entry:*

1. An initiator wants to introduce a change process within an organization.
2. The initiator identifies the system, determines the need for change, and obtains support from administrators.
3. The initiator identifies the constituent groups who will be affected by change.
4. Members of the organization agree to use the systems change model, and then develop a statement of need.

*Mobilization:*

1. A facilitator agrees to work with the initiator and selected participants in the change process.
2. Participants form a steering committee to guide the process.
3. Participants establish a communication system.
4. Participants define their roles and responsibilities.
5. Participants ratify a mission statement and formulate goals.

6. Participants formulate and ratify measurable objectives that reflect progress toward the larger goals.
7. Participants analyze baseline data in order to select priorities for action.
8. Participants agree upon which issues to address.

*Planning:*

1. Participants in the change process develop and ratify action plans and timelines for initiating change.
2. The steering committee devises a system to monitor and review the implementation of action plans.
3. The steering committee develops an evaluation plan to measure the effectiveness of the changes made.

*Implementation:*

1. Members of the organization implement the action plans.
2. The steering committee monitors implementation of the action plans and makes adjustments as needed.
3. The steering committee communicates all changes in the plans to those who will be affected by them.

*Review:*

1. Participants evaluate the effectiveness of the changes made.
2. Participants evaluate the usefulness of the systems change model.
3. Participants determine where to re-enter the mobilization phase in order to continue the change process.

## IMPLEMENTING CHANGE: PREPARING THE ORGANIZATION

Integration is one of the more complex innovations on the current educational scene. It requires the same many-dimensional change process and the same persistence in the face of difficulties as any major educational reform. It requires accepting new beliefs and values; cognitively understanding the interrelationship between philosophical principles and concrete diagnosis and treatment; and changing the roles and role relationships between regular classroom teachers and special education teachers, and between school personnel and community members and professionals outside the school (Fullan, 1982). It requires reviewing curriculum materials and technologies, learning new teaching strategies, and changing the assumptions of education staff about students with disabilities.

To assure a smooth transition in the integration of these students into regular educational programs, there are two aspects of the change process that should receive particular attention: the preparing of an organization for change and the finding of a facilitator with skills to help the educational system make the intended integrated changes. We now look at some of the preparatory activities of the change process.

### Establishing a Mission Statement

Before engaging in any actual outreach to other district constituents, it is critical for the initiators of change to develop a mission statement which summarizes the proposed change. Because the change process is one of continual negotiation—and sometimes frequent compromise—it is important that change advocates have a statement which can always be used to assess the status of the change process. While goals and objectives taken to achieve an integrated education model may, on occasion, be negotiated or compromised, a mission statement should never be compromised. It is, in essence, the standard against which your efforts will be measured.

An example of a mission statement to guide a systems change effort for integrated education might read:

> It will be the policy of _____ School District that all children with moderate, severe, and profound disabilities will receive their education on regular education school campuses. It will also be the policy of _____ School District that children with moderate, severe, and profound disabilities will be educated in regular education classrooms to the maximum extent possible.

Having such a mission statement in writing from the onset of change activities will always keep the constituents focused on the desired outcome. Once the goal of creating an integrated educational model within the district is achieved, it may be possible to place the mission statement into the district's set of special education policies and procedures.

### The Initiator

Any successful change process depends largely upon the skills of the initiators of change. An initiator can be any member in an organization who wants to take responsibility for introducing a change process within the organization (Heggelund et al., 1984). It may be more than one person; frequently the role is filled by several key administrators.

While any individual can theoretically initiate a change process, the chance of that change being successful will increase if the initiator:

- has the standing within the organization to initiate the change alone
- has the confidence and respect of administrators, teachers, support services personnel, and parents
- has the ability to call and conduct meetings
- has a commitment to using a systematic, goal-oriented, participatory process for improving the organization

The actual position of the initiator within the organization (e.g., regular education adminstrator, special education administrator, special education or regular education teacher, support services staff member) is less important than that the initiator possess the requisite stature and personality characteristics.

If the initiator does not possess the necessary personal characteristics or is not perceived as holding power or authority, it would be advantageous to have a co-initiator. Co-initiators may also be drawn from a variety of positions (e.g., special education administrators, regular administrators, program managers). The co-initiators must work well with one another and have complementary skills. Each co-initiator should have major supervisory responsibility for a significant number of people involved in implementing the change or affected by the change.

## Using District Organization to Support Change

Initiators should analyze the decision-making structure of their district so as to effectively implement change processes. A first analysis must determine which constituencies ought to be involved in the change process. Many of the affected constituencies will be obvious; others will be less so. It is critical, though, that sufficient attention be allotted to identifying all potentially affected groups. The development of such a listing will allow the change agent to take these constituencies into account in early planning, thus giving them a sense of investment in the projected changes.

In moving towards an integrated service model, some of the obvious constituencies might include:

- administrators of the buildings in question
- central office administrators

- special education and regular education teachers affected by the proposed changes
- parents of students in those same programs

Some of the less obvious constituencies might include:

- other district administrators
- parents of younger handicapped children who will enter the district's programs in the future
- representatives of local social service agencies who have frequent contact with the students and their families
- higher-education faculty involved in the training of future district teachers
- community advocates for students with developmental disabilities and their families

It is not our intent or expectation that all such groups should necessarily be equally involved in early planning. But we do believe that any constituency with the power to hinder or block change efforts must be treated respectfully, possibly even courted for inclusion as a participant in early planning.

It is also important to assess both the formal and the informal lines of decision-making within the district. Formal lines of decision making are usually shown by a district's set of organizational charts. Informal lines of authority are often less apparent. Analyzing these lines will allow change agents to understand which constituencies are involved in actual decision making versus which are only theoretically involved. Frequently constituencies that are outside the formal lines of power actually possess significant input into—and sometimes veto power over—certain types of special education policy decisions.

Analyzing formal lines of decision making within a district can be done by a relative newcomer to the system. Analyzing informal lines requires a deeper understanding of the dynamics of both the district and its surrounding community. This type of analysis requires the insight of those who have worked within the district for an extended period of time and understand the intricacies of the various relationships. If the initiator does not have this background, it is recommended that a co-initiator be found who does.

After identifying all constituencies and assessing the formal and informal decision-making lines of authority, integration proponents are able to identify the usual form of decision making that occurs when special education changes are introduced into the district. They know who actually makes the decisions to implement innovations, understand timelines for district decision making, and anticipate potential political and fiscal roadblocks. In short, the integration effort will have a greater chance for success because of this background preparation.

Proponents are now ready to develop their beginning strategies for moving towards an integrated service model. It will also be necessary to plan for any alterations in the way that the model is routed through the usual district decision-making process. For example, there are some situations where it is permissible to approach a variety of administrators about proposed changes. In this case, it would be best to initially approach those individuals thought to be most receptive to the idea of integrated education. It is also important to determine what type of argument (stressing, e.g., fiscal or educational benefits, or the importance of compliance with state and federal intent) would be most effective with each particular administrator who is approached for support.

The next step in the change process is to seek the authority from the appropriate administrator to convene a steering committee. Rather than continuing to place the entire burden on oneself or on a small group of co-initiators, it is time to increase the number of people helping implement the change by inviting others to serve on the steering committee. Those people invited to serve should be in essential agreement with the mission statement. They should represent all significant formal constituencies affected by the proposed change and at least some of the informal groups that will be indirectly affected.

Members of this committee will need to have credibility within the district and the larger community. After all, these people are the ones who will eventually reach out to their own constituencies and "sell" the idea of integrated education. They will have to be carefully chosen so that they form a group that can function cohesively and make quality recommendations. At the same time, they need to be individuals able to articulate constructively their own or their constituency's reservations or criticism about the proposed changes. Their mere ideological commitment to an abstract concept such as integrated service does not guarantee that they will be able to work together over the prolonged period of time during which the changes are being planned and implemented.

## Feasibility For Change

All organizations vary in their ability to undertake change. In order to determine an organization's readiness for change, the initiator must informally assess the existing human, physical, and financial resources to see if they are adequate for the implementation of an integrated model. The Feasibility Questionnaire (see Exhibit 4-1) is a tool to help the initiator answer questions related to the organization's cohesiveness, ability to support a change, attitudes about change, past experiences, participation, power structure, leadership, facilitation and internal communication system.

The purpose of the questionnaire is to help clarify and identify potential problems or concerns prior to publicly announcing a desire to implement change. The initiator can rather quickly discover if the climate is conducive to change or if preparation in certain areas is needed to make the climate con-

---

Exhibit 4-1  Feasibility Questionnaire

*Cohesiveness*
1. Do the participants agree on the need for change? Do they feel a problem exists?
2. Do they have the same perceptions and expectations concerning the change process?

*Support*
3. Do all levels of the school's hierarchy support change?
4. Is there adequate time to carry out the change process?
5. Are there direct and concrete benefits for the participants?

*Attitudes/past experience*
6. Do the potential participants have positive attitudes toward change?
7. Do all the levels of the organization share the same perceptions and expectations?
8. Are the personalities of those to be involved open-minded and willing to experiment?
9. Has the organization undergone successful change in the past?

*Participation/power*
10. Will those affected be able to participate in the decision-making process?
11. Will participants have the opportunity to meet and work cooperatively with one another?
12. Is the organizational climate an open one?

*Leadership/facilitation*
13. Is there someone who can provide leadership within the district?
14. If there is not someone within the district who can facilitate the change, does the school or district have funds to hire an outside facilitator?

*Communication*
15. Is two-way, face-to-face communication possible among the participants at all levels?

---

Source: *The DISCO Manual: A Design for Implementing Systems Change in Organizations.* Inservice Training and Program Development Systems, University of Washington, Seattle, Washington. (Based on "Change Processes at the Elementary, Secondary, and Post-secondary Levels of Education" by D.A. Paul. In N. Nash & J. Culbertson (Eds.) *Linking Processes in Educational Improvement: Concepts and Applications.* Columbus, Ohio: University Council for Educational Administration, 1977.)

ducive. If a number of questions are answered negatively, the climate is not proper for implementing a system change.

Note that adequate time given to preparing an organization for change will be time well spent, for the results will reflect the preparatory efforts. This entire preparation stage is essential because it generates a commitment from all the participants, a sense of ownership with respect to the goals and the process, and sets the stage for successful movement toward the goal of integrating students with moderate to severe disabilities.

## CHOOSING THE FACILITATOR

Once the organization has prepared itself to begin the integration of students with moderate to severe disabilities, the initiator must consider and utilize every method that will insure success. One such method is to enlist the services of a consultant/facilitator—a person who is charged with the responsibility of orchestrating an organization through the change process.

The ideal facilitator is a person who understands the technical content of a proposed change in addition to the change process needed to achieve the specific goal. There are some instances, though, when a highly skilled facilitator can still successfully accomplish change without a detailed knowledge of special education or mainstreaming concepts. In this type of situation, the process for change is the facilitator's responsibility while the content of the change is the participant's responsibility.

The facilitator should avoid the problem-solving and advice-giving aspects of a consultant's role, and concentrate on helping the organization establish a process for change. Organization members must not perceive this person as having a bias toward any particular constituent group, solution to a problem, or style of programming. The facilitator should have credibility in the school district, and ideally should be financially, socially, and emotionally neutral in order to take the needed risks for the sake of the organization's overall mission.

Exhibit 4-2 can be used an as initiator's guide to match up the skills of a facilitator with the needs of the organization.

A facilitator should be willing and prepared to train others for continuing the process after the facilitator has left. Facilitators do their clients a great service if they plan for a mutually satisfying termination of the working relationship that leaves the organization with skills and the momentum necessary to continue with the change process on its own. A listing of responsibilities met by the facilitator is provided in Exhibit 4-3.

In selecting a facilitator whose skills are appropriate to the needs of the organization, the initiator should determine whether to use a facilitator from

---

**Exhibit 4-2** A Checklist for Selecting a Facilitator

*Characteristics*

_____ 1. Flexible
_____ 2. Ethical
_____ 3. Tolerates ambiguity
_____ 4. Open and sincere
_____ 5. Enjoys working with people
_____ 6. Optimistic and supportive
_____ 7. Good listener
_____ 8. Builds trust

*Skills/competencies*

_____ 9. Experience consulting
        _____ 9.1. communication
        _____ 9.2. team building
        _____ 9.3. problem solving
        _____ 9.4. conflict resolution
        _____ 9.5. planning
        _____ 9.6. motivation
        _____ 9.7. managing processes
        _____ 9.8. asking difficult questions
_____ 10. Experience diagnosing
        _____ 10.1. data collection and analysis
        _____ 10.2. evaluation
_____ 11. Experience educating
        _____ 11.1. training
        _____ 11.2. giving and receiving feedback
_____ 12. Experience establishing credibility across levels of the hierarchy
_____ 13. Experience as a linker
        _____ 13.1. identification of resources
        _____ 13.2. referral
_____ 14. Experience with group dynamics

*Experience*

_____ 15. Experience as a change agent facilitator
_____ 16. Experience implementing change
_____ 17. Experience with our system

---

*Source: The DISCO Manual: A Design for Implementing Systems Change in Organizations* by M. Heggelund, V. Lynch, J. Pruess, S. Soltman, and N. Zodrow, 1984, Seattle, WA: University of Washington. Unpublished manuscript.

**Exhibit 4-3** Responsibilities of the Facilitator

1. The facilitator provides leadership during meetings
   1.1 Provides structure for the process
   1.2 Maximizes participation of members
   1.3 Keeps group on task
2. The facilitator observes the process of systems change
   2.1 Observes and analyzes working groups
   2.2 Offers constructive feedback on both process and products
3. The facilitator communicates with others effectively and strengthens communication within the group
   3.1 Facilitates communication among participants
   3.2 Helps the group establish and institutionalize communication structures
4. The facilitator aids participants in problem solving
   4.1 Aids in data collection and analysis
   4.2 Facilitates decision making and hypothesis testing
   4.3 Provides assistance in evaluation
5. The facilitator aids the group in conflict resolution
6. The facilitator disengages from the change process and helps participants at the site take over functions
7. The facilitator educates the organization's members

*Source: The DISCO Manual: A Design for Implementing Systems Change in Organizations* by M. Heggelund, V. Lynch, J. Pruess, S. Soltman, and N. Zodrow, 1984, Seattle, WA: University of Washington. Unpublished manuscript.

outside or inside the system. There is no single best answer, as there are advantages and disadvantages in using either type.

An *internal facilitator* is employed on a full-time salary by the organization, yet is not part of the organization undergoing the change. In the case of a school district, for example, this might be someone with facilitation skills working within the district, but not in the department targeted for change.

On the one hand, an internal facilitator will have more knowledge about the organization than an outsider, including informal knowledge about the workings of the system that may be inaccessible to an outside facilitator. An insider probably also has more opportunity for continuous observation of activity within the organization, is better able to secure feedback at strategic points, and may be able to see where addditional support is needed to maintain the change process. And such a person is a logical choice if there are no funds to hire an external facilitator.

On the other hand, an internal facilitator may be more cautious in making suggestions, avoiding those areas that may threaten his or her own job within the larger organization or agency. Organization members may suspect a facilitator's objectivity because of perceived vested interests, and they may not be able to establish an open and trusting relationship with an insider perceived as having power within the organization. An internal facilitator has a biased insider's perspective, and thus may not be able to come up with fresh ideas; yet in seeking greater objectivity, an internal facilitator may become too detached from the needs and concerns of the group undergoing change. Finally, the role of facilitator may be an additional job responsibility and not be able to claim a person's full attention.

There are also advantages and disadvantages in regard to an external facilitator—one who is not a member of the organization undergoing change and therefore who probably does not have a vested interest in the change process. This person, because not directly affected by the change, can remain impartial and objective. Such a person can focus totally on moving constituents through the change process and developing their skills so that they can assume a greater responsibility at later stages of the change process.

On the other hand, an external facilitator, unless well prepared and perceptive, lacks familiarity with the context and history of the organization and its operational procedures. This individual cannot always be present when important decisions need to be made or when important issues arise. Finally, there is an expense involved in hiring an outside consultant as opposed to using an internal facilitator.

In summary, an internal facilitator understands the workings of the organization and may have a built-in rapport with the initiator, but also may be too close to the situation and the participants. An external facilitator brings a fresher, wider perspective and the promise of greater objectivity, but is deficient in knowledge about the organization and initially lacks rapport with the key players. The best solution would be to utilize an external facilitator for the initial stages of the change process and then have this person train an internal facilitator who can oversee the process after it has been instituted.

When looking for an internal facilitator, it is important to choose someone who works outside your department, program, or unit. Such a person might come from one of the following groups:

- school district consultants
- counselors
- department supervisors or coordinators (from other departments)
- special education coordinators
- teachers or parents with facilitation skills
- support personnel from other departments
- curriculum coordinators

- representatives of school district multidisciplinary teams
- someone whose responsibilities or job title has been changed to fill this role

An external facilitator could come from one of the following:

- faculty in colleges and universities in education or special education programs who do field consulting
- staff of special projects at colleges and universities that provide consultation, technical assistance, and facilitation to special education school personnel
- personnel with facilitation skills from regional education programs
- directors of federal programs
- state education department personnel and state department curriculum consultants
- personnel in staff development or program development
- school personnel with facilitation skills from another school district

## A Note About Timelines

A major factor in the change process is the element of time. A change that is to become habitual will require a major investment of time. Three to five years is not an unrealistic timeline to expect before a viable integrated model becomes routinized within a school organization. Because the lack of time may always be used as an easy excuse to resist innovation, it is good to establish timelines for any change within an organization. Establishing set timelines and sticking to them will alleviate frustration, disillusionment, burnout, and apathy among the participants in the change effort. Preparing the organization for change will require careful planning and enough time to answer the many questions and concerns of those most involved in the change, as well as increasing their comfort with the proposed change. Finding a facilitator who works well with your organization and establishing a rapport with the members will also take time. Some individuals may be able to change quickly, but a large organization probably will not.

## SUMMARY

Integration of students with moderate to severe disabilities into regular education settings can directly affect many staff members who may—or may not— feel adequately skilled to meet the special needs of these students. In order to lessen resistance and to build a sense of ownership in the integrated model, several steps are suggested, especially preparation of the school organization for change, and the use of a systematic and participatory change process.

Assessing your school district's feasibility for change will help identify any potential barriers that may impede the progress of implementation of an integrated model of service delivery for students with special needs. Additionally, the support and guidance of a facilitator who is skilled in organizational change processes is strongly recommended.

This chapter discussed several ways to insure the careful planning of the successful transition of moderately and severely disabled students from a self-contained educational setting into an integrated educational program. This attention to the details of preparing for change is an accurate reflection of the importance of planning in a change process.

## REFERENCES

Fullan, M. (1982). *The meaning of educational change.* New York: Teachers College Press.

Heggelund, M., Lynch, V., Pruess, J., Soltman, S., & Zodrow, N. G. Haring, Principal Investigator. (1984). *The DISCO manual: a design for implementing systems change in organizations.* Unpublished manuscript, Inservice Training and Program Development Systems, University of Washington, Seattle.

Heggelund, M., Haring, N.H., Lynch, V., Pruess, J., Soltman, S., & Zodrow, N. (1985). Systems change: A case study. *Remedial and Special Education, 6*(3), 44-51.

Paul, D.A. (1977). Change processes at the elementary, secondary, and post-secondary levels of education. In N. Nash & J. Culbertson (Eds.), *Linking processes in educational improvement: Concepts and applications.* Columbus, OH: University Council for Educational Administration.

I wish to thank Valerie Lynch, James Pruess, Zelalem Yilma, and Michael Berres for their guidance, editorial contributions, and very helpful comments.

Chapter 5

# Integration of Students with Severe Disabilities in the Madison Metropolitan School District

*Eileen F. McCarthy,* with *Michael Shoultz*

The Madison Metropolitan School District (MMSD) has been involved in the integration of students with severe handicaps for many years. Through the years, the district has moved from an exclusionary to inclusionary service delivery system. Currently the MMSD's total school population is approximately 22,000; of this number over 2,000 students receive special education services, ranging from minor modifications in the regular education program to self-contained special education placement. All students, regardless of the severity of their handicap, are served within regular education buildings. Of the approximately 2,000 special education students in the district, 220 are considered to have severe handicaps. *Severely handicapped* has been defined by the MMSD as:

> functioning in the lowest 1% of the population and whose primary disability is mental retardation at the moderate, severe, or profound level with or without accompanying disabilities in the areas of vision, hearing, communication, autism, physical anomalies, emotional disturbance, and/or medical problems. (Loomis, 1982, p. 1)

The purpose of this chapter is to describe the processes and strategies that have led to the MMSD's shift from an exclusionary to an inclusionary service delivery system. It is expected that program administrators may utilize this information in their own efforts toward integrating students with severe handicaps. A chronology of events that led to the initial inclusion of students with severe disabilities in the MMSD is provided, followed by a discussion of the factors that led to their integration. There is then a discussion of continued integration efforts and the lessons that were learned throughout the process. Finally, evaluation efforts and dissemination practices are examined in light of their implications for the program manager.

## HISTORICAL PERSPECTIVE

### From Exclusion to Inclusion

Special education programs have existed in Madison since the early 1900's. These programs operated under Wisconsin's long-standing permissive legislation (1918-1973). However, the students who initially received the benefit of public education were those with handicaps traditionally considered more mild. It was not until the late 1960's that educational programming was provided for students with moderate to severe disabilities. These programs and services were provided through a medical model which segregated these students in specialized environments "in the belief that they could not benefit from regular education or even in proximity of heterogeneous groupings of students" (Gruenewald and Loomis, in press). The early 1970's saw greater inclusion of students with severe and profound disabilities.

During the late 1960's, the district's programs for students with moderate to severe disabilities were located in two facilities: Sunnyside School and Lapham Elementary School. Sunnyside School was a segregated facility that housed most of the district's programs for students with moderate to severe mental retardation. Lapham Elementary was a regular elementary school with a separate wing which housed the district's program for students with orthopedic handicaps, regardless of age or functioning level, as well as a few units for students with moderate mental retardation. All other special education programs were provided in regular public schools with varying degrees of isolation depending on the number of students involved and the severity of the handicap. However, by and large the district's special education programs operated as a parallel system to the regular education program. The separation was due to "funding patterns, public and professional attitudes, and a first level of satisfaction on the part of parents that at least their children were in school and not at home or in an institution" (Loomis, 1982, p. 3).

In 1970, Sunnyside School was condemned and the district was forced to search for another facility. At this same time, a neighborhood school, Badger, was to close because of declining enrollments. Initially, Badger had been slated to become the district's maintenance garage for equipment. However, those involved in searching for a new facility to replace Sunnyside School were very much interested in Badger. It was seen as a favorable site since it was relatively new and accessible. It looked good to parents whose children had been attending a condemned building.

In 1970, Sunnyside School was closed and eight units for students classified as trainable mentally retarded were relocated at Badger. Students with the more severe disabilities continued to be excluded. It was not until the 1972–73 school year, when the district obtained a small Title VI grant from the Wisconsin Department of Public Instruction, that students with the most severe disabilities were included in Madison's special education system. This grant allowed for the inclusion of two classes for young students with sensory or orthopedic deficits, severe mental retardation, or behavioral problems. These classrooms were also housed in Badger School.

The inclusion of these two classes at Badger was important for at least two reasons. First of all, it marked the first attempt to include students who had been historically exluded from public education. And, of equal importance, a working relationship between the Madison Metropolitan School District and the University of Wisconsin-Madison's Department of Studies in Behavioral Disabilities was initiated.

In 1969, Professor Lou Brown became a faculty member at the university and established a training program for teachers of students with severe and profound handicaps. Professor Brown's major focus at that time was the development of housing and vocational opportunities in the community in order to prevent the need for institutionalization. Hence, in 1972, when teachers were sought to teach two new classes for students with severe disabilities that were being provided at Badger through the Title VI grant, graduates from Professor Brown's training program were hired. This began the "infusion of new blood" into Madison's special education teaching staff and became one of the first major links between the school district and the university (Muoio, 1983, p. 70).

In 1974, a three-year federal grant, Madison's Alternative to Zero Exclusion (MAZE), was awarded jointly to the MMSD and the university for the development of curriculum and expansion of services for students with severe handicaps. It is important to note that during this same period (1973–1975), both state and federal legislation mandated the provision of educational services to all students regardless of the severity of their handicaps.

Thus, through the influx of federal money, as well as the support of state and federal mandates, the provision of programs and services aimed at zero rejection were well underway. Consequently, the program at Badger School continued to grow, and as all the available space gradually became utilized, the district found there was a need for expansion (Muoio, 1983).

## Expansion Throughout the System: Early Integration Efforts

With the inclusion of more students with severe and profound disabilities in Badger School, staff began to feel the constraints of limited space. Yet while Badger lacked sufficient space, other schools in the district were facing declining enrollments. Consequently, due to the combination of declining enrollments, overcrowded conditions at Badger, the infusion of university influences (teachers and curriculum), and parental concerns regarding educational outcomes, early integration efforts within the MMSD began.

In 1971, one class of five-year old students with Down's syndrome from Badger School was placed in a regular education elementary school. It was felt that this would be the best place to start, since these students were young and had no physical or emotional disabilities. Subsequently, the success of this first attempt was followed by the integration of three other classes into regular schools. The progression of the integration started at the elementary level (1971–1975), then moved to the middle school level (1975–1976) and lastly the high school level (1976–1977), at which point classes were located on each side of town.

In some cases, the classes of students with moderate mental retardation were placed in buildings which already housed students with mild mental retardation; in other cases, the class of students with moderate mental retardation was the first class for students with retardation in the building. It is important to note that district administrators concluded that no particular advantage attaches to either sequence.

The integration of students with mild to moderate disabilities was so successful that by 1976, only 46 students—those with severe and profound mental retardation and other severe disabilities—remained at Badger. In 1977, due to a complex of factors, the decision was made to close Badger. At this time 30 students were integrated into Glendale Elementary. The remaining 16 students, primarily older nonambulatory students with severe disabilities, were placed in the orthopedic wing of Lapham Elementary.

## Integration of Students with Severe Disabilities: The Closing of Badger

Although the decision to close Badger School was not final until 1977, the process actually took place over several years (1971–1977). With each group to leave the segregated facility, more and more sophisticated and successful strategies were developed. One of the most successful strategies was the mobilization of several constituencies, including parents, teachers, and administrators. As a result, the thrust to move came from several different directions.

In 1977, when the decision was made to close Badger School, six classes for students with severe disabilities were assigned to Glendale School. The challenge that faced the MMSD was to take self-contained classes that had been accommodated in a school with an institutional-type setting and move them into a regular education setting, and do it in such a way as to benefit everyone involved. In describing this process of change, it is important to note that no one person can be identified as primarily responsible for the transition from an exclusionary to inclusionary model of service delivery. Certain actors clearly played key roles. As mentioned earlier, Professor Lou Brown of the University of Wisconsin was quite influential. A former MMSD coordinator of special education and principal of Badger School, who had left Madison to take a position with the federal agency responsible for special education (formerly the Bureau for the Educationally Handicapped [BEH] and now the Office of Special Education Programs [OSEP]) was a key influencer. However, in addition to these key actors, other general factors should be viewed as particularly influential in the integration of students with severe disabilities. A discussion of each follows.

*Management Decisions and Support*

The strategies for change involved support from high-level administrators and the development of linkages and interrelationships, bringing together implementers on a person-to-person basis. The decision to provide educational services within regular education buildings to all students, regardless of the severity of their handicaps, did not occur as a result of strong parental or advocacy pressure. As Stetson (1979a) noted:

> . . . it was motivated instead by a strong departmental commitment to the principles of normalization, to a system-wide belief that interaction between handicapped students is beneficial to both groups, and to strong superintendent support for a search for alternatives. (p. 54)

*The Role of the Superintendent*

Throughout the late 1960's and 1970's, the superintendent of schools demonstrated strong professional leadership with regard to special education and to integration throughout the system. This is evidenced not only by his search for a solution to declining enrollments, but also by his support for the commissioning of a study on accessibility for students with handicaps as required by Section 504 of the Rehabilitation Act of 1973 and by his decision to shift building administrators within the district.

*Declining enrollments.* Due to district-wide declining enrollment, the superintendent of schools recommended to the board of education that a number of schools be closed. A school closing plan was proposed and adopted by the board. Although a number of options were available, the superintendent decided to close, among others, Badger School and Lapham Elementary, which housed the orthopedic wing. An additional impetus for closing both Badger and Lapham came from the success of earlier integration efforts. Thus, this decision to close Badger and Lapham, partly due to the success of integration, resulted in the further promotion of integration of students with severe disabilities.

*504 study.* In the fall of 1977, the superintendent gave support to developing an accessibility study in order to implement Section 504 of the Rehabilitation Act of 1973. A district-wide task force made recommendations to the board of education which were adopted in early 1978. This resulted in the designation of 17 schools (of the district's 40) to become accessible and in the provision for their subsequent remodeling over the next three years.

Among the recommendations of the task force were the following: the development of physically accessible school sites for students at all instructional levels, the provisions of a range of support services at these sites in order to enable students with physical handicaps to participate with their chronological and instructional age peers in curricular and extracurricular activities, the provision of continued staff development and training, and the comunication of the district 504 Plan to the community. As a result, a series of inservice workshops were developed which targeted all administrators, regular and special education staff, and parents. The recommendations of the task force were a major factor in integration efforts over the next several years.

*Administrative shifts and changes.* An additional event of great impact, which occurred simultaneously with the district's school closings, was the superintendent's decision to shift building administrators in order to develop a closer match between their interests, skills, competencies, and the needs of the students to be served. As a result, thirteen administrators were shifted. In making these changes, the superintendent informed those involved that he would be asking the Director of Specialized Educational Services (now Integrated Student Services) for recommendations. Gruenewald and Loomis (in press) state that it was an unprecedented move for him to make such an announcement. Furthermore, "it was a tremendous declaration of support for a recognition of the significance of the handicapped population to be served" (p. 57).

## The Role of the Director of Special Education

During the late 1960's, the level of dissatisfaction from parents and professionals within the system regarding the outcomes of special education was so great that the superintendent dismissed virtually all of the special education administrators. This led to redesigning the system and developing a new philosophy. Efforts to diminish the separate system of special education were undertaken with the hiring of a new director in 1972 and a new set of special education administrators. Perhaps one of the most significant accomplishments during 1972–76 was the adoption of a set of clear goals designed by the director and adopted by the board of education that would set the stage and provide the legitimation of the integration efforts discussed throughout this chapter. These goals have undergone minor changes over the years, but they are the foundation for the system's present philosophical conception of "one instructional program that provides appropriate options to meet the needs of all students" (Gruenewald and Schroeder, 1979, p. 4). These goals called for the development of the following:

1. A comprehensive but flexible range of service options that will provide appropriate educational services to the full spectrum of children with handicapping conditions. This spectrum should encompass all children with handicapping conditions from severe through mild.
2. Systems of support to the regular or ordinary educational system designed to help it teach and manage a broader range of individual differences, thereby preventing undue labeling and segregation of children with handicapping conditions.
3. Closer working relationships with the community and its agencies to prepare the community to receive and understand persons with handicapping conditions. Efforts will also be made to coordinate school programs with other community programs to insure the continuity of education and development of the individual and to reduce unilateral and duplicative services.
4. Closer working relationships with parents of children with handicapping conditions to insure that appropriate and meaningful services are provided to all students and parents.
5. Evaluation mechanisms for describing and measuring positive student changes as the primary intended outcome of all services. (Madison Metropolitan School District, 1973)

It was also during this time that the director demonstrated support for inclusion of students with severe disabilities by his endorsement of a collaborative effort between the MMSD and the university in the sumbission of the MAZE grant.

At the time of appointment of the current director in 1976, initial integration efforts were well underway. With the demonstration that students with severe disabilities could be in regular schools, the role of the school as "caretaker" diminished rapidly. While curricular development had begun in segregated facilities through the MAZE grant, it became clear that greater attention needed to be focused on curriculum and instruction for this population in the regular schools. The director has clearly supported and fostered this progression through even stronger university collaboration.

Through his participatory management style and expertise as a problem solver, continued integration efforts have been extremely successful. The parallel systems of special and regular education have been dissolved through formal changes in the organizational structure brought about by the director's strong commitment to "one integrating instructional program with options for all students." This philosophical conception is based upon the following beliefs:

1. No student is too handicapped for placement in an appropriate educational program. All students have the right to be educated in the least restrictive environment.
2. Handicapped students should participate to the maximum extent possible in the regular education program: the academic component, the non-academic component, and the extracurricular program.
3. The special education programs should be a part of the school district's total instructional program—not a parallel system! We believe in one instructional program with options for all students.
4. All students should be in chronological age appropriate environments.
5. All necessary related services a student needs to fully participate should be provided.
6. There must be a scope and sequence of the curriculum, grades K-12, ages 3–21.
7. Programs for the handicapped must be geographically distributed within the district.
8. Placements of students in special education programs must be determined by multidisciplinary assessment of a student's educational needs.
9. Parent involved must be emphasized in the assessment and instruction of handicapped students.
10. Segregation versus nonsegregation: Segregated service delivery models are disadvantageous for the following reasons: (a) Exposure to nonhandicapped student models is absent or minimal. (b) Handicapped students tend to learn handicapping skills, attitudes and values. (c) Teachers tend to strive for the resolution of handicapping problems at the expense of developing functional community reference skills. (d) Lack of exposure to handicapped students limits the probability that skills, attitudes, and values of nonhandicapped

students will become constructive, tolerant, and appropriate.

11. Interactions with nonhandicapped aged peers: Upon completion of school, handicapped persons will live in public, minimally segregated, heterogeneous communities. Therefore, they will have constant exposure to nonhandicapped citizens. It seems imperative that the educational experience should be representative in preparing the handicapped students as well as the nonhandicapped students to function independently.

12. Architectural barriers and building facilities: In the not too distant future, the majority of public buildings will be modified for accessibility to handicapped persons. Since this is one of the legal mandates of the federal government, building segregated special school facilities will no longer be a necessity.

13. A functional and naturalized curriculum: For moderately and severely handicapped students it is essential that educators plan a longitudinal education curriculum that prepares them to function as independently as possible in desegregated, post-school, social, recreational, vocational and domestic environments. (Gruenewald and Schroeder, 1979, pp. 1–2)

These 13 beliefs have been promulgated and extensively supported by the director. They are the foundation and justification for integration efforts and for having one instructional program.

### The Role of the Principal

The role of the building principal cannot be underestimated. As was seen with the final move from Badger to Glendale, the initial success of integration was largely due to the fact that the principal was hand-picked by the superintendent for his ability to solve problems and change work. While a supportive principal does not ensure success, a nonsupportive principal almost ensures failure.

### Preparation of the Larger School Environment

The move to an integrated educational setting from Badger to Glendale was preceded by careful planning and preparation. The combined leadership of an enthusiastic principal in both the sending and the receiving school, as well as the availability of a full semester of planning time, enabled those involved to systematically implement the transition strategies. The following anecdotal chronology was provided by the program support teacher who was an integral part of the process.

Prior to the transition from Badger, the principal, a representative group of teachers, and the steering committee from Glendale observed the program at Badger and talked with staff in order to better understand their needs and priorities. Following these observations, three levels of inservice were planned. The first level was to inservice professionals in both buildings, the second was to inservice the parents and the community, and the third was to inservice the students.

Professional inservice began with each classroom teacher from Glendale having the opportunity to spend an afternoon observing at Badger School. Each teacher was also asked to take a parent from the community with them when they went to visit. A total of seven groups ranging from four to seven people in each group took advantage of that observation opportunity. Following the visit by the Glendale staff, the Badger staff then had an opportunity to come to Glendale School to observe classes and tour the building.

Shortly after these observations, two afternoon inservice programs were planned. The first inservice program was held at Badger for the Glendale staff. All Badger staff members had an opportunity to share their job responsibilities as well as the educational programs and skill levels of the students in their class. Glendale staff had an opportunity to interact, ask questions, and obtain points of clarification. That inservice program was followed by a similar program at Glendale School, where staff from Badger had an opportunity to ask questions in order to gain an understanding of Glendale's needs and of their program.

Parents from both schools were involved in these inservice programs. The principal met with the steering committee of parents from Badger School in order to preview some of their concerns and answer some questions. He met as well with his own parent steering committee at Glendale School. An evening meeting was held for all parents who would be sending children to Glendale School the next school year. The principal reviewed exactly what Glendale School's program design looked like for that current year, and then reviewed with the parents the changes and the program design for the following year. The parents attending were then divided into small discussion groups. A staff member from each categorical and grade level area also joined each small group in order to answer parents' questions.

At the beginning of the new school year, the instructional design was implemented. At the same time, staff developed an inservice design for children in grades K–5. A teacher of the severely handicapped program and a support staff member from that unit were assigned to each grade level. They, in turn, teamed up to design a plan for sharing appropriate information regarding this new program with the specific grade levels. Because of the cooperation between regular educators and special educators, this information was presented very successfully at all grade levels. The teachers of the severely handicapped students and the support staff presented to the children the positive aspects of what the handicapped students could do. Questions from children at the different grade levels indicated the need for information appropriate to each level. Questions for kindergarten students often focused on matter-of-fact ideas: "How does he get on the bus?" "How does the wheelchair work?" "Will I catch it?" The sophistication of the fifth graders emerged in other questions: "Was it hereditary?" "Does he have brain damage?" "What are the possibilities for improvement?"

The joint planning and process development that occurred in these first inservices continue to be part of the ongoing program, for teams of teachers (regular education and special education) still need to plan appropriate and meaningful activities for all students. Gruenewald and Loomis (in press) state that "such training continues to provide the impetus for a problem-solving approach to student learning and behavior versus the avoidance behavior of referring the child out of the classroom" (p. 57).

## Additional Factors

In addition to the management decisions and support and the preparation of the larger school environment described above, the following factors also have been instrumental in facilitating the integration of students with severe disabilities: (i) university collaboration, (ii) parent involvement, and (iii) state and federal legislation.

### University Collaboration

From the early 1970's, the board of education has supported the application for federally-funded projects that focus on the development of new approaches for the education of students with moderate to severe retardation. Many of these have been in conjunction with the University of Wisconsin-Madison. The still vital partnership between the MMSD and the university has been mutually beneficial and has provided the mechanism for exchanging ideas, training future staff, demonstrating new instructional technology, and conducting specific research in the area of education of students with handicaps (Gruenewald and Loomis, in press).

As a result of the working relationship between the university and the MMSD cooperative grant and research activities, it became increasingly evident that the educational programs being provided to students with severe disabilities did not prepare them adequately to be independent young adults. The gains made in school did not relate to gains in nonschool environments. This realization led to a major reorientation in the development of curriculum and in the instructional models used for teaching students with severe disabilities in the Madison schools. Consequently, the curriculum and instructional strategies described by Brown et al. (1978) came into being and substantially altered the delivery of special education in the MMSD. Clearer alternatives to the nonfunctional "readiness" curriculum had been developed. It became less acceptable to plan curriculum based on readiness skills for or the developmental approach to academic, social, language and vocational skills, especially for the adolescent (J. Schroeder, Personal Communication, September 17, 1985). Strategies for determining what to teach and how to teach relate directly to four functional domains: vocational, domestic, recreational/leisure, and community functioning skills. Clearly what evolved in Madison was an instructional competence and a clear direction for meeting the educational needs of students with severe handicaps.

*Parent Involvement*

The extent of parent involvement and support in planning for the education of students with severe disabilities was critical. From the beginning, parent groups at Badger were active; many of these parents continue to serve as parent group leaders in the schools that their children now attend. The roles that they play have been, and are, numerous. Parents act as advocates, state legislation developers, and participants in study groups and task forces. Loomis (1982) indicates that in Madison, parents have been instrumental in working with professional staff, community resources, and employers to refine, adjust, improve, and expand programs in order to obtain the ultimate goals for students. Furthermore, professional staff are committed to resolving problems by maintaining close communication with parents. "Parent pressure, although constant, is generally healthy, constructive, and encouraging. The fact that participation in program development has been mandated is somewhat irrelevant in this district" (p. 6).

*State and Federal Legislation*

Another force which gave further impetus to integration efforts was the implementation of both state and federal laws. At the time that Public Law 94–142 and Wisconsin's state legislation (Chapter 115) were passed, 1975 and 1973 respectively, Madison had initiated educational programming for all students regardless of severity of handicapping condition. With the implementation of the small Title VI grant and the MAZE grant, the district had embarked upon extending services to those students who once were excluded. Thus the passage of both Chapter 115 and PL 94–142 can be viewed as providing legitimization to the district's service delivery system (Loomis, 1982).

## CONTINUED INTEGRATION EFFORTS

### Further Program Expansion

A particular event had implications that aided the expansion of the program after the initial move from Badger. When Badger closed in 1977, the 16 students who were not moved to Glendale but rather to the orthopedic wing of Lapham and then the following year to LaFollette High School provided the impetus for the integration of students from Central Wisconsin Center (CWC), an institution within the boundaries of the MMSD, in 1979. The primary reason that these 16 students were moved to the orthopedic wing of a regular elementary school for one year was their age and severity of disability. Plainly stated, these were the older students who were nonambulatory and more severely disabled and who required a physically accessible building. Except for Glendale Elementary, Lapham Elementary was the only accessible school; thus, students with orthopedic disabilities, regardless of their functional age level, were housed there.

At that time, the 504 Task Force was convened in order to devise the plan which would result in structural accessibility throughout the MMSD. Since there weren't any accessible middle schools or high schools for students who were nonambulatory, the orthopedic wing had become the holding place until the recommendations devised by the 504 Task Force were implemented. The 504 Task Force recommendations included the modification of LaFollette High School and required "substantial resources from both regular and exceptional education for curricular development, development of appropriate instructional space, materials and equipment, and staff development" (Madison Metropolitan School District, 1978, p. 10). Once the 16 students with severe disabilities were located in the high school and the appropriate staff development undertaken, the ground had been broken for the inclusion of those students living at CWC, which took place a few years later.

### Staff Development

Through the years, the MMSD has been extremely active in providing needed training and development activities to school personnel as well as to parents, students, and the community at large. This is evidenced by the planning and preparation involving both staff and the larger school community during the time of Badger's closing. However, continually ensuring that all staff (teachers, aides, and related service personnel) are knowledgeable in up-to-date educational approaches and curricula poses a challenge for any program providing services for students with severe disabilities. The MMSD has met this challenge by supporting program development and expansion through on-going staff development and inservice training.

The MMSD has an extensive staff development program that provides two inservice training days per year for all teaching staff. Furthermore, the district requires that all school personnel complete six academic credits every four years. In fulfilling this requirement, personnel can enroll in courses at the university, design independent study courses that relate to students needs, or take courses in the district's inservice training project, the Madison Exchange. The Madison Exchange offers courses taught by teachers, university personnel, and others. A wide range of subject matter is covered, from issues specific to students with handicapping conditions to general courses on report writing and educational problem solving. Courses for teachers serving students with severe disabilities have included Strategies for Longitudinal Curriculum Development for Students with Severe Handicaps, Designing Individualized Communication Programs for Students with Severe Handicaps, and Intermediate Sign Language.

As has been the case in most other areas discussed in this chapter, the influence of the university in these efforts has been significant. Many of the teachers are graduates from the university's Department of Studies in Behavioral Disabilities. However, university personnel are also active in other areas related to staff and program development, such as providing consultation to teachers and other staff, participating on various task forces on curriculum and instructional strategies for students with severe disabilities, and teaching courses through the Madison Exchange. From initial integration efforts to today's continuing efforts, staff and program development activities have been instrumental in ensuring meaningful and appropriate educational programming for students with severe disabilities.

Finally, the MMSD has been particularly proactive in its focus on the transition from school to work, instruction in nonschool environments, and follow-up of graduates from programs for students with severe disabilities. It was only after the MMSD focused upon these activities that other districts across the nation began to do likewise and federal support and intervention for these initiatives developed.

## LESSONS LEARNED

During the evolution from an exclusionary to an inclusionary special education system, the MMSD did not have a model to follow, so certain practices that were attempted did not always result in the intended consequences. However, the lessons learned from the earlier integration attempts have helped expand the program after its initial implementation. More specifically, the closing of Badger helped integration proponents realize that certain circumstances should be avoided in the future. Among these are the following.

- The movement of 30 students at one time to one school (Badger to Glendale) tended to create a "ghetto effect" or a school within a school. The number of students with handicaps in a given building should not exceed the natural proportion, i.e., the proportion of students with severe disabilities at any single school setting should not greatly exceed their proportion in the general school population.
- The movement of handicapped students to a school without regard to the chronological age appropriateness of the placement could further isolate those students from other students, who might be considerably younger or older.
- When new programs encroach on physical space and are perceived as reducing current or future resources, great resistance is encountered.

The MMSD staff has learned from these situations. Throughout the change process, the presence of a clear direction, provided by the articulation of goals by the Director of Special Education during the 1973–76 period, enabled the system to plan for change and proved to be an invaluable foundation.

## Implications for the Program Manager

In reflecting upon the chronology of events that led to the closing of Badger School and the subsequent integration of students with severe disabilities, it is evident that many considerations need to be addressed by principals and program coordinators when placing and managing programs in a school building, including the following (Loomis, 1982, pp. 10–11):

1. Handicapped students should be in physically accessible schools that are chronological age appropriate.
2. Handicapped students should be placed in instructional groupings which match their learning level and style.
3. The number of severely handicapped students in a building should not far exceed the normal proportion of handicapped in the community population.

4. Physical, occupational, and speech and language therapy services should be integrated into the instructional program.

5. Classrooms should not be segregated within the building but assigned throughout the building with the same considerations which apply to areas assigned to the nonhandicapped so as to avoid a ghetto effect.

6. Student schedules should contribute to the integration of handicapped and nonhandicapped students in all instructional and extracurricular activities.

7. Adaptive allocations must be provided as necessary; team teaching is frequently appropriate; resources for instructional supplies in mainstream classes must be provided.

8. Opportunities for heterogeneous grouping with higher functioning students must be systematically sought and provided.

9. Opportunities for interaction with nonhandicapped students must be systematically sought and provided.

10. Student and staff and parent orientation must be provided.

11. Transition staffings are essential when individual students progress from one school to another; orientation should be provided for groups of students progressing from one school to another.

12. Adequate paraprofessional resources must be available; volunteer resources can be used to advantage.

13. Special staff must recognize they are an integral part of the total staff and assume the range of responsibility and assignments in committees, club sponsorships, and coaching that are necessary for school operations.

These considerations are not exhaustive. Furthermore, they have changed through the years as integration became more and more successful. The program manager should attend to these considerations or strategies in collaboration with the building principal to make integration work and to avoid some of the unintended consequences encountered by the MMSD.

## EVALUATION EFFORTS

### Internal Evaluation

A key component vital to continued improvement of programs is systematic evaluation which may take many forms. Evaluations may be conducted internally in an ongoing manner, both formally and informally, or they may take the form of empirical research conducted by external sources.

One measure of the effectiveness of any educational program is the performance of its graduates in their subsequent environments, i.e., the domestic, vocational, and recreational environments of the larger adult society. Through a contract awarded by the United States Department of Education, Office of Special Education, Division of Innovation and Development to the University of Wisconsin-Madison and the Madison Metropolitan School District in 1979, a follow-up study (VanDeventer et al., 1981) of students with severe handicaps who were formerly enrolled in educational programs offered by the district was conducted. In an attempt to at least assume partial accountability, information secured during 1979 about the current life situations of severely handicapped graduates of the years 1971-1978 (Badger) was analyzed to determine whether the preparatory educational programs to which those persons were exposed were the most appropriate. The intent of this evaluation was to determine what improvements or modifications in education service delivery models, curricula, etc., might be warranted, so that beneficial changes could be made as soon as possible.

In the years 1971-1978, 53 students with moderate to severe handicaps graduated from the MMSD. Of that number, only one is currently working in the community. In the years from 1979-85, 68 students graduated—54 of these are currently working in the community. This demonstrates that those students who were educated in a segregated facility via a caretaker model (1971-78) continued to need to be taken care of after graduation. If only one graduate of those years is working in the community compared with 54 of 68 graduates of integrated settings (utilizing curricular strategies that are functional in nature), the evidence in support of integration is overwhelming.

While vocational strategies continue to be developed and refined, evaluation of living arrangements of graduates have pointed to the need for further emphasis on curriculum strategies related to the domestic and recreation/leisure domains. It should be noted that the results of analysis of follow-up data has effected improvements in curricular strategies across all domains. Through work with parents, optimum goals for students are determined, resulting in the development of appropriate individualized curriculum to achieve those goals.

Aside from the follow-up study of graduates, evaluation of the impact of integration on students has been primarily through informal or subjective sources. A multitude of informal and anecdotal reports are consistently encouraging, while complaints from the community, staff, or parents are limited, quite specific, and resolved promptly. According to the Program Coordinator for Mental Retardation Programs, informal feedback shows there is more acceptance of the severely handicapped than of students with less severe learning problems. For instance, it is more likely that the high school principal will have to deal with nonhandicapped students ridiculing the behaviors of the emotionally disturbed or mildly retarded students than with any harassment of a student with severe disabilities. More students of any age volunteer to work or play with students with disabilities than complain about sitting near such students in the lunch room (Loomis, 1982).

## External Evaluation

In addition to the internal evaluation described above, the MMSD underwent an external evaluation (conducted in 1982 by Steven Taylor of Syracuse University) of programs for children with severe disabilities. He stated that the MMSD, with the support and assistance of the University of Wisconsin-Madison, had implemented a number of innovative strategies that prepared children with severe handicaps to live in their home communities and participate in normal patterns of life. These strategies included the following (p. 1):

- integration of children with severe disabilities in regular schools
- a functional, community-referenced curriculum
- integrated vocational placements for middle and high school students
- program support for teachers and other school personnel
- educating institutionalized children in local public schools
- administrative leadership and support for integration

In addition to the Taylor evaluation, several case studies have been written about the events in Madison, two of which are of particular significance here. The Bureau of Education for the Handicapped and the Office of Civil Rights funded a project to examine six sites considered successful in implementing the least restrictive environment for students with severe disabilities. The MMSD was one of the six. As a result of her study, Stetson (1979b) identified seven administrative factors as critical in serving students with severe disabilities in the least restrictive environment. A critical administrative factor is defined as "an element within the school or the community which is under the focus of control of an administrator and is deemed necessary for the successful inclusion of severely handicapped students in the least restrictive environment" (p. 25). These factors are:

1. an appropriate service delivery plan for students with severe disabilities
2. organizational support for the education of students with severe disabilities

3. personnel assigned for the provision of administrative assistance and instructional leadership
4. positive attitudes among school personnel toward students with severe disabilities
5. a responsive staff development program
6. acceptance of the concept of integration and the least restrictive environment by the nonhandicapped community
7. acceptance of the concept of integration and least restrictive environment by parents of students with severe disabilities

In reflecting upon these seven factors, Stetson (1979b) concluded the following regarding the MMSD:

> The Madison Metropolitan School District offers an excellent example of the positive impact of strong, consistent, and well informed administrative leadership on the acceptance of severely handicapped students into the Least Restrictive Environment. . . . Careful cooperative planning occurs before any major move is taken; decisions are accompanied by attention to the underlying concepts and processes; actions are evaluated. . . . With its strong administrative support for the concept of the Least Restrictive Environment and with its creative, long-range planning to guide the implementation of this complex concept, the Madison Metropolitan School District deserves its reputation for programming excellence. (p. 70)

The second case study (Brinker, 1982) was funded by the Office of Education and conducted by the Educational Testing Service to evaluate the integration of students with severe disabilities into regular education and community settings. The MMSD was among fourteen school districts located in nine states involved in this study. The purpose was to describe the degree and quality of integration in terms of the interactions between handicapped and nonhandicapped students; to explore the educational context which influenced the degree and quality of integration; and to determine whether integration had an impact on the education of students with severe disabilities and on the attitudes of nonhandicapped students towards students with severe disabilities. The results of the study provided statistically significant evidence of the following (Madison Metropolitan School District, 1983, p. 2):

1. Social interactions with other students occur at a higher rate in integrated settings when compared to the same students' rate of interaction in segregated settings.

2. These interactions are more frequently reinforced by nonhandicapped students than by handicapped students.
3. Social interactions of severely handicapped students in integrated settings are influenced more by antecedent and concurrent features of the educational contents than by the degree of severity of these students' handicaps.
4. The rate of interaction with nonhandicapped students is significantly related to the proportion of educational objectives achieved at the end of the year, even when the severity of the students' handicap is controlled for statistically.
5. The amount of interaction between severely handicapped students in integrated settings is a significant negative predictor of the attitudes of nonhandicapped students in integrated schools.

The internal evaluation efforts described have assessed the impact of the program on specific students and the effectiveness of the program as a whole. The evaluations by Stetson, Brinker, and Taylor concern larger issues of program effectiveness (utilizing both qualitative and quantitative methodologies), and serve as examples for other administrators who may wish to evaluate ongoing efforts.


## DISSEMINATION PRACTICES

The MMSD is committed to the dissemination of information regarding the education of students with severe disabilities. The district has been particularly successful in implementing the following dissemination practices: (1) site visitation coupled with opportunities for discussions, and (2) sharing of curriculum products and strategies. A brief description of each follows.

Visitation to various MMSD sites in which students with severe disabilities are educated take place daily. It is felt that these visitations, coupled with the opportunity for discussion, are extremely effective in disseminating information and helping to change other systems' service delivery models for students with severe disabilities. Visitations are coordinated by the MMSD and university personnel and are usually requested by administrators, parents, teachers, and government officials. Included have been representatives from most of the 50 states, several European countries, and Australia and New Zealand.

The sharing of curriculum products and strategies has taken place mainly through developing written materials and giving presentations across the country and around the world. Since 1971, the University of Wisconsin-Madison and the MMSD have produced 15 volumes of curricular information related to the provision of educational services to students with severe disabilities. Many of the papers contained in the volumes have been revised and republished in various professional journals and books. Furthermore, several research, policy, and vocational strategy papers have been developed in conjunction with university personnel.

Presentations by university staff and the MMSD staff have frequently taken place at national, state, and local conferences. In addition, numerous requests are received from education agencies, universities, and parent organizations for on-site technical assistance and consultation concerning the education of students with severe disabilities. At least 50 on-site consultations are done by university and MMSD personnel yearly, reaching a wide variety of audiences. Papers have been presented to international audiences as well. Slide presentations which picture students with severe disabilities engaged in activities which demonstrate the success of curricular strategies have been developed for dissemination.

These activities are an integral part of dissemination and are encouraged by personnel from both the MMSD and the university. Informal and formal feedback from around the country and the world on the effects of dissemination practices continue to be positive.

## CONCLUSION

While certain events and processes described throughout the chapter cannot be replicated, many can be. Particular attention should be paid to the establishment of a philosophy for integration concomitant with the adoption of goal statements, thereby providing a basis and clear direction for change. The administrator should recognize the importance of organizational structure to the implementation of change. The establishment of linkages and interrelationships is critical: lines of communication must be well established and it must be evident that the program has the support of higher-level management. Furthermore, the professionalism of the staff must be recognized and supported through extensive ongoing staff development and training.

REFERENCES

Brinker, R.P. (1982, October). *The rate and quality of social behavior of severely handicapped students in integrated and nonintegrated settings.* Paper presented at the Integration Evaluation Project Conference, Educational Testing Service, Princeton, NJ.

Brown, L., Hamre-Nietupski, S., Lyon, S., Branston, M.B., Falvey, M., & Gruenewald, L. (Eds.) (1978). *Curricular strategies for developing longitudinal interactions between severely handicapped students and others and curricular strategies for teaching severely handicapped students to ac-*

*quire and perform skills in response to naturally-occurring cues and correction procedures.* (Volume 8, Pt. 1). Madison, WI: Madison Metropolitan School District.

Gruenewald, L.J., & Loomis, R. (in press). Evolving organizational structures in special education: The Madison example. In E.F. McCarthy, & D.D. Sage (Eds.), *Proceedings of the University Council for Educational Administration, Council on the Study of Leadership Behavior and Field Practices in Special Education Administration, Career Devlopment Seminar on Evolving Organization Structures in Special Education* (pp. 47-70). Cambridge, MA: Connections Information Service.

Gruenewald, L.J., & Schroeder, J. (1979, November). *Integration of moderately and severely handicapped students in public schools.* Paper presented at the Organization for Economic Cooperation and Development Conference, Paris, France.

Loomis, R. (1982, October). *Integration of severely handicapped students in the Madison Metropolitan School District.* Paper presented at the Integration Evaluation Project Conference, Educational Testing Service, Princeton, NJ.

Madison Metropolitan School District (1973). *Program document: Specialized educational services.* Madison, WI: Author.

Madison Metropolitan School District (1978). *Task force report on Section 504, Subpart D—Preschool, elementary, and secondary education.* Madison, WI: Author.

Madison Metropolitan School District (1983, December 1). *Evaluation of the integration of severely handicapped students in regular education and community settings.* (Instructional Services Division Report). Madison, WI: Author.

Muoio, G.T. (1983). *A case study of innovation adoption: The integration of severely handicapped children into typical public schools.* Unpublished doctoral dissertation, Syracuse University, Syracuse, NY.

Stetson, F.E. (1979a). *Critical administrative factors which facilitate the successful inclusion of severely handicapped students in the least restrictive environment.* Unpublished doctoral dissertation, University of Maryland, College Park, MD.

Stetson, F.E. (1979b). *Critical administrative factors which facilitate the successful inclusion of severely handicapped students in the least restrictive environment.* Washington, DC: Office of Civil Rights and Bureau of Education for the Handicapped.

Taylor, S.T. (1981). *Making integration work: Strategies for educating students with severe disabilities in regular schools.* Syracuse, NY: Syracuse University, Special Education Resource Center.

Taylor, S.T. (1982). *Metropolitan Madison Public Schools—A model integrated program for children with severe disabilities.* Syracuse, NY: Syracuse University, Special Education Resource Center.

VanDeventer, P., Yelinek, N., Brown, L., Schroeder, J., Loomis, R., & Gruenewald, L. (1981). A follow-up examination of severely handicapped graduates of the Madison Metropolitan School District from 1971-78. In L. Brown, D. Baumgart, I. Pumpian, J. Nisbet, A. Ford, R. Loomis, & J. Schroeder (Eds.), *Educational programs for severely handicapped students* (Vol. 11). Madison, WI: Madison Metropolitan School District.

---

The authors are indebted to the following persons from the Madison Metropolitan School District who provided valuable input for this chapter: Dr. Lee Gruenewald, Director of Integrated Services; Jack Schroeder, Coordinator of Student Services; Ruth Loomis, former Coordinator of Student Services; and Pat VanDeventer, Program Support Teacher.

Chapter 6

# Educating Students with Severe Handicapping Conditions "Side-by-Side"

Jo Thomason

## HISTORICAL REVIEW

The Albuquerque Public Schools (APS), located in the middle Rio Grande Valley, serve one-third of New Mexico's school-aged population. The district's 78,000 students attend 116 schools in a geographical area larger than the state of Rhode Island. Its students have rich and diverse cultural backgrounds, and come from all socioeconomic levels. Approximately 37.8% of the student body are of Hispanic origin, 3.4% are Black, 1.5% Asian, 2.5% Indian, and 54.6% Anglo. A great many different languages and dialects are spoken by these students in their homes. Faculty and staff have the same rich heritage as do the 12,000 students in special education programs for students with handicaps.

Special education is relatively new to Albuquerque and to New Mexico. The first special education class in the APS was opened in 1955 and served children diagnosed as trainable mentally handicapped. The program grew slowly through the 1950's and 1960's. The 1970's was a period of rapid growth, produced by pressure from strong parent groups, by litigation, local Board support, and legislative changes. In the 1980's, growth, with the exception of programs for gifted students, slowed dramatically, and in 1985 it appeared to level off at approximately 967 programs serving both students who are handicapped and those who are gifted.

In 1970, Buena Vista School was opened as a segregated facility designed to serve students with a diagnosis of mental retardation. Most students were in the trainable mentally handicapped range of intelligence and were both ambulatory and toilet trained. Children with more severe handicapping conditions were placed at the state institution or remained at home. They were not served by any educational program. As the city of Albuquerque grew geographically, a number of parents in the northeast section became concerned with the busing distance and time to Buena Vista School and they requested that a program be opened closer to their home. In response to their request, a class for elementary age students was opened in a neighborhood school. The preparation of the school and community was not sufficient, and the small numbers of students in a geographically large district limited the amount of support available from district-level personnel. The class and its students remained isolated within the school, and students were not integrated into the social or academic activities of the school. As a result, the principal found that there were heavy demands on his time and insufficient technical assistance was available to the teacher. At the end of that academic year, the program was closed with concurrence from both parents and administration.

There was, however, a commitment from both the district and the parents to "try again," but with a different model. These events were the impetus for the conceptualization and implementation of the Side-by-Side model still in use in the APS. The term *Side-by-Side* was selected in an effort to convey to parents, staff, and community that students with handicaps would not be "dumped" into regular classes without support, but that they would enter an individualized special education program while attending school with their nonhandicapped peers.

The Side-by-Side component at McCollum Elementary School was opened in the fall of 1973. Many of the basic components of the model introduced at that time are still integral to the program today. A special educator was selected to be the assistant principal. The appointment of a trained special educator as assistant principal assures the availability of on-site technical assistance for the staff, and it enables the principal, while also involved in the special education program, to have sufficient time to manage the entire school and deal with all parents and students. This ensures that the quality of the general education program is positively, rather than negatively, impacted by the special education program.

Advance preparation of the school staff, student body, and community was conducted. General education teachers were offered an opportunity to transfer to another school should they feel unable to work comfortably in a total school environment which included children with moderate to severe handicapping conditions. While no teachers requested such a transfer, they expressed appreciation that such an offer had been made.

The school plant was minimally remodeled to provide additional and accessible bathrooms, an indoor area for physical education, and expanded office space for the school nurse (who came five instead of two days per week), a speech therapist, and the assistant principal. McCollum, typical of Albuquerque elementary schools, is a one-story facility, so additional remodeling for accessibility was not necessary. All classrooms have doors opening directly to the outside, thus simplifying disaster evacuation procedures.

The program opened in the fall of 1973 and served approximately 40 students in 7 classrooms, each staffed with a teacher and an aide. The original remodeling of the site at McCollum provided classrooms for moderately and severely handicapped students in one wing of the building. Administrators and support services for the program were in the same wing. Thus, interaction between children who were handicapped and those who were not was somewhat impeded. Interaction did occur in the lunchroom, on the playground, and at assemblies. Classroom integration began slowly and was accomplished on a student-by-student basis. Most such integration was arranged by classroom teachers who approached a regular classroom teacher to suggest integration of a special class student.

## EXPANSION

Over the next three years, the program at McCollum grew in numbers. Parents were offered a choice, for elementary age students, between placement in the program at Buena Vista and the one at McCollum. Increasing numbers of parents selected placement at McCollum. At the same time, some program elements began to be refined. Some special classes were moved out of the original wing and regular classes moved into their place. Thus, in a gradual manner, the special classes began to be dispersed throughout the school. Classroom integration was increased and regular classroom students began coming to the special classes for a portion of their school day, creating the first formal model of reverse integration used in the APS.

The impetus for program expansion to the midschool level was, again, provided by parents, who requested an age-appropriate regular school campus for children becoming too old to continue at McCollum (Brown et al., 1983). This request was made in the spring of 1976. A midschool site, Madison, was selected, remodeled over the summer, and a Side-by-Side program started the following fall. The same steps to prepare parents, staff, and community were followed as had been used at McCollum. As our level of sophistication had increased, at least slightly, the preparation of personnel was accomplished somewhat more smoothly.

At the Madison site, we did encounter some new problems. At that time all midschools were impacted in terms of student body size. Because of limited space in the main building, a large number of portables had to be moved onto the campus. Portable buildings were utilized by both regular and special classes while some special classes were housed in the main building.

Remodeling portable buildings in order to provide bathroom facilities and access by students with physical disabilities proved expensive and has never been as satisfactory as the remodeling of classrooms in a permanent building. Problems of access to outlying buildings are exacerbated because New Mexico's climate and water scarcity dictates dirt playgrounds, which become muddy during periods of rain or snow and dusty during high winds.

In 1978, the continued aging of students at both McCollum and Madison dictated the need for expansion to an age-appropriate high-school campus. The decision to open a program at Manzano High School initiated the most difficult phase of the Side-by-Side program. At the time the decision was made, the program configuration was as follows. The Side-by-Side component at McCollum was overcrowded for two reasons: more and more parents were requesting an integrated rather than a segregated site, and students were being "held back" from midschool due to overcrowding at Madison. Another elementary school, Mark Twain, was serving as an integrated site, but the special education component was not conceptually a Side-by-Side program, had no special education administrator, and was beginning to negatively impact the regular school program. Finally, Madison was overcrowded because more parents were selecting an integrated program and students were being held on the midschool campus for lack of a high-school program.

At the same time the student population at the segregated site, Buena Vista, had declined as parents opted for a less restrictive environment. The elementary age population was about 15 students and the midschool age population was approximately 40. Conversely, all high-school age students with moderate to severe retardation were being served at Buena Vista, with the exception of a few older students who were being held at Madison. The large majority of older students at Buena Vista had never attended school on a regular school campus. During the years of program initiation at McCollum and Madison, the parents of these students had selected a segregated site and, in addition, were a part of the parent group who first fought for public school services for their children. Many were veterans of the days when their children had been turned away from the public schools because no services were available. The city, and the school district, were in a growth period and the geographical expansion of both was increasing busing time and distance for some students. Some parents of students at Buena Vista were requesting an integrated program site for their children.

Analysis of the student population remaining at Buena Vista indicated that opening a high-school program and removing all students whose parents had requested an age-appropriate program would reduce the Buena Vista population to the point that maintaining a quality program at a segregated site would no longer be feasible. The analysis was based on student counts, the residential locations of all students in all programs, and discussions with parents, advocacy groups, and the school administration. Following this analysis, the Special Education Department made recommendations to the administration and the Board of Education. The recommendations were that a second elementary site be opened across town from McCollum at Atrisco School, a second midschool site to be opened across town from Madison at Taft School, a high-school program be opened at Manzano, and Buena Vista be closed.

All of these recommendations had strong support from a majority of parents, from advocacy groups such as the local Association for Retarded Citizens (ARC), and from the school administration. The recommendation to close Buena Vista School, however, created serious concern among a group of parents of older students. First, they were worried that if the program at Manzano was not successful, it would be closed. Then, since Buena Vista would have been closed, they would once more face a school district with no program available for their children. Second, they were worried about the safety of their children. They feared that their children might be teased, hit, sexually assaulted, victims of drug dealers, bewildered, frightened, or lost. They saw the move as a move not only from a more to a less restricted environment, but also from a more to a less protected one. Third, they were concerned about program quality. At Buena Vista School, an entire school and its curriculum had been geared to the special needs of their children. They were worried that at a large urban high school of close to 3,000 students, the uniqueness of their children's program would be lost and that quality would suffer.

Within the parent community of Manzano, a small group of parents of nonhandicapped students expressed surprisingly similar concerns. They, too, feared for the safety of their children and were concerned that the students transferring from Buena Vista might hit, tease, sexually assault, or sell drugs to their children. They, too, worried that program quality might suffer with the influx of students from Buena Vista.

Discussion (and, indeed, arguments) went on for several months and reached a climax on the night the Board of Education met to make a decision on the issue. One group of parents picketed the meeting and their concern was so great that they were considering legal action against the Board and had even started a fund to finance such action. The Board of Education, which had previously demonstrated major support for its special education programs and administration, voted to accept all of the recommendations. Steps toward program implementation began.

Planning and preparation of students, parents, staff, and community had, of course, started well in advance of the Board decision and continued through the summer and fall. For all three new program sites, the preparation steps which are now a standard procedure were followed; they will be discussed later in this chapter. Due to the strong concerns expressed by parents of students moving to Manzano, a number of additional efforts were made with this population. During the spring, regular classroom students from Manzano visited Buena Vista and decided to establish a club whose purpose would be to assign "buddies" for entering Buena Vista students, to assist them in their transition to a new school, and to facilitate their participation in the campus life.

New components were added to the special education curriculum to familiarize the entering students with their new sports teams, school colors, yearbook, and the myriad details that constitute a comprehensive high school. Buena Vista students were taken on the customary introductory visits to Manzano so they could see the school they would attend in the fall.

In addition to the standard large and small group meetings with parents, the special education assistant principal met with each parent for a one to three hour meeting during the summer. The payoff was outstanding. The program opened smoothly in the fall. With the exception of some minor teasing from both old and new students, no fears were realized, and by midwinter the parents contemplating litigation had donated their fund to a newly formed booster club.

## ADDITIONAL CHANGE

Shortly after the opening of the new Side-by-Side programs at Manzano, Taft, and Atrisco, another change came about for the program. Up to this time the program had served students with moderate and severe retardation. Children with profoundly handicapping conditions remained at home or in the state institution. In October of that year, the Special Education District office received a child find referral from Casa Angelica, a private residential facility within the District's boundaries run by a Catholic order of nuns. The administrator at Casa Angelica requested educational services for all of their 24 school age residents.

At the time of referral, the majority of these 24 residents were nonambulatory and 22 were classified as severely profoundly mentally retarded. Because the request for funding came late in the fall, there were no operational dollars available to start an educational program. Application was made for a small state grant, and an educational program was developed in cooperation with personnel from the University of New Mexico. Service delivery began in early January immediately following the winter break. During that semester and over the summer, all services were delivered on-site at Casa Angelica. The majority of these students had never participated in an educational program. Hence, program goals in the first month were highly structured and specific. One goal for all students was the preparation of students for entrance into a regular school program. The first students began attending classes on an age-appropriate campus in the fall. Over the course of the next year, the on-site program was phased out and students were moved to schools with Side-by-Side programs (Arkell, Thomason, and Haring, 1980).

The success of the Side-by-Side model for service delivery to students with severe retardation led to the adoption of the same model for students with some other severe to profound handicapping conditions. In subsequent years, elementary Side-by-Side programs were opened for students with severe communication disorders (including students diagnosed as autistic) and for students with the most severe behavior disorders. In addition, the program for students with severe physical impairments became a full fledged Side-by-Side program with appropriate support.

## CRITICAL PROGRAM AND SUPPORT ELEMENTS

### Administrative Support

There are a variety of factors critical to the successful integration of students with severe handicapping conditions on regular school campuses. Each of these factors should be analyzed with regard to potential impact on a program under development in a local education agency (LEA)(Stetson, 1984).

Administrative support for the Side-by-Side program has been a critical element in its success. When upper administration was first approached regarding the possibility of moving larger numbers of students with more severe handicapping conditions onto regular school campuses, some administrators expressed serious reservations. To address these concerns, staff members first gathered data from integrated sites in other states, made site visits to see such programs, and brought administrators from districts with successful integration into the district as consultants. These initial activities provided a rich bank of supportive data that became the basis for discussion with the administration. Through this process, staff were able to secure administrative support and determined that it was appropriate to go to the Board of Education to seek their approval.

It is important to differentiate between two stages of obtaining critical administrative support. Initial support for program initiation can be secured using the kinds of activities outlined above. A combination of data-based information and information on best educational practices and child development theory can be utilized effectively at this stage.

The second stage is equally important and more often neglected. Strategies need to change at this point. Data-based information becomes even more important and now needs to include such things as child-progress data from within the district, cost-effectiveness data, as well as case-history and testimonial information. Other strategies can also be brought into play at this time. Top administrators should be taken for site visits to see the programs in action. These same administrators need to be highlighted in press releases, television coverage, and public recognition events. Any visitors from other agencies or areas should have an opportunity not only to tour schools and visit with special education and school personnel, but should also have an exit interview with top administrators. The administration should be notified of any recognition received by the program and should get copies of all pertinent publications. A number of these same activities are appropriate for local Board of Education members as well. For the purposes of program support it is useful to think of Board members and top administrators as a target unit. Appropriate strategies for dissemination of information will vary according to local rules and customs, but whatever the strategies, the two groups usually require the same kinds of information and recognition.

## Community Support

Community support, similar to administrative support, must be both developed and maintained. In urban settings, it may also be useful to think of the "community" as really two communities: the immediate school community and the larger urban community.

Both initial and ongoing community support often begins with educational efforts. Large segments of any population have limited awareness of the needs and rights of children with handicaps. Knowledge of the potential of children with handicaps is even more limited. Thus, the educational campaign needs to focus on basic characteristics, needs, and rights, and it needs to highlight the achievements and potential of children with severe handicapping conditions. It is critical that this campaign be extended to council members and legislators on the local and state level. These groups will also need opportunities to visit programs, understand funding requirements, and observe the progress of students in the special classes for which they provide the funding.

Those in the immediate school community will need the same information that is provided to the public at large for developing awareness. However, it is beneficial to make available to the school community more in-depth activities to promote a higher level of knowledge. These activities may include student presentations at PTA or similar parent meetings, classroom or program open houses and tours, and regular inclusion of information regarding the special education program in the school newsletter.

At the time of program inception there needs to be a carefully planned educational campaign both for the immediate school community and, to a lesser degree, for the public at large. Enough information must be provided to make community members receptive to the program without "overselling." Excessive publicity can create the impression that the program is unduly expensive and parents may become concerned that so much emphasis given to special programs may result in the regular classroom program receiving inadequate attention.

An additional point is that, as with administrators, efforts must be ongoing. When dealing with the public, the concept of maintenance is even more important. Each year there are new community members who are unfamiliar with the program, citizens who did not see the previous year's campaign, and new program elements that need to be brought to the attention of the community.

Finally, there are some community members who have the time to become volunteers. Volunteer activities can range from daily tutoring in the classroom to assisting at one special event. It has been our experience that the two critical components in building community support are adequate information and an opportunity for involvement.

## Parent Support

Developing and maintaining the support of parents of nonhandicapped children in the school community can be achieved in essentially the same manner described for developing and maintaining community support. When students with severe handicaps first move to a regular school campus, it is helpful to conduct an awareness campaign and to address such potential concerns as loss of program quality for their children. It has been our experience that, as the community has become more accustomed to the Side-by-Side model, the need for extensive preparation has decreased and can usually be accomplished in a few group meetings.

Maintenance of the support of parents of regular education students can be facilitated by additional activities. Parent-school groups, whether PTA or some other school-based group, have been particularly helpful. Such groups can sponsor awareness activities and can be encouraged to include parents of students with handicaps in their activities. The opportunity for these two groups of parents to come to know each other and to share their many common experiences, concerns, and hopes can do much to achieve ongoing program support from parents of regular education students. It is useful to organize school visitation days and parent nights in such a way that all parents visit a cross section of classrooms and thus develop an understanding and appreciation for the total school program.

Parents of special education students will have some unique needs to be addressed. If the move is to be their first experience with a regular school campus, those needs will be more intense and will require more exhaustive preparation (see section on *Expansion.*) However, any change in school program, whether dictated by a geographic move or because a student has advanced to midschool or high school, can cause family stress and concern. When the student has a severe handicapping condition, this stress and concern is exacerbated. Thus, any such move requires support from school personnel. Parents must be offered an opportunity to visit and tour the new school, to meet personnel who will be involved with their child, and, if possible, to meet parents of both special and regular education students at the new location.

Inclusion of parents of special education students in PTA or other school parent groups is particularly important. Students with severe handicaps are often bused to a school outside their neighborhood. It can be difficult for them to identify with the school and to feel a part of its community. Participation by their parents in school groups can help to overcome this barrier, and it enables the parents to assist the total school program.

While parent participation in general school activities is highly desirable, it is often necessary to establish special education parent meetings as well. Parents of students with severe handicaps do have concerns and needs not typically shared by parents of regular education students. These may include such issues as other agency resources, death and dying, guardianship, group home living, institutionalization, special sex education, and a host of similar topics. Parents may wish to develop support groups in order to share similar concerns and solutions.

## Staff Support

Support from both regular and special education staff can help to ensure program success. Obtaining initial support from both groups is primarily a matter of disseminating information and providing appropriate inservice. We have found that staff on a regular school campus experience some apprehension over the inclusion of students with severe and profound handicapping conditions. Awareness level information delivered through inservice can alleviate a part of this apprehension. Special education administrators in our district have found it helpful to act as substitute teachers in regular classrooms in schools about to receive Side-by-Side programs. Serving as substitute teachers enables regular classroom personnel to spend a day on site at an existing Side-by-Side program. Inservice can provide some information, but actual site visits and especially meetings with regular classroom teachers who have worked in such a setting are the most critical factors in building regular staff support for the program.

When Buena Vista, the segregated site, was closed, we also encountered concerns from special education staff. This was more true at the high school level than among elementary or midschool teachers. It is easy to overlook the importance of providing inservice and site visits for special education staff about to move to a regular school campus for the first time! However, the provision of such services can do much to relieve staff anxiety over the change.

Maintenance of staff support requires some activities which are substantially different from those needed prior to program implementation. The initial services provided to special education staff would rarely need to be continued. Ongoing awareness inservice will need to be provided for regular education staff, although content and format must be changed to maintain the interest of continuing staff members. New activities must be introduced to maintain regular staff support. We have found that providing aide assistance or materials to regular classroom teachers who are integrating students with severe to profound handicapping conditions is appreciated.

Both regular and special education teachers need to develop respect for each other's jobs as well as for the roles played by other members of the staff. It is natural for regular education teachers to feel that the reduced caseload of special education teachers makes theirs an easier job. Special class teachers, required to do parent meetings, Individualized Educational Plans (IEPs), and accountability reports, may feel that they are the hardest working members of the staff and that indeed it is the regular class teachers who have the easier job.

We have found it an effective inservice technique to have all building personnel trade jobs for a day. The first insight inevitably occurs during the planning for such an inservice day, for there are some staff who cannot participate in the job trade, including the school janitor, the nurse, the secretary, and the aides serving students with severe to profound handicapping conditions. Following such a job trade, staff have a heightened awareness and appreciation of the difficulty and importance of the role played by each. Staff support can also be maintained through cooperative efforts at improving the total educational program of the school, for teachers can contribute their own expertise and benefit from the expertise of others.

Maintenance of special education staff support for an integrated service delivery model is not difficult. Most staff are positively reinforced by the progress they see in students and by working in a natural environment. Their support can be further maintained through the provision of ongoing technical assistance. It is also important to ensure that special education staff, particularly ancillary staff, feel they are an integral part of the school. There are occasions when this is difficult to achieve. Ancillary staff are frequently in short supply and it may prove a poor use of their limited time to assign them to those extra duties that mainly help to make a staff more unified. When this is true, it will be especially important to utilize such vehicles as relevant staff committees and judicious assignment of room locations to achieve a positive working environment for all staff members.

### Student Support

Developing and maintaining the support of regular education students is vital to the successful integration of students with severe handicapping conditions on a regular school campus. Strategies will vary according to the age group of the students, but fortunately students of all ages are generally accepting of their peers with handicaps.

When a new program moves to a site, general awareness sessions in individual classrooms are good. We have also found it beneficial to facilitate high school student visitations to schools already serving students with severe handicaps. A number of our sites have initiated student buddy systems to help new students to feel more welcome and to adapt to their new environment. One note of caution is appropriate in this regard. Elementary age children are often *too* solicitous of children with severe handicaps, and they need to be reminded that "Johnny can open the door, put on his coat, pick up his book, etc., for himself."

After program initiation, we have found it useful to encourage regular awareness activities. Very Special Arts Festivals, Handicap Simulation Day, and able-bodied student participation in wheelchair tennis or beeper baseball have helped students to appreciate the experiences of students with handicaps and have proved to be enjoyable as well. Those which center on sports, games, and other leisure time activities also help to promote student integration on the playground, in lunchrooms, and on the campus in general.

It has been our experience that special class students are extremely supportive of the Side-by-Side model, and those who moved from a segregated site report that they much prefer attending school on a regular campus. Students for whom it is a new experience or who are changing schools are likely to feel some apprehension. An opportunity to visit the campus before school begins has been found to greatly alleviate some of those concerns. The buddy system mentioned earlier has also been helpful in this regard, particularly with older students.

## ADMINISTRATION AND BUILDING ISSUES

### Dispersement and Clustering of Classes

The Albuquerque Side-by-Side model utilizes both clustering of classes in selected schools and dispersement of classes within each school (Thomason and Arkell, 1980). Integration of students with severe handicaps can be greatly facilitated when it is possible to disperse special classes throughout the school. At the initial site developed in Albuquerque, McCollum school, the entire Side-by-Side program was housed in one wing. We found that not only did such placement inhibit the natural intermingling of students, but equally importantly it decreased potential interaction between special and regular education staff.

It required a period of several years to disperse the classes at McCollum throughout the building. In subsequent sites, where classes were dispersed from the onset, integration was achieved more rapidly. Dispersement of classes at high school sites remains more of a problem. High schools in Albuquerque, as in many other cities, are highly departmentalized. Departments are frequently clustered within the building. This has obvious convenience and communication benefits for most departments. However, in the case of a special education department, such clustering inhibits integration of faculty and students.

### Size of Population with Handicaps

Integration is also promoted when the size of the population of students with handicaps is not unduly overrepresented when compared to the population of students without handicaps. However, the Side-by-Side model used by the APS dictates a higher percentage of students with handicaps in schools housing such programs than would be found should each student attend their neighborhood school. We have found that the advantages of such a delivery model are so significant that they outweigh the potential advantage of having each student in his or her neighborhood school.

The primary advantage we have found to the clustering of students is with respect to related services. When students are dispersed throughout the system, related services are delivered on an itinerant basis. Students with mild and moderate handicaps receive ancillary services under such a delivery system. Students with severe and profound handicapping conditions often require a multiplicity of such services. Itinerant therapists and other ancillary service providers find it difficult to coordinate services and typically do not meet frequently with teaching staff in group planning sessions. The Side-by-Side model permits the full time assignment of related service personnel to each program. All staff involved with a specific student are thus able to meet together biweekly or triweekly, which ensures that all services are co-ordinated.

Clustering also facilitates parent and student support. Students are able to work and learn with their nonhandicapped peers but are also able to interact with peers who have similar experiences as theirs. At the midschool and high school level, clustering enables a degree of departmentalization, so that teachers may specialize in a specific area of the curriculum.

Despite these advantages, we have found it important to limit the size of each Side-by-Side program. When this has not been done, the program negatively impacts the school by overloading elective and other regular classes, and placing stress on school health, cafeteria, and janitorial staff.

## On-Site Administration

One of the most critical factors contributing to the success of the Side-by-Side model is the provision for an on-site special education administrator in each program. A special educator is assigned as an assistant principal in each school with a Side-by-Side program. This additional administrative staff permits maintenance of program quality for the school as a whole.

The building principal, while responsible for all the educational programs in the school, does not need to attend each IEP meeting, meet with each parent, attend daily educational team meetings, and assume sole responsibility for supervising a large number of additional staff. The special education administrator assumes primary responsibility for each of these tasks, and is available for on-site technical assistance to staff and parents, also providing expertise to regular class teachers both in the integration of students with severe handicaps and in designing programs for regular class students who are experiencing some difficulty.

## Architectural Issues

When a Side-by-Side program is moved into an existing building, some architectural renovation is required. In some cases, renovation will involve ramping and other basic access modifications. More unique remodeling will also be required when students with severe handicapping conditions are to be served. The majority of such renovation is required in the bathrooms. Provision will usually need to be made for washdowns, changing tables, a washer and dryer, a shower, and diaper disposal, in addition to accessible toilet stalls.

Some modification of playground equipment is usually needed at elementary school sites where students with physical limitations are in attendance. When such modifications are thoughtfully done, they can greatly facilitate integration by making accessible equipment and areas attractive enough to all students to promote joint usage. For example, it has been our experience that lowered basketball hoops, accessible to students in wheelchairs, are equally enjoyed by younger (and shorter) students, who also find them "accessible."

In general, the APS has made a distinction between making sites accessible and making them barrier free. While each site is, of course, accessible, they are not free of all barriers found in nonschool environments. We regard our job as one of preparing students to live in the community, and hence feel that a part of our curriculum should teach students how to overcome some of the barriers they will encounter in their daily lives.

It is important to recognize that architectural design affects not only physical integration but student and staff interaction as well. We have found that architectural design has a major impact on programs. The dispersement of classes throughout the building and the combining of special education and regular education administrative offices in one area are a means of conveying the message that it is a total school program. Similarly, if additional health care professionals are added to the staff, it is beneficial to locate such services in or adjacent to existing offices.

There is a temptation, when adding additional staff, to add separate workrooms and teacher lounge space. Such a design promotes separation. Enlargement of existing spaces or designation of space usage on some other basis, such as smoking/nonsmoking, will enhance communication and integration.

Programs are also influenced by the design of therapy areas. Large, well-equipped rooms for occupational, physical, and speech therapy will promote the delivery of such services in assigned areas. However, should the administrator prefer that the majority of ancillary services be delivered in the classroom or community, then less adequate therapy rooms are called for (Sternat et al., 1977). It is important that each architectural design decision be made consciously and the design be developed in such a way that desired program outcomes are facilitated.

## Janitorial Services

In most school districts, the movement of students with severe handicapping conditions from a segregated site to a regular school will require increased janitorial services at the new site. The same level of service per student that was required on a segregated site will be needed on an integrated site. Such service will ensure the maintenance of cleanliness standards needed for health reasons and will also aid in preventing offensive odors that greatly inhibit the acceptance of students with severe handicaps.

## Medical Support

Many school districts, including the APS, do not typically provide full-time nursing services in smaller schools. It has been our policy that all schools housing a Side-by-Side program would be provided such services. The presence of a full-time nurse is felt to be necessary for the health and safety of those students with serious, or potentially serious, medical problems. An additional benefit is the increased comfort of parents and administrative staff, who know that a competent professional is on hand should a medical emergency arise. Program acceptance is also enhanced through increased nursing services, since all schools would like to have a higher level of service than is generally available.

Preparation for medical emergencies is necessary. For example, Albuquerque provides a resuscitator and suction device at each site where medically at-risk students are served. This equipment is very rarely needed, but again parents and staff are reassured to know that it is at hand in case of an emergency. It is also wise to alert, and provide inservice for, emergency personnel close to the school. Hospital staff are often not familiar with the unique needs of special education students, but have proven eager to provide needed services when they understand the requirements. A staff member or parent should accompany any child who requires emergency hospitalization in order to be sure than nonverbal communication is understood.

## THE FUTURE FOR SIDE-BY-SIDE

### A Noncategorical Side-by-Side

Since its inception, the Side-by-Side service delivery model has continued to evolve. Until 1984 all of the Side-by-Side programs had been, at least to some degree, categorical in nature. In 1982 the Albuquerque Board of Education requested than a new elementary school, Chaparral, be designed to include a Side-by-Side program. This was the first such request initiated by the Board and was the first time that a Side-by-Side program would move into a new school designed to accommodate students with severe handicaps.

Staff members and parents worked with both building and playground architects through each phase of the design process. Our previous experiences had taught us things we would do differently if we could—and suddenly we could! We learned that when features for handicapped students are included in the original design, they are less obvious to the student body and the environment therefore appears more natural than in some of the renovated sites. There was very little additional cost to provide these features, and costs were substantially less than those of renovation.

During the planning phase, staff also met to discuss program design at the new school. Chaparral was somewhat geographically removed from other Side-by-Side programs. Partially for that reason and because staff felt that there were benefits to serving a more diverse population, it was decided that the Chaparral program would be a noncategorical one. The geographical boundaries of the Side-by-Side program are larger than for the regular education program. Within the larger boundaries, Chaparral is able to address the needs of all exceptional students other than the sensorally impaired, who are provided with special class placement.

The Chaparral program utilizes precision teaching in both regular and special classes. Data obtained to date indicates that use of a common technique, in this case precision teaching, in both regular and special class settings greatly facilitates integration efforts. It has provided teachers with communication tools, as well as permitted regular class teachers to increase individualization in their classrooms.

## Movement to Community

In addition to piloting its first noncategorical model, the Side-by-Side model is also evolving into a more community-based program. The model was initially fairly traditional, for the program that was offered to students on a regular campus was very similar to that which had been offered in a segregated setting.

The first steps in moving toward a community-based setting began some years ago as teachers and staff developed a more functional and vocational orientation. Not only were students integrated into other classroom and social settings on campus, but they also had prevocational and vocational assignments that took them to the cafeteria, the grounds, hallways, and offices. Next, teachers began taking students off campus, not only for therapeutic swimming and field trips, but also for visits to work environments.

The move to on-site training was accelerated when the state began its participation in PL 94-142. Federal funds have been used to hire a job developer whose primary focus is students with severe handicaps. These moves were also used to increase student access to career exploration activities, exposing them to a wider variety of job options.

## Model Benefits

As has been discussed throughout this chapter, parents and professionals in Albuquerque have found the Side-by-Side model to be a beneficial one for students with severe handicapping conditions. Generally, both staff and parents find marked improvement in special education students' social behavior. The students who moved from a segregated to an integrated campus themselves reported preferring the opportunity to go to a regular school.

When we talk about the Side-by-Side program, usually the focus is, as it should be, on the effects of such a program on students with handicaps. We have found an additional benefit, however, which is seldom explored. That benefit is the effect of such a program on students who do not have a handicapping condition. Regular class students have reported to us that they have learned to see people with severe handicapping conditions as full-fledged people, seeing beyond the disability or condition. They feel it has increased their sensitivity to, and respect for, differences in people. Parents of these students have also reported advantages they have seen for their children in attending a school which includes students with severe handicaps.

The following letter is an eloquent example of such a report. It was written by the mother of a regular education student at Taft middle school upon the graduation of her daughter. When the letter was written to the Taft Assistant Principal in 1983, the APS had just announced plans for a second high school Side-by-Side program at Valley High School.

---

November 2, 1983

Rae Ann Ray
Taft Middle School

Dear Ms. Ray,
   After reading the Taft News, I decided to write a short note in complete support of the new Side-by-Side to be opened at Valley next year. One of the most pleasing experiences my child has had at Taft has been working with the Side-by-Side children. It has offered her the opportunity to expand her knowledge of others and their situations in an existence that often overlooks interest in the "other" person. My daughter may even elect a career in a related field because of her interaction with these children.
   I have every hope that in her high school years at Valley she will be given more opportunities to work in this very valuable program.

Thank you very much

Susan Sowell

## REFERENCES

Arkell, C., Thomason, J., & Haring, N. (1980). Deinstitutionalization of a residential facility. *Journal of the Association of the Severely Handicapped, 5*(2), 107-120.

Brown, L., Ford, A., Nisbet, J., Sweet, M., Donnellan, A., & Gruenewald, L. (1983). Opportunities available when severely handicapped students attend chronological age appropriate regular schools. *Journal of the Association for the Severely Handicapped, 8*(1), 16-24.

Sternat, J., Messina, R., Nietupski, J., Lyon, S., & Brown, L. (1977). Occupational and physical therapy services for severely handicapped students: Toward a naturalized public school service delivery model. In E. Sontag, J. Smith, & N. Certo (Eds.), *Educational programing for the severely and profoundly handicapped* (pp. 263-278). Reston, VA: Council for Exceptional Children.

Stetson, F. (1984). Critical factors that facilitate integration. In N.Certo, N. Haring, & R. York (Eds.), *Public school integration of severely handicapped students* (pp. 65-81). Baltimore: Brookes.

Thomason, J., & Arkell, C. (1980). Educating the severely/profoundly handicapped in the public schools: A side-by-side approach. *Exceptional Children, 47,* 114-122.

# Chapter 7

# Mainstreaming a Student Who is Visually Impaired

*Kristine E. Davis, Ellen J. Knight, and Marilyn Patterson*

## THE EARLY YEARS

Other than a seeming obstinacy about being born, there was nothing about the pregnancy or Eric's birth that indicated blindness. His eyes appeared normal. At three months of age, Eric's parents first began to have concerns about his eyesight. Sometimes he did not appear to notice objects placed in front of him. There seemed to be no attempt to track objects. And there were occasions when both eyes appeared to be looking in different directions.

When he was five months old, his parents' concern warranted a special trip to their pediatrician. The physician noticed an abnormality in Eric's eyes and arranged for an appointment with an ophthalmologist that same afternoon. While waiting for the appointment, his parents' imaginations ran wild. The precise diagnosis was optical atrophy—that is, Eric's optical nerve had not developed.

The diagnosis had a highly emotional impact on the family. Each parent dealt with the situation in his or her own way. Marilyn, Eric's mother, would rock him, play with him, and cry. Bill, Eric's father, would spend time talking and playing with Eric, and then retreat into the depths of his home workshop. Both wondered how to present the news of Eric's visual impairment to the rest of their family. They decided to write to their parents before trying to talk about it on the phone. They agreed that they had to be positive and decided to focus on what Eric *could* do, and how he was going to do it. At this early stage, Eric's parents were haunted by the possibility that he might have to go to the School for the Blind—250 miles away in Salem, Oregon— as they were unaware of local resources. About this time they were contacted by the coordinator of the Southern Oregon Program for the Visually Impaired (PVI)—a regional program established to provide educational services to the visually impaired from birth to the age of 21. Local school districts within six counties in southern Oregon contract services from PVI, since blindness and visual impairment occur at such a low incidence that individual school districts could not justify providing services on their own. Services from PVI can be initiated by a variety of people: parents, medical personnel, educators, or other social service agency representatives.

Bill and Marilyn were reluctant to accept professional advice on parenting, especially before they had the knowledge to gauge the appropriateness of any advice. They began reading everything they could find about blindness, but found the material in the local library severely limited; most of it consisted of autobiographical accounts. Contact was made with the Program for the Visually Impaired to borrow books. It was through this quest for information that a relationship between Eric's parents and the coordinator of PVI grew.

Three months after the visit to the ophthalmologist, the coordinator of PVI was invited to Eric's home. Weekly visits were set up for her to observe and play with Eric and help Eric's parents keep track of his development. Her intent was to help Eric's parents maximize their son's sensorimotor development by exploring, experiencing, and manipulating his world.

Early in his life it became evident that some of Eric's unique personality quirks were going to cause him almost as many problems as his blindness. An adamant refusal to do something until it was his decision marked much of his development. This obstinacy turned seemingly innocuous incidents into prodigious events. One bad experience with any activity or object, especially if it was a first one, created extraordinary resistance to a second experience. Consequently, sessions with the PVI coordinator were spent deciding not only where Eric was developmentally and where he was going next, but also how to introduce the next step to meet the least resistance from Eric.

When he was almost three, Eric began attending a parent-tot experience group, sponsored by a local church. Eric dealt with this socialization experience with increasing resistance. Marilyn remembers this program as more beneficial for her than for Eric, as it helped her gauge her own expectations and gave her ideas for activities to do with Eric. Watching other children of Eric's age, she had the opportunity to see what toys might interest him and how the other children played.

Despite her participation in the parent-tot group and assistance from the PVI coordinator, Marilyn found Eric's second through fourth years to be overwhelming and emotionally exhausting. With Eric the only blind child of his age in the area, typical support systems from other mothers were unavailable. During this time, home visits from an itinerant teacher from PVI provided Marilyn with some encouragement and support, as the teacher helped to brainstorm and exchanged ideas on ways to work with Eric.

Eric's parents sought help from additional community sources in an attempt to mitigate problems they saw ahead and to try to understand Eric's extreme reluctance to initiate activities. A speech therapist was consulted, for example, on how to help Eric learn the appropriate use of personal pronouns—an area that is difficult for many children with visual impairments. A psychologist was asked for advice on how to get more cooperation from Eric during instruction on daily tasks and how to encourage Eric's interaction with his peers. These initial encounters with various professionals were disappointing to Eric's parents. While the professionals seemed very knowledgeable in their general fields, they did not have a specific awareness as to how blindness complicates the developmental processes.

Bill and Marilyn found that it would be impossible and inappropriate to implement every suggestion that came from the professionals. Frequently, because these suggestions were presented as formal lessons, they needed to be adapted to the family's routine for daily living. Eric's parents couldn't be expected to be training him twenty-four hours a day; priorities needed to be set.

Services provided by PVI had placed an emphasis on training Eric in self-help skills, but as he appproached school age, a shift was made to the acquisition of academic skills. In the attempt to prepare Eric for attending public school, instruction was provided in the following areas: Braille reading and writing, concept development, gross and fine motor development, and auditory and tactile development. This instruction was provided in a 1:1 tutorial by an itinerant teacher from PVI. Lessons in orientation and mobility were provided by a specialist from the same program.

The itinerant teacher at that time was confident that Eric had the ability to participate in a regular classroom. She arranged to give Eric some lessons in a kindergarten room that was empty during the afternoon so that he would be somewhat familiar with the school when he began kindergarten. Eric was to be the first totally blind student to begin formal instruction in the Medford School District.

By the time Eric was school-age, his right to a free and appropriate public education in the least restrictive environment (LRE) was protected by PL 94–142 and Oregon state regulations. Eric's parents had decided early that he would attend public school in his own community rather than be sent to the School for the Blind in Salem. To ensure this, they became involved as advocates in state level meetings regarding future funding for the Southern Oregon Program for the Visually Impaired. They knew that without PVI resources would not be available to support Eric's attendance in the local public school system.

## MAINSTREAMING: THE PUBLIC SCHOOL EXPERIENCE

Attempting to arrive at workable definitions of *integration, least restrictive environment,* and *mainstreaming* is always a difficult task. This was certainly true for PVI as it grappled with providing Eric an appropriate education within the Medford school system. During the process of reviewing Eric's public school experience, we discovered that there seemed to be a significant difference between his initial school experiences from 1980 to 1984 and his experience during the 1984–1985 school year. The latter experience seemed to more clearly fit definitions of most appropriate and least restrictive that were in the full spirit of PL 94–142.

### Kindergarten: Ready or Not?

Eric entered public school in 1980 and was well prepared to meet many of the academic challenges of the kindergarten program. Due to the instructional priorities of his previous PVI teacher, he was more advanced than the rest of his peers in the areas of phonics, reading readiness, and math concepts. However, his social experiences were more limited, based primarily on family interaction (with scant peer involvement at the preschool).

Compared to the preschool experience, the longer school day and large number of students were both confusing and physically demanding for Eric. In addition, he was assigned a new PVI itinerant teacher who had no previous experience in mainstreaming. This lack of experience, along with only minimal communication with Eric's previous itinerant teacher, led to serious misconceptions about his readiness abilities.

Itinerant PVI services were available to the classroom teacher through a contractual agreement between the Medford School District and PVI. Once a student such as Eric was referred to the program, an itinerant teacher would be assigned to provide support, materials, inservice to the classroom teacher, and an Individualized Educational Plan (IEP).

Eric's IEP was written by the itinerant teacher prior to the IEP meeting. The primary goals addressed in the IEP were academic and it stressed Braille reading and writing skills. The meeting was conducted by the itinerant teacher and attended by the classroom teacher, the building principal, the orientation and mobility instructor, and Eric's parents. For the first time, Eric's parents felt as though they were not a part of the planning of their son's education program. The public school personnel had little idea of the input they could have in the development and implementation of the IEP.

Although Eric's kindergarten teacher had no formal training or preparation in dealing with children who were visually impaired, she was willing to include Eric in all appropriate classroom activities. Eric attended the entire classroom session and continued to receive compensatory instruction from the itinerant teacher and the mobility specialist before and after school. The itinerant PVI teacher was available to work with Eric in the classroom during special projects and in the gym for physical education activities as she determined appropriate.

The kindergarten teacher was essentially responsible for planning Eric's classroom instruction, whereas the itinerant teacher provided the materials necessary for this instruction. Coordination of the curriculum and the materials necessary required lengthy daily communication between the two teachers. The kindergarten teacher used a wide variety of worksheets that required explanation before they could be transcribed for Eric. Most of the kindergarten activities and games had to be modified so that Eric could participate, and discussion was necessary to determine what adaptations the classroom teacher needed to develop.

The question of Eric's participation in certain classroom activities was addressed but not resolved. The itinerant teacher assumed the position that all the classroom activities were appropriate for Eric's participation, even when the classroom teacher questioned the relevance to Eric of some of the activities. This was especially true of art activities such as coloring, cutting, and pasting. Whereas the goal of these activities—to develop fine motor coordination, language skills, and general concepts—was a reasonable one, the classroom teacher felt this goal could have been met in ways more appropriate to a blind student.

Eric was experiencing academic success at this point, but his progress was hindered by his delayed social development, lack of interaction with his peers, and his small size, which combined to encourage the other children to treat him as though he were much younger. The classroom teacher and Eric's parents decided that Eric needed a second year in kindergarten to improve his social skills.

### Kindergarten Again!

In 1981, Eric returned to kindergarten with the same classroom and itinerant instructors. Basically, the roles of the two teachers remained the same as the previous year, with the classroom teacher responsible for planning the curriculum and the itinerant teacher providing 1:1 academic instruction.

The orientation and mobility specialist provided instruction in the classroom in an attempt to facilitate more appropriate interaction and to foster Eric's independence. The IEP process was handled the same as the previous year, with the classroom teacher and the parents reviewing the finished document but having little involvement in the decision making. The instruction of social skills was not addressed on Eric's IEP, although this had been the reason for his retention. Concern was voiced over this matter, but it was argued that since social skills are difficult to measure objectively, instruction of social skills should not be done formally.

Eric continued to acquire academic skills that put him ahead of his classmates. Socially, he failed to make the progress that his classroom teacher and parents had anticipated with his retention. He did not seem to view himself as a member of the group and often needed special attention from the classroom teacher in order to follow directions given to the class or to complete an assigned task. He failed to make friends with his peers and seemed to perceive them as his helpers. It was concluded that another year in kindergarten would not solve his delayed social development.

## First Grade

The IEP process for first grade was conducted as it had been in the past. The classroom teacher had little opportunity to voice her concerns regarding the appropriateness of materials and activities, the amount of itinerant instructional time in the classroom and on a 1:1 basis, the availability of math worksheets, and the need for available assistance and support in the classroom.

Like his kindergarten teacher, Eric's first grade teacher had no formal preparation and was not provided with opportunities through staff development or inservice to develop the skills for instructing a totally blind student in her classroom. She was willing to assume responsibility for his instruction provided that the itinerant teacher be responsible for the appropriate adaptation of materials and assistance during such activities as art and physical education, and at other times when Eric could not function independently.

As the year progressed, the classroom teacher found herself responsible for Eric's entire school day with no itinerant assistance. The itinerant teacher spent much of her time in the exact transcription of materials for Eric's use in the classroom. She felt that in order for Eric to be mainstreamed, he needed to be doing exactly what the other students were doing. This included answering worksheets by drawing lines, circling words, and coloring the correct answer—tasks which were impossible for Eric to monitor. It was only after numerous requests from the classroom teacher and intervention by the parents that some help was made available for Eric during the period when handwriting instruction was given.

The classroom teacher became quite frustrated by the lack of support both from administration and from PVI. She lacked a goal or sense of purpose for her instructional efforts with Eric. She felt that she was required to handle the problems and responsibilities of developing this program on her own, and she derived none of the benefits that come from working on a team. She felt isolated in and unprepared for the role of appropriately serving Eric. Nothing in her educational background had prepared her for dealing with the problems of mainstreaming. She questioned whether Eric benefited from the program. She spent a great deal of time assisting Eric with activities that had not been modified to fit his needs. She was continually frustrated by faulty equipment. Because she did not understand Brailled materials, she had difficulty monitoring Eric's progress. She did not view Eric as being fully integrated into the classroom. Because of Eric's failure to follow directions and the disturbance created by his lack of mobility skills, she realized that the mere physical placement of this student in her classroom was not a true example of mainstreaming.

A meeting was held at the end of first grade in an attempt to clarify roles for the next year and addresss some concerns about Eric's program. However, with the intervention of summer vacation and a new principal, there was little follow-through into the next year.

## Second Grade

Eric was placed in a second grade classroom with a teacher who had previous experience working with a blind student and involvement with PVI. Even so, the teacher did not feel completely capable of making judgements regarding the translation of her program to fit Eric's needs. It was her expectation that Eric would participate in all the learning processes that the other students underwent, but with the emphasis on goals and not specifics. For example, drawing lines on a matching activity posed practical problems for Eric, since he could not monitor what he had done. She felt that the itinerant teacher should determine what practical and realistic modifications were needed so that she could evaluate his understanding of the concept being tested without having to bother about his skill at drawing.

Eric's next IEP was developed at the end of September. Because she had worked with Eric for only 3–4 weeks, the classroom teacher felt she was unable to contribute much information and essentially complied with what had already been written by the itinerant teacher.

The second grade teacher felt her preparation was limited in spite of her prior experience four years earlier. She was upset by a variety of programmatic concerns. She was unable to help Eric with his Braille writer since she had been given no training in how to load and unload it. Questions concerning blindness and practical information regarding how to integrate Eric were not answered satisfactorily by the itinerant teacher. Materials and supplies were frequently not provided by the itinerant teacher. While the classroom teacher wanted to have Eric's Brailled books interlined so that she could monitor his participation, this was rarely done except through the volunteer efforts of Eric's mother. Consumable materials, such as Braille paper, were in short supply.

Eric's parents felt the program was not working as it should. They had difficulty identifying the cause of their dissatisfaction, despite frequent discussions with Eric's teacher and visits to the classroom. They were concerned about their son's frustrations and increasing resistance to attending school.

A complete breakdown in the communication between the classroom teacher and the itinerant teacher over support, services, roles, and responsibilities necessitated the involvement of the supervisor of PVI, an assisting teacher from PVI, and the school principal. Meetings were held in an attempt to resolve the difficulties, and as the end of the year approached, it was determined that a change in itinerant teachers would be necessary.

Communication was the crucial element that seemed to be missing from the mainstreaming process in Eric's early school years. Classroom teachers and Eric's parents felt their needs and questions were not being addressed. Expressed concerns over the appropriateness of specific classroom materials and activities for Eric were met with little explanation and consideration. The itinerant teacher chose to emphasize the acquisition of academic skills on a 1:1 basis but ignored the increasing gap between Eric's academic abilities and the mechanical means to use those academic skills quickly and efficiently in the classroom. In addition, Eric's poorly developed classroom survival skills (those needed for successful participation in classroom routines) and his lagging social development made it increasingly difficult for Eric to be adequately mainstreamed.

The classroom teachers, having little or no experience with integrating a child like Eric, were hesitant about making their concerns widely known. They naively assumed that the difficulties necessarily attended having a special needs student in their classrooms and that there was little that could be done. It was somehow forgotten during the first four years of Eric's public school experience that mainstreaming is far more complicated than the mere adaptation of materials and the physical placement of a special needs student in a regular classroom.

## Third Grade

As a result of complaints from the classroom teachers and the dissatisfaction expressed by Eric's parents to the supervisor of PVI, a different itinerant teacher was assigned to Eric. This new teacher began working with the third grade classroom teacher to set up an arrangement which benefited the classroom teacher, satisfied the parents, and began to deal with Eric's social inadequacies, which had previously been ignored. This was able to happen, however, not because of any structural changes in the supervision by PVI or the school administration, but because teachers within PVI have a great deal of freedom to determine how students are served, which can result in drastically different programs for students depending on the itinerant teacher assigned. In this particular situation, program change would result from the concern of parents and teachers rather than from any changes in administrative style or philosophy.

Elements were incorporated into the program which made it more successful for Eric, more enjoyable for his classroom teacher, more edifying for his peers, and more in line with a full definition of mainstreaming. Among the changes were the following:

- The newly assigned itinerant teacher defined her role as functioning as a support service to the classroom teacher and identifying and instructing Eric in any area which would help him fit in and function more independently and efficiently.
- Eric was taught independent daily classroom survival skills such as:
  —following oral or written direction;
  —understanding when to raise his hand in response to a general question and when to lower it after someone else had been called for the answer;
  —learning alternate response systems for directions inappropriate to the visually impaired, such as marking an answer with a sticker instead of circling it or writing an answer rather than drawing lines for matching; and
  —learning to decide which system provided the quickest means to indicate a response.
- So as to enhance interactions between himself and his teachers and peers, Eric was taught social skills such as:
  —discriminating their voices and learning to address them by name;
  —responding when spoken to;
  —soliciting aid in a polite manner;
  —learning games and jokes to share with others; and
  —controlling unacceptable social mannerisms, such as picking his nose in public, engaging in verbal outbursts, and putting his head in inappropriate positions.
- Instruction was provided in the classroom and on a 1:1 basis by the itinerant teacher or aide in the following compensatory skills:

—learning the use of an abacus for math calculations

—refining both literary Braille and Nemeth Braille codes for reading and writing;

—beginning instruction on the computer using a voice synthesizer and with the goal of providing a printed copy for the sighted classroom teacher;

—learning to use an Optacon (optical-to-tactile converter) which enables a blind individual to read printed materials

—developing skill in the use of a slate and stylus for note-taking without using a Braille writer; and

—acquiring information or directions using tape-recorded materials available free for the blind and physically handicapped from the Library of Congress.

• To increase the opportunity for generalization, instruction in orientation and mobility was implemented throughout Eric's day rather than limited to isolated lessons.

Eric's third grade teacher believed that the role of the classroom teacher was to take students as far as possible by maintaining a high level of student motivation for the learning process. He initially felt somewhat intimidated by the idea of serving a blind student in his classroom, especially since he thought Eric would be his complete responsibility. He was relieved to find that this was to be a shared responsibility, with the classroom teacher determining the content and the itinerant teacher determining the method of instruction. He also discovered that support services would be readily available and could be changed depending on his perception of what Eric needed to function within that specific classroom.

The classroom teacher and Eric's parents found that their concerns and ideas were respected. They felt they were an integral part of the IEP process. One major IEP change was that time spent by the itinerant teacher or aide with Eric would be increased to three hours per day, with the majority of that time spent in the classroom.

The decision as to what areas of instruction Eric could afford to miss in order to make time for individual lessons was a difficult one. One area which he missed quite frequently was physical education; however, the only one who saw this as beneficial was Eric! His lack of interest and skills in physical activity meant that he was excluded from many of the extracurricular activities offered at his school.

That year, materials for Eric seemed to be adequate. Most of Eric's textbooks came from the Portland Regional Library for the Visually Impaired. The itinerant teacher made time available to Braille any supplemental materials requried on short notice by the classroom teacher. When the math text failed to arrive on time, for example, itinerant support was provided to interpret the printed material to Eric as he listened to his classroom teacher's math lesson. When other materials or activities needed to be adapted, the emphasis was to find the best way to modify them to ensure that Eric would be successful.

Previously, Eric's sighted peers had been given only minimal instruction about blindness. To enhance their interaction with Eric, 16 inservice sessions were conducted by the itinerant teacher, assisted by Eric's mother and an itinerant PVI aide. The students were taught ways of describing objects without using visual characteristics. They engaged in independent living activities (e.g., eating, drinking, finding their coats, tying their shoes) while blindfolded. They traveled around the school blindfolded while using a sighted guide. They experimented with various adaptive devices, such as the talking calculator, the talking computer, the Braille writer, the slate and stylus, the abacus, the talking alarm clock, the Braille watch, and the Optacon. A blind adult who used a Seeing Eye dog visited the class and answered many questions. The students experimented with senses other than sight in voice and object identification. They tried to determine a sequence of events by utilizing their listening skills. They played many games while blindfolded. The students seemed to enjoy the activities and indicated a desire to participate in additional inservice activities the following year.

Questionnaires given before and after showed that the students had developed a greater awareness and knowledge about blindness. The inservice sessions appeared to help Eric's peers to gain an understanding of the difference between sympathy and empathy, to develop positive and appropriate ways of interacting with him, and to develop a greater appreciation of their own sight and other senses.

## EVALUATING THE EXPERIENCE

The lack of well-defined goals and objectives makes it difficult to give an objective evaluation of the effectiveness of PVI's services and of Eric's educational plan. However, the principal's, the parents', and the classroom teacher's perceptions were seen as more positive after the shift to a more fully integrated program was initiated beginning with third grade.

The building principal has expressed the view that the mainstreaming program has been a growth experience for all concerned. He stated that adjustments had to be made by the individuals involved with the program, but he thought that the benefits of the program were increasingly positive and that the experiences in sharing and being helpful were particularly profitable for the children directly involved with Eric. He also noted a significant difference in emphasis during discussions with Eric's parents. Rather than mainly voicing concern about whether the school system was doing an adequate job with their son's educational program, they now have confidence in the existing program and are active supporters of the total school program.

The greatest change that Eric's parents noticed was in his attitude toward school. He had been emotionally guarded or cautious as a first and second grade student. He had many fears about doing his corrections, because he did not appear to understand his mistakes. He was afraid to do his homework when he was not sure what was required of him. He cried frequently and resisted going to school in the mornings. His parents initially thought this was related to the obstinacy in Eric's personality, a characteristic that had been evident since preschool years. However, with the changes in the program in third grade, Eric was more relaxed, easier to reason with, less resistant, and more independent about doing his homework. He looked forward to going to school and seemed to enjoy sharing school experiences with his family.

In an informal evaluation of the third grade program, the classroom teacher felt that the year had been beneficial to Eric. He saw that Eric was able to make significant academic *and* social gains when direction was provided within the classroom setting. He observed that Eric had learned to function more independently during the year. Finally, he noted that Eric had developed into a more active member of the class.

Eric's school records show that his grades improved in four subjects: arithmetic, English, reading, and social studies. High test scores for that year on the Brailled version of the Stanford Achievement Test correlated with his classroom performance in the areas of math, language, spelling, and word study skills.

At the beginning of the third grade, Eric had exhibited continuous disruptive or negative vocalizations about errors in his work, the amount of work required of him, or changes in the classroom schedule. He also did not follow directions well, did not raise his hand, and often shouted out without consideration for others. Following implementation of a new behavior program developed by the new itinerant teacher, those disruptive behaviors were reduced to the point that he no longer required extra attention from the classroom teacher for behavioral concerns.

Although Eric was not always happy about the amount of work required of him, he came to realize that he was a part of the class and expected to do the work. He became aware that there were events taking place in the classroom that he was missing when he was being given individualized instruction and expressed concern about this to his parents. He participated in an informal discussion group every morning with the other boys in the class. He eagerly related items of interest from these discussions to his parents, who felt he had a greater sense of belonging to the group than he had had in his previous school years. Towards the end of the year, Eric was selected by his classmates to receive the "Sunny Award," an award given for friendliness, good attitudes, and cheerful disposition presented by the principal at a school assembly.

With his increasing social awareness, Eric was developing a better understanding of appropriate behavior and of people's expectations of him. He expressed it well himself. When he was reminded of a correction needed for inappropriate behavior, he replied, "Oh, you mean you want me to be a regular guy."

An evaluation of Eric's mainstreaming program must note the following benefits realized by Eric:

- He is able to remain at home with his family and attend the neighborhood school.
- He enjoys many of the benefits afforded the other children at his school.
- He is in an atmosphere where his blindness is not the focal point.
- He is learning to make the adjustments necessary to live in the sighted world.
- He is learning to function more independently.

## MAINSTREAMING: QUALITATIVE INTEGRATION

Defining integration and mainstreaming as keeping a special needs child with his or her regular education peers as much as possible is not sufficient. It is more than the quantity of time spent in the regular classroom or around normal peers. It is more than being in the cafeteria and eating lunch at the same time. It is more than sharing the same recess time and being out on the playground together. It is the quality of such interaction that is important. It is having friends to talk to while in class or eating lunch or playing outside that is critical to a quality integration program. It is watching students interacting and not seeing the special needs child being treated differently by his peers but as an individual with his or her own strengths and weaknesses.

Currently the means exist for referring, evaluating, and identifying students with special needs. The IEP process addresses the educational needs of those students. However, once identified, there are no guidelines or policies either from most states or most local administrative sectors as to how quality of the integration is to be enhanced. Consequently, the existing individual programs vary depending on how the direct service staff view their roles. Programs may change because of how teachers are assigned, not necessarily because students' needs change.

In the process of attempting to describe a quality integration program, we compiled a list of critical guidelines that we feel would assist future integration efforts for visually impaired and blind students within the PVI. The considerations fall into two major areas: administrative considerations and teacher-related concerns. While a few of the following concerns are specific to the PVI or the Medford School District, we believe that most would be applicable to any district trying to implement quality integrated services, especially for moderately and severely involved children.

## Administrative Considerations

1. Administrative policy and procedures are needed for determining which students are to be integrated and the extent to which this will occur. The overall policy, though, should stress that all disabled children should be served on regular campuses and that almost all special needs students should be served for at least part of their day in regular classrooms. Careful consideration should be given to the ease with which students with various types of special needs (e.g., academic deficits versus social deficits) can be incorporated within a regular classroom program and to the type and amount of support the student needs to function within that setting.

2. The general goals for mainstreaming a particular student need to be clearly defined and agreed to by those staff working with the student.

3. There should be a clear definition of the roles, responsibilities, and working relationships of the following personnel: classroom teachers, the building administrators, special education administrators, instructional specialists, aides, and other special services staff. There should be established protocol for addressing questions, concerns, and problems related to the services provided by these personnel.

4. The mainstreamed student needs to be assigned to experienced and competent personnel who maintain flexibility and open-mindedness toward all aspects of the program.

5. The classroom assignment of special needs students should be made as early as possible in the spring to allow for the commencement of staff development, awareness activities for regular education students, and easier acquisition of materials needed for the following year.

6. Principals responsible for supervision of the classroom teacher should be knowledgeable in integration philosophy and practice.

7. Supervision of itinerant staff should be by someone with expertise in the integrated student's primary disability area, with adequate time available for observation and consultation.

8. Administrators need to be cognizant of the additional time required of the classroom teacher in a mainstreaming program and to make adjustments as necessary. It is important that administrators try to provide teachers with adequate preparation time and support for incorporating a special needs child into their classroom. Class size and distribution of students must to be carefully planned.

9. There needs to be a community awareness program designed to reach the larger school environment (other students, all staff members, parents, administrators, school board members, and the community) and facilitate a better understanding of the personal and educational needs of exceptional children.

## Teacher-Related Concerns

1. There needs to be adequate teacher preparation prior to the first day of school to alleviate apprehension, perhaps including observation of the student. This preparation should involve both regular and special educators.

2. To foster open communication among all team members, adequate time should be available for consultation involving classroom teachers, itinerant staff, and parents.

3. Itinerants may have little or no contact with one another on a day-to-day basis and time needs to be made available for discussion of specific problems or for sharing ideas and information.

4. Itinerants need to maintain flexible schedules to be available to observe and provide assistance for those problems which occur at times other than during their regular assigned times.

5. Adequate and appropriate materials need to be readily available. This is particularly true when trying to integrate a student with a low-incidence disability in a mainstreamed setting not normally equipped to serve such a student. For a blind student, acquisition and preparation of materials is the primary responsibility of the itinerant teacher, with the classroom teacher providing information and ideas.

6. When integrating a blind student using Brailled materials, there needs to be immediate translation from Braille to print for feedback to the teacher and the student.

7. There needs to be ongoing inservice for the classroom teacher and classmates of handicapped students, rather than a one-time awareness session that occurs at the beginning of the school year. While inservice or staff development opportunities are often given a low priority when integrating a low-incidence child, these experiences are critical for allowing the teacher to feel as though he or she is being supported in the long-term effort.

## SUMMARY

Constructing an appropriate educational program for Eric was not an easy task. Not only did the program teach some things to Eric, but Eric clearly taught his educators many things about effective educational programming. However, it was discovered that almost anything is possible if those involved are willing to continue to solve problems and recognize their own strengths and weaknesses. Many benefits can be derived from the development of an exemplary integrated program such as Eric's, including the development and enhancement of teaching skills, the edification of the other students, and the greater ability of a school system to provide quality services to other special needs students in the future. It is hoped that the information contained in this chapter will prove beneficial to those who are meeting the challenges of mainstreaming the special needs student.

# Chapter 8

# A Model for Public School Programming for Hearing Impaired Students

*Marianne K. Hesseltine*

## TRADITIONAL SERVICE MODELS FOR HEARING IMPAIRED CHILDREN

According to statistics published in 1940 in the *American Annals of the Deaf,* more than 90% of all hearing impaired (HI) children in the United States and Canada were educated in residential schools for the deaf or in large day schools and programs specifically for HI students. The latter were typically located in large metropolitan areas, where a sufficient number of HI students made such programming possible.

As recently as 1979, Craig described the residential school as "a facility with a total commitment to deaf young people as opposed to a facility primarily designed for hearing students" (Craig, 1979, p. 277). His emphasis on readily available specialized personnel, technical resources, relevant curricula, and spacious grounds was shared by many researchers and practitioners.

The low incidence of this handicapping condition (Brill, 1978), particularly in rural and suburban areas, and the costly technological support devices required to establish and maintain such programs were factors that limited local administrators' interest in integration. Administrators were also faced with the task of mobilizing staff to take on the academic demands of teaching children whose communicative and linguistic needs posed enormous challenges despite their average to above average intelligence. The few large scale models that appeared successful did not offer administrators on local levels much hope for replication, since these programs had large student bodies and could thus justify a variety of specialized personnel, support services, technological devices, and technicians. Members of the deaf community as well as community agencies seving deaf adults also viewed the problems of serving HI children as best met by a residential center, with its substantial, specialized resources.

## FORCES AFFECTING INCREASED INTEGRATION

Despite these concerns and the strong support for residential placement, the percentage of HI students educated in residential and day schools dropped from 90% in 1940 to 30% by 1979. The transition was not without problems. In many instances, the reaction from administrators in residential and large day schools for HI children was both critical and defensive. Negative reactions also came from unprepared regular educators and concerned administrators. While the concept of mainstreaming HI students was viewed positively, there was a strong need for guidelines.

The most dramatic impetus for change in placement options for HI children was the enactment of PL 94-142 in 1975. Although the interpretation of this law was varied and not always consistent, the law did raise the issue of integration for HI children as a possible placement option. Up until this time, children with unilateral, fluctuating, or mild to moderate hearing losses were the only HI students automatically included in regular school programming. Given the outwardly intact speech of these children, the assumption was that language and auditory skills were similarly adequate. A number of researchers (Ross and Nober, 1981; Davis, 1977, etc.) have questioned this assumption and have discussed the unmet needs of these children (even if the placement option itself was not seen as detrimental). Also at this time a subtle change began to take place in the description of this population of children. The term *deaf* was gradually replaced by the term *hearing-impaired*, a subtle but significant change. This modification in terminology reflected the growing awareness of a continuum of hearing loss and a range of auditory functioning even among the profoundly impaired.

Legislation also influenced the development and growth of advocacy and information centers to serve the needs of families with an HI child. These centers offered parents guidance, support, and encouragement in selecting a program that best suited their child's needs. The legislative support gained by parents through PL 94-142 and the development of information centers gave them renewed status in integrative programming.

One positive result of legislation was the movement to serve HI children from birth to 3 years. The availability of funding through early intervention programming further strengthened the role parents played in determining educational placement for their child. Parents with early intervention training felt better prepared to make decisions concerning their child. These programs also fostered confidence in the parents' own ability to meet the demands of a hearing loss in their child as opposed to relying mainly on experts.

Sophistication in the area of amplification resulted in the capability of personal hearing aids to maximize residual hearing and the ability to detect and assess hearing loss at much earlier ages. The critical learning period from birth to 3 years was often spent with an undetected loss or a misdiagnosis of the child's actual learning difficulties. The participation of families in early intervention programs enabled children to be better trained to respond to sound stimuli through play audiometry techniques. The increased accuracy of their responses allowed audiologists to fit the child with appropriate amplification at a much earlier age.

Better usage of residual hearing through amplification, even for the child with a severe or profound hearing impairment, resulted in improved development of communication skills. Speech development remained delayed for many children, but more importantly the development of a usable language system helped minimize the communication barrier between parent and child. Whether language was shared through natural gestures, homemade or formal signs, was not as important as the fact that a meaningful communicative bond could exist between parents and their HI children.

Concurrently, society began to attach less of a stigma to the use of manual communication and the sound of deaf speech. Sesame Street taught thousands of preschoolers and their families that signs were fun. Established groups such as the Boy Scouts and Girl Scouts learned signing, and local school districts offered signing classes as part of their continuing education programs. Street signs cautioning "Deaf Children at Play" became increasingly frequent. Training of personnel to serve as interpreters became a priority at community colleges and some four-year institutions as the need for interpreters in public school classes grew. The increased availability of trained interpreters provided administrators with personnel to bridge the communication barrier between the classroom teacher and the HI student.

## SERVICE TO HI STUDENTS IN NEW YORK STATE

In New York State, there exists an educational agency known as BOCES—an acronym for Board of Cooperative Educational Services. This agency for "shared services" was established in 1948 to enable smaller or rural school districts to join together in requesting similar services from a larger unit. Districts are able to pool their resources in requesting a particular service from the BOCES in their region. The means of obtaining desired services is through a mutually agreed upon shared service contract that specifies the tuition to be paid for the amount of service requested. While a larger school district is able to procure necessary services and resources on its own, smaller districts are able to obtain a part or parts of necessary services. The needs of several school districts can be economically supported through BOCES agencies, which are reimbursed for providing the total service. Not only are overall costs minimized, the individuality of each district remains intact while duplication of services is avoided.

Involvement of BOCES in educating hearing impaired children originated long before the enactment of PL 94-142. In 1970, a pilot program was begun between the Monroe County BOCES and the Rochester School for the Deaf for the purpose of expanding occupational training (Hehir, 1973). This initial effort resulted in similar attempts by the New York State School for the Deaf in Rome and Mill Neck Manor School for the Deaf. By 1972, five of the eight residential deaf schools in New York State were utilizing the services of BOCES occupational centers for integrating secondary deaf students. Hehir concluded that "the deaf student in New York State can receive adequate occupational training in integrated BOCES centers with essential support services being provided by the specialized schools for the deaf." Munson and Miller (1979) conducted an extensive three-year study from 1976 to 1979 to evaluate the mainstreaming of secondary students in four schools for the deaf in New York State with the corresponding BOCES in their county. On the basis of this study, Munson and Miller urged that administrators establish educational policies based on the common needs of all young people whether handicapped or not. Their feeling was that past efforts have encouraged separatism and "resulted in educational efforts for the handicapped that emphasize their deficiencies and limitations" (p. 313). A survey of all BOCES organizations (Hesseltine, 1980) found that almost 65% of the respondents were serving hearing-impaired students. The growth of services between 1965 and 1980 remained fairly constant despite the enactment of PL 94-142. Between 1965 and 1969, six programs were initiated while eight new programs were begun for each of the periods 1970-1974 and 1975-1979. Thus, a varied history of service to HI students existed at the time the program to be described was established.

## GETTING STARTED

### Forces in Oswego County

There are areas in most states that are not in proximity to metropolitan centers and thus have limited resources. In these areas, programming for children with special needs poses particular challenges. In upstate New York, Oswego County is such an area.

The geographical boundaries of Oswego County enclose 964 square miles, yet the 1980 census reports a population of approximately 114,000 people. In contrast, Onondaga County, which is adjacent to Oswego, covers 794 square miles but supports a population of about 464,000 people. These demographic figures illustrate the largely rural nature of Oswego County.

Prior to the establishment of the HI program in 1977, two groups were concurrently moving toward initiating such a program. The families of five HI children (ages five and six) in Oswego County all shared similar concerns, even though they initially had no contact with each other. At the same time, administrators at Oswego BOCES were becoming increasingly aware of the growing desire of these families to initiate an appropriate program within the county. The forces within each group, and especially after their subsequent joining, provided the impetus for establishing the first HI class in September 1977.

The New York State School for the Deaf in Rome is the nearest residential facility. Although available to the families and recommended by various Committees on the Handicapped (COH), each family rejected the school as a placement option. (A COH functions in each school district as a child placement board responsible for making placement recommendations for all handicapped children in their district.) One mother who visited the School during the fall of 1976 at the request of the COH, rejected this placement because "there was no speech. I felt he could learn to talk, so I was really against Rome." Her son could possibly have commuted to the school as a day student, but she felt it was too far. The other families lived much further from the school, making residential status mandatory.

Another family was initially advised to sent their son to a local program for the mentally retarded or to kindergarten at age five. When it was obvious neither option was satisfactory to them, local administrators recommended the State School for the Deaf. Although this family was coaxed into visiting the school in Rome, they had no intention of sending their son there. The mother remembers the school as "dingy, with gray walls and no atmosphere." Communication was another concern: "When I saw the kids, all I could see was signing—no talking at all—and I didn't want that for my son. I knew he could talk."

A third mother was strongly encouraged to send her son to the School for the Deaf. She recalled that "if there were deaf kids around, they usually went to Rome." Although advised to visit Rome, she never went because she just "couldn't see sending him there."

One mother also visited the Sherwood Hearing-Impaired Program in nearby Onondaga County shortly after her visit to the School for the Deaf in the fall of 1976. The BOCES sponsored program had been established in 1974 in a public school setting. This option was viewed more favorably than the State School for the Deaf, even though mileage was still a concern. During the one year her son attended the program, at the age of five, he left home at 6:00 A.M. and did not return until 5:30 P.M. or later. If a direct bus route could have been arranged, he would have traveled 65-70 miles one way. As it was, he was "bused all over the county." Further, the lack of programming for HI children in Oswego County made parent participation in the child's schooling difficult. Conferences were difficult to arrange and the long school day gave families minimal contact with their child during their waking hours. The growing concern felt by this family for the traveling their son had to do (especially during winter months) led them to regularly pressure the director of special education at Oswego County BOCES.

Two of the hearing impaired children were also enrolled in the Sherwood program at this time. One mother was concerned about the Sherwood program because it seemed as if her son wasn't made to feel a part of the school. She also sensed some disinterest on the part of the regular staff. The parents of the second child, on the other hand, felt the classes were fine, but they knew there were other HI children in Oswego County and wondered why a program couldn't be started there. One mother met another mother at a school function and learned of the latter's repeated efforts to have a program begun in Oswego County. This contact strengthened the first mother's efforts to persuade the director of special education to begin a county program. Networking between the two families was an important initial step in the growth of parent advocacy as a meaningful force.

Administrators at Oswego BOCES were becoming concerned with the apparent need to resolve problems associated with serving HI children in their county. On a district level, individual children were typically recommended and accepted for residential placement. In some instances, children were bused to the next county for programming. The number of HI children identified had been few, with most of them not discovered until near school age. Thus, the need to develop an integrated program in the county had not reached any measurable level until this time.

Pressure from one particular family was another factor. The assistant Superintendent of Oswego BOCES stated that "this family was instrumental in requesting that something be done to shorten the boy's ride, which meant that you had to have a school closer to his residence somehow." In order to examine the possibility of starting such a program, Oswego BOCES first conducted a needs assessment to investigate how many students in the county would take advantage of such a program. Once they determined that there were five such students (all of whom were five and six years old), the assistant superintendent and the director of special education decided the numbers justified starting a program.

Their next priority was how and where to adequately serve the HI students. BOCES administrators were aware that parents wanted assurances the new program would be comparable before they agreed to leave an established placement. The fact that an existing program was in place in nearby Onondaga County was viewed as highly beneficial for implementing a new program. As a second step in the program planning process, the director and the assistant superintendent visited the Sherwood program. Both administrators spoke with the staff and administrators of the Sherwood Program to discuss problems involved and gain information on how best to set up such a program. The Sherwood staff and administrators were very helpful, not only in sharing potential problem areas, but also in making specific recommendations, which included having a maximum class size of eight, carpeting rooms to enhance acoustical needs, and placing the program in a school with an accommodating administration. They encouraged keeping the program as much a part of the school as possible and fostering parents' involvement.

Oswego BOCES had a past history of innovative programming for children with special needs. While they did not see the State School for the Deaf as a bad option, they did consider it a limited one and felt confident they could offer parents a quality program in their own county. The newly appointed director of special education was eager to try new challenges. He felt that "programs like this start best when it's a challenge to administrators." There were no obstacles within the BOCES administrative board to setting up the program. Also, as he indicated, "If you go along in small enough steps, you don't get so overcommitted that you can't back away."

A third group involved in these preliminary steps were the school districts from which the students came. It was necessary for Oswego BOCES to convince the districts that it could offer comparable programming. The districts had settled contracts with Onondaga County to serve the HI children, but as the director of special education said, "With schools, it's relatively easy—it's financial. A less expensive way of doing something is the easier way—especially if you can provide the same thing." Among other things, the reduction in transportation costs would be a major plus if comparable quality programming bcame available.

## Selecting a Site and Administration

The next phase of planning addressed the question of where the program would have the best chance to succeed. Options in rural Oswego County were somewhat limited, but classroom space was available in three districts. One district was eliminated early in the planning because the administration was not enthusiastic about having an HI program in their building. The assistant superintendent of Oswego BOCES had been an administrator in one of the remaining two districts prior to his move to BOCES. In his former position, he had had consistent success in placing new or innovative programs in the Bradford Elementary School under the direction of the building principal. Success in this building occurred because of the receptiveness of everyone from the principal down to the cafeteria and maintenance staff. The assistant superintendent described Bradford as "the best building in the district, the most creative, the most successful, the most stimulating." A major BOCES criterion for placing the program in a building was that the parents and HI students be accepted as residents of that school community and be welcomed in all school activities and organizations. Given this criterion and the past tradition of successful programming at Bradford, the school was selected as the new program site.

The building principal was very active in preschool and early childhood programming, had a creative emphasis on staff inservice, and utilized a participatory management style. Having a building principal with a commitment to staff development, an interest in innovative programming, and a desire to be personally involved was essential for the success of the HI program. The director of special education stated, "I think it can only work if you've got a building principal who wants to take the program."

With the groundwork laid for placement of the new program, the director contacted all five families in March, 1977, to tour the building and meet the principal. Parents were also given the opportunity to visit the available building in the other district initially considered. Their impressions of the principal and the Bradford school were highly favorable, more so than their impressions of the other available facility. Although Bradford was not centrally located within Oswego County, the parents' enthusiasm for Bradford outweighed any remaining distance concerns. One student would still travel 33 miles, but the choice of Bradford was more than acceptable to his family.

The building principal felt confident from the start, even though he admitted he wasn't familiar with this type of programming. He felt the Bradford staff would do their best in providing the right setting for the trained personnel to be brought in by BOCES. During the initial visit, he tried to help parents and BOCES administrators "get the beat of the school, the pulse, the attitudes." He assured parents that their children wouldn't be singled out as being different. It was clear to him that BOCES was looking not only for physical accomodations, but a supportive climate as well. In order to achieve a positive school climate, the principal routinely took this goal into consideration in the recruitment process. Credentials were important to him, but he felt an administrator had to "probe the person, because a teacher teaches what they are." Any of various teaching styles was acceptable at Bradford as long as certain conditions were met, namely, that the requisite material was covered effectively and that the students showed evidence of significant learning.

A second meeting was held at the Bradford School in April, this time in the evening to allow the Bradford staff to attend. It was an informal meeting designed to demonstrate to families the supportiveness of the staff. Issues such as mainstreaming, signing, and general communication with the HI children were identified as positive interest areas by the staff. Prior to this meeting, the principal had scheduled a faculty meeting to discuss having the hearing-impaired program in the building. Most reactions were highly favorable, particularly at the primary level. There were some concerns voiced as to how it would affect individual teachers, and a few teachers at the intermediate level expressed a desire not to take sign language. The principal assured his staff that for the most part trained personnel would work directly with the HI students, while interpreters would be available should the need arise.

### Hiring HI Program Staff

The director of special education was particularly interested in recruiting a teacher with sufficient expertise to intitiate the program, because he himself had no experience in HI programming. The Sherwood program provided him with a roster of teachers from their files. In addition, ads were placed in local papers. He felt that the location of Bradford was an asset to his recruitment efforts, because it bordered on Onondaga County, which contains Syracuse. Proximity to a large metropolitan area would be helpful, because "if you're going to place a program in a remote, rural area even if it's the best school—your recruiting will suffer and you'll reduce your choices."

A selective paper screening of applicants combined with personal interviews resulted in the tentative appointment of a teacher for the HI class. On her recommendation, a part-time speech pathologist was also appointed. The assistant superintendent and the director of special education scheduled a third meeting with parents in May, 1977, to give them the opportunity to meet and interview the teacher and the speech pathologist. Both administrators felt the involvement of parents in confirming teacher appointments would reduce remaining concerns (if any) and pave the way for positive future interactions between the staff and families. All were in favor of the appointments and eager to get underway.

## PROGRAM IMPLEMENTATION

### Preliminary Preparations

Once appointed to initiate the program, the teacher of the HI class moved quickly in a number of areas to make the transition smooth for administrators and staff at Bradford and BOCES and for the five families. Following the May interview, personal thank-you letters were sent to each parent and the building principal, along with information on a fall signing class and a parent newsletter. This teacher was currently employed by an HI program near Washington, D.C. and utilized resources in that area to determine audiological needs, classroom acoustical modifications, specialized curricular materials, and speech therapy devices and materials by consulting with a number of individuals and agencies knowledgeable about the needs of hearing-impaired children. These contacts enabled her to submit requisitions to Oswego BOCES for up-to-date and appropriate audiological, curricular, and speech-related materials and devices.

The assistant superintendent enlisted the aid of a woman in Oswego County who had deaf parents and was a fluent signer to teach basic sign language to interested staff over the summer. The principal, the school nurse, a bus driver, and the cafeteria manager, as well as teachers, attended these weekly sessions. A spirit of hopeful expectation developed among the Bradford staff for the new program.

The teacher of the HI class made an effort to set up fall schedules with the principal in late June. She was eager to set in motion the students' schedules for the coming year. The assistant superintendent advised her that the principal didn't make those plans until early August for his building and that she should comply with his administrative style. As a personal friend of the principal, the assistant superintendent was well aware of the need to respect this administrator's management policies; one could count on his full support in return. An awkward confrontation was avoided through this sound advice.

The teacher requested the right to interview and hire the full-time assistant who would also interpret for the children as needed. The director of special education made potential applicant files available to her in August in order to allow time for inservice of this assistant. One individual had a Bachelor's degree in home economics and was very interested in the position. She had no previous signing experience, but was willing to become fluent. Although the teacher would have preferred an assistant with signing fluency, someone with such skills would not be easily located.

## Selecting the Classroom

The space available for the HI program at Bradford was currently being used as a continuing education room for senior citizens among other functions. The principal made his office available for the senior citizens on Friday afternoons so they could continue their weekly card games. The uncarpeted classroom posed an immediate acoustical problem with 26 metal lockers across the back of the room. Removal of the lockers was structurally and fiscally impossible, so plans were made to cover the lockers with cork, felt, or some other suitable substance to reduce sound reverberation. Oswego BOCES had agreed to carpet the large room, and cotton drapes replaced fiberglass drapes to better absorb sound.

The most impressive feature of the room was its location. Situated in the main lobby adjacent to the front office, the HI classroom was in the center of all school activities. Other primary classrooms were contiguous to it on the primary wing. All primary classes passed by the room to reach the gym, cafeteria, and main lobby. The nurse's office was situated directly across the hall. Visitors entering the school or parents picking up regular students were routinely exposed to the program and to information about it posted on the corridor outside the room.

Although various pieces of furniture and instructional materials had been ordered by Oswego BOCES, nothing had arrived when school began. The principal managed to locate five small student desks and a teacher's desk so that the five children and two adults were able to begin functioning in the large, newly carpeted room. His administrative support and guidance was especially valuable given the 30 mile distance between the new program and Oswego BOCES administrators. The Bradford Elementary School secretary was equally helpful in providing an array of bulk supplies to enable the teacher to welcome the young children to their new room. The school nurse was eager to use her new signing ability to help the children feel comfortable should they need to see her.

### Inservice: Staff

A variety of formal and informal means were used by the teacher to promote an awareness of deafness and the specialized learning needs of the HI students. She had spoken to the principal about the need to begin "social" mainstreaming of the HI children in as many areas as possible. The primary contact the children had had with normal hearing peers at Sherwood Elementary was through the gym class. It was mutually decided by the principal and the teacher that the students would formally attend art and gym classes with one of the first grade classes. Although there were two other first-grade classes in the school, the principal felt that the first-grade teacher was the most receptive of the three and would be better able to make the experience a positive one. She had attended signing classes during the summer and was planning to teach her first graders what she had learned. The art and gym teachers had some concerns about how to best serve the students, but were willing to go ahead with the program. The gym teacher was relieved to know an interpreter would explain his directions and rules for various games. The art teacher, though, initially preferred not to have another adult present in the room. The teacher of the HI class spent time each week explaining the role of the interpreter and how her intent would simply be to transmit the message the art teacher conveyed. After a few weeks, the art teacher agreed to try the interpreter and quickly became comfortable with her in the room. Because the HI students did not wear their hearing aids to gym, the teacher did not need to wear the corresponding microphone. However, in art class the children wore their aids and needed the teacher's specific instructions. The art teacher willingly wore a microphone, particularly as he gained the sense they were responding to him as their teacher. Until the teaching assistant acquired sufficient signing skills, the teacher of the HI class attended art and gym classes with her students and served as the interpreter. She thus had the opportunity each week to walk to and from art class with the regular classroom teacher. These informal talks not only built a friendship, but also facilitated discussions about hearing loss. Other teachers would often ask the regular teacher how things were going, and she was better able to accurately increase their understanding of hearing loss.

Sign language classes were begun shortly after school started and were open to anyone employed at Bradford. Participants from the summer class were joined by cafeteria workers, school aides, a bus driver, and related staff (district psychologist, LD teacher). Since the classes were held in the HI classroom, there was an opportunity for staff members to informally raise questions about some instructional focus seen in the room or about hearing loss in general.

The faculty room where teachers shared lunch provided another informal opportunity to increase the awareness of hearing loss. Not all these contacts were positive experiences for the teacher of the HI class, who occasionally heard comments such as "I wouldn't mind teaching five kids with a full-time aide—no matter what their problem was!" She also heard comments such as "How is one person supposed to manage five reading groups?" It was tempting for her to sympathize by saying she faced the same problem. But it was clear to all staff members in the HI program that under no circumstances could they voice similar frustrations and not have it misinterpreted. Instead, they each waited for open-ended questions that allowed them to describe in a general way the subtle, but devastating, consequences of a profound hearing loss. Over time, the avoidance of complaints combined with simply stated answers to direct questions changed the resistance of most teachers in the school. Often, a regular teacher who grasped some of the realities of a hearing loss was better able to convey this information to colleagues.

Efforts were made to provide certain members of the school community with signs specifically needed by them, such as cafeteria workers, bus drivers, and the school nurse. The acknowledgement of their job related specialization gave them a communicative linkage that fostered usage.

One of the most critical areas of inservice related to the amplification devices worn by students and teachers in the HI program. In addition to personal hearing aids, each child had a Phonic Ear FM auditory trainer for use in school. Based on the same principles as an FM radio frequency, an FM auditory trainer allowed each child to "tune in" only to their teacher or to an environmental microphone. It was advantageous to have auditory equipment that minimized extraneous noises such as feet shuffling, chairs being moved, and objects dropping. The students' personal hearing aids, although powerful, did not have this minimization capacity. When the students were integrated in art class, the teacher quickly became aware of the power and screening features of the device. The lack of carpeting in art class and throughout the school increased the need for an FM system. In the HI classroom, when the environmental setting could be used, HI students had direct input from their classmates as well. The ability of the device to minimize extraneous sounds was a primary justification for having Oswego BOCES purchase the system. Teachers and other staff who informally asked about the device were encouraged to listen to the different input provided by the system. These individuals spread information to those less inclined to ask.

## Inservice: Normal Hearing and HI Students

In general, the students were much more receptive to information and much less concerned about how or what they asked than the staff. Many of the normal hearing students received direct inservice from their own teachers, particularly those attending signing classes. Others came directly to staff members in the HI program to ask why a student didn't respond when they spelled "Hi." There was only one girl in the HI class who was the subject of fierce competition by other girls in gym and art class wanting to sit next to her. She frequently returned from class hand-in-hand with two other little girls. Two of the HI boys were particularly athletic and became favorite choices in setting up teams. The motivation of the normal hearing children to communicate with the HI students was so strong that they would use any and all means to get their point across. The teaching assistant was able to readily supply them not only with a particular sign, but also general communication strategies such as facing the person directly, minimizing interference from light sources, and speaking naturally.

More formal, school-based inservice followed in the next few months, but the informal contacts that normal hearing and HI students shared at school in the first few weeks were highly meaningful to them. On the playground, children other than the first-grade class with whom the HI class had regular contact were given the opportunity to play together and ask questions of their teachers and the HI staff. Some teachers utilized their students' questions to gain answers for themselves. The teacher of the HI class attempted to keep her answers brief, nontechnical, and to-the-point to encourage future interest.

Lunchtime was not as opportune a period for either group of children to relax. In fact, one mother was concerned abut the relative segregation of classes at lunchtime, where intact classes determined seating. Her son was also upset because he was often told to just eat and not talk, eliminating a possibility for socialization.

A factor which made it difficult for normal hearing and HI children to establish friendships after school was the distance traveled by each HI child to reach the Bradford School. Building neighborhood ties and riding a common bus route were not possible given the county-based program. It remained up to the families to encourage some form of integration after school and on weekends.

The HI students gained a sense of belonging from the principal. They were well aware that he was the school's principal and, like the other classes, received a brief visit from him every morning. The habit of greeting each class every morning made the principal a highly visible administrator.

The first-grade teacher and another teacher at Bradford made plans to visit the local zoo and invited the HI class to join them. Other less structured activities became common, such as sharing lunch outside together on a nice day or having a joint end-of-the-year party.

The teacher of the HI class would frequently use questions asked by the normal hearing students as a means for preparing the HI students about others' perception of hearing loss. In many social as well as academic situations, the HI students would not know how to interpret or respond to a hearing peer. By discussing these communicative gaps as they occurred, the HI students were more quickly prepared to deal with new situations.

### Inservice: School-Based

A long-standing tradition at Bradford Elementary School was the school-wide celebration of Flag Day. Each spring, essay contests would be held, poster contests begun, and everyone would participate in a ceremony in the gym. The teacher of the HI class sent a flyer to each teacher in the school offering to instruct their class in signing the Pledge of Allegiance over a three-week period of their choice. Out of 18 teachers in the school, only 2 teachers declined. The teacher of the HI class and her assistant took turns going into the various classes with two or three HI student "helpers." Over the three-week period, the HI students would go into a classroom with their teacher or teaching assistant for 15 to 20 minutes at the end of the day. After the three-week instructional period, the classroom teacher would then continue to sign the Pledge with her class each morning. When the ceremony was held in late spring, it was difficult to determine which group was most proud—parents, teachers, students, or administrators.

Shortly after the school year began, the teacher of the HI class posted a sign-up sheet outside her classroom and sent a flyer to each teacher inviting them to visit the classroom for a 30-minute period to learn about hearing loss and the Phonic Ear equipment. Each HI student was assigned a duty ranging from handing out "I love you" stickers in sign language to sharing signed English books. All staff members in the HI program assisted each class and their teacher as they listened through the Phonic Ear equipment and learned about the parts and their functions. Response to the invitation was favorable, with only two or three classes not participating.

Each holiday season, all classes in the school participated in a Christmas program, each class performing a skit, play, or other form of entertainment. The HI class performed a short play based on *'Twas the Night before Christmas.* Students with intelligible speech narrated the story while other students acted out scenes. At the end of the play, the class led the school in singing and signing Christmas carols. Practice sessions had been held with interested classes and their teachers to show them how to sign the songs before the holiday program. Teachers who participated in the practice sessions said they enjoyed the experience more than they had in the past.

### Inservice: Parents of Normally Hearing and HI Students

The first grade students who had mainstreamed with the HI class had the most direct experience with the HI students. Thus, their parents were immediately made aware of the new program. The first-grade teacher reported that most parents mentioned the program when visiting the school or attending parent conferences and seemed very impressed with the experience for their child.

The principal held a "Meet the Teachers Night" early in the school year to introduce all teachers to the Parent Teacher Organization. He made a special effort to welcome the new program and briefly described its focus. His enthusiasm was transmitted to the parent organization as well. Parents of the HI students felt an even stronger bond with their new school. One parent recalled how the principal at Sherwood had not seemed personally involved in the program, but "the minute I walked into Bradford, I felt comfortable." She sensed that this principal really wanted the HI students in the building. Another parent described the principal as someone who "bent over backwards to go out of his way."

Throughout the school year, parents of the HI students were members of the regularly scheduled signing class. Attendance at the classes by teachers at Bradford, the principal, and others made a strong, positive impression on them. One mother looked back on the situation as one in which "we really felt welcomed—right from day one. It was like they had always known us."

The assistant superintendent at BOCES was a parent at the school. Even though he had been one of the chief administrators in starting the program, the skills of his son in signing the Pledge of Allegiance made a deep impression on him as well. His knowledge of the program and personal involvement enabled him to share a unique perspective with other BOCES administrators.

Parents of all children at the school were invited to attend special events, such as the Flag Day ceremony, the Christmas program, and seasonal parties. It was difficult for parents of the HI children to be involved in these activities because of distance. However, the HI class went on field trips regularly with parents invited to attend on a rotating basis.

Grandparents Day was another Bradford tradition that usually resulted in visits by many grandparents. Frequently they would stop in the HI class for a visit after learning about the program from the principal. In this way extended family members as well as parents of normal hearing children became more aware of the existence and functioning of the program.

### Inservice: Community

Regularly scheduled field trips to the Fire and Police Departments, Post Office, and even a dentist office were more successful than would seem possible. In order for each facility to accomodate the needs of the group, they needed to acquire a knowledge of hearing impairment. The teacher of the HI class discussed the visit arrangements ahead of time with each agency and then followed through at the site.

A radio interview with the teacher of the HI class took place in November, 1977. The interviewer prepared by discussing the issues with her to better understand what questions to raise. The 30-minute interview was aired on a major station in Oswego County, resulting in several follow-up calls for more information.

Newspaper coverage occurred at regular intervals over the next three-year period with accompanying pictures to illustrate features of the program. One article entitled "Sign in, please, at Bradford" described a signing course offered at Bradford. Other articles focused on the type of schooling offered to hearing-impaired students in Oswego County through these specialized programs. Both radio and newspaper coverage were effective tools in reaching individuals in rural Oswego County.

The Oswego BOCES Board of Trustees was given a brief overview of the program by the HI staff and two of the families. At one of their regularly scheduled meetings, the assistant superintendent scheduled a presentation to give the Trustees a more direct exposure to the newly established program.

Administrators from each of the four school districts who had contracted with Oswego BOCES to provide a program for HI students from their districts met individually with the teacher of the HI class. Most of the administrators felt that district monies were being properly spent, even though per pupil costs were much higher than for other special needs students. However, administrators from one school district appeared reluctant to give their approval for fiscal support since a program at the School for the Deaf at Rome could be utilized at no cost to them. At one point, an individual questioned the merits of the new program, suggesting it was a "band-aid operation" that didn't compare in quality with the State School. The teacher of the HI class responded to these and other concerns by supporting the rights of parents to have their child live at home and receive appropriate schooling and the right of each student to have an appropriate placement option available to them. In addition, she stressed the merits of integrating HI children in a supportive environment that allows them regular contact and association with normal hearing peers. All administrators were welcomed to visit the program to see first-hand the positive gains already achieved.

## PROGRAM EXPANSION

From 1977 to 1985, a variety of issues surfaced affecting the management and maintenance of the HI program. Four issues were especially important. They are: mainstreaming, inservice, discipline, and administration. Obstacles faced in each issue area and attempts to resolve them are discussed below.

### Mainstreaming

Every aspect of this issue raised more questions than it answered. While no one questioned the merits of mainstreaming the HI students, specific details on why, when, and how to do it remained unclear, even for individuals directly involved. The philosophy of Oswego BOCES in starting the program was that HI students become fully integrated into their school community. It was also the desire of parents that their children not be excluded from normal hearing peers. The principal supported the concept of having the HI program function as a part of the existing Bradford structure. The HI staff placed great emphasis and importance on inservice training at a variety of levels to facilitate integration of the students and enhance understanding of deafness.

Implementation of the mainstreaming program relied heavily on the support of the building principal and the willingness of the regular classroom teachers to have HI students in their classes. Initial efforts were focused on social mainstreaming in addition to having HI students in art and gym classes with their hearing peers. Except for some initial questions as to where to situate the interpreter and HI students, how to accept the presence of a second adult, and what the FM microphone actually did, the transition for the first three years was relatively smooth. Since chronological age was the primary determining factor for lunch, gym, art, and even music, scheduling in these areas was accomplished through the building principal.

Academic placement was more complex, requiring finer diagnostic assessment for appropriate placement. It also necessitated direct instruction in a content area by regular teachers, who would then be responsible for grading the HI student. The principal was instrumental in negotiating contacts by going "behind the scenes, probing around, and encouraging a teacher who seemed receptive to the idea."

Even though finding a willing teacher hadn't been a concern when the program began, the director of special education at Oswego BOCES later decided they were fortunate to have chosen Bradford, where several classes existed at each level. He advised not choosing a building "so small that if you have a problem at a grade level, you can't work around it. With only one section at a level, you don't have choices."

The principal faced a situation where no teachers were willing to take the HI students at the 5th grade level and he resorted to "administrative finessing." He described these negotiations as "politics with a small p. This is where they help you, then later you help them." He attempted to talk mildly reluctant teachers into accepting the student(s) as a challenge.

Despite all these previously successful techniques, no teacher would willingly accept the HI students at the 5th grade level, and one finally had to be assigned. Three HI students were scheduled to be with the teacher for math for one period each day. She reacted to this pressure by refusing to tell the HI teacher ahead of time when math was taught. Frequently, she'd send a student to the HI class and announce math was starting then. Both the speech pathologist and the HI teacher juggled their work with the students in order to accommodate this sporadic schedule. Once a relative pattern seemed to be established, the teacher would then not have math for a few days saying they had just had "review sessions." The situation continued into January, at which time the relationship between the two teachers became more companionable. As their friendship increased, problems in math scheduling gradually decreased. The HI teacher offered to tutor some of the regular students who had difficulty in math. This arrangement and the growing friendship between the two teachers lent stability to an otherwise non-productive situation. Over the years, it became increasingly clear that informal teacher contacts and negotiations were the foundation for successful mainstreaming.

The following year, mainstreaming two HI students into 6th grade math and social studies classes was necessary. The principal suggested that the teacher of the HI students make personal contact with available teachers at that level. One teacher thanked her for "thinking of her" but said she wasn't interested. While the second teacher didn't feel comfortable with the integration either, she agreed to the arrangement on a trial basis. The subsequent success of this placement ws largely due to the positive interaction and flexibility between the teachers. The following year, the regular teacher described her concerns, fears, and eventual satisfaction with the placement at an inservice workshop.

Existence of more than one section at a grade level, although beneficial, was not a guarantee of availability. Once a teacher had accepted HI students for a year or two, an attitude developed that their "duty was done." Related to this problem was the growing tendency for other administrators or supervisors to resent the intrusion on their teachers' time and energy.

The principal's reaction was to become less directly involved. The complexities increased rapidly and without direction from Oswego BOCES or his own district administrators, he was reluctant to arbitrarily force teachers to accept HI students. A resolution currently under consideration is to have the Bradford school district, in combination with administrators at Oswego BOCES and the local Committee on the Handicapped, draw up guidelines and recommendations for mainstreaming HI students. All administrators feel this effort will minimize conflicts, promote a positive attitude, and curtail counterproductive activities by persons not directly involved in programming. The director of special education described BOCES programs as tenants in someone else's building. He stressed that "sometimes it's hard to know who the landlord is." Therefore, it becomes necessary for teachers and administrators to consider conflicts individually in order to find resolutions.

## Inservice

During the first year of operation, the teacher of the HI class provided extensive inservice for teachers, staff, students, parents, and the community. As time passed, the need for inservice became more specific, particularly given the staff changes in the HI program. The original HI teacher left the program at the end of the 1979-80 academic year. She was replaced in the fall of 1980 and a second HI teacher was also hired that fall to teach a second class of younger HI children.

The Lion's Club contacted the school to obtain information on hearing impairment and were offered an inservice workshop by these two teachers. The two teachers brought auditory equipment to the Lion's next meeting, showed a movie introducing deafness, described their classes, and discussed sign language. The following year the Lion's Club donated money to the junior high HI class to support their trip to Washington, D.C.

The local fire department had numerous contacts with the HI program through field trips. They requested assistance with emergency and medical signs, and received drawings of appropriate signs which were later posted in the ambulances and the firehouse.

When six HI students were ready to move to the junior high level, their teacher provided an inservice workshop to junior high personnel in the spring of the year before. She was supported by school administrators, who made attendance at the full-day workshop mandatory. They felt it was important and would affect all personnel at some level. The guidance counselor, a pivotal person at the junior high, helped the HI class teacher get in touch with teachers most receptive to the students. He also listed the HI students in computer records at the levels recommended by their teacher for the following year. This linkage and the early contact with teachers made the students' transition to the junior high level a smooth one.

In the fall of 1983, a third teacher was added to the HI staff as the program extended to the preschool level. She met with the principal during the summer and at a follow-up meeting brought in a few parents to talk to the principal and ask questions. Once school started, she and her assistant provided a workshop for teachers. They described the Phonic Ear equipment, how the students lost their hearing, and the communication difficulties imposed by deafness. When the HI class teacher noticed that the somewhat noisy walking and talking of her three and four year olds in the hall was bothering some of the other teachers, she took time to explain why these areas were problematic for them. By providing an explanation before formal complaints were made, this teacher gained greater acceptance of her students.

One potential source of conflict for this teacher was the regular field trips taken by her class. Lack of district monies and the nature of curricular needs resulted in few field trips for the regular classes. This teacher, however, needed to expose her students to as many experiences as possible, and had the backing of Oswego BOCES for these trips. Near the end of the school year, one of the two kindergarten teachers invited the HI class on a field trip with her and the other kindergarten class. The teacher of the HI class obtained permission forms and made arrangements to go, but she began to sense friction from the other teacher. When she realized that this teacher did not want the HI class to participate in the field trip, the HI class teacher cancelled plans for the trip to avoid making the situation worse. When asked by this teacher why she didn't go, the HI class teacher explained they "really needed to catch up on a lot of work."

Inservice was also provided to individuals who unknowingly created conflicts. The HI class was the youngest group of children in the school and seemed especially appealing to the cafeteria manager, who couldn't resist giving them preferential treatment. On Halloween, she gave candy to them but to no other group. At Christmas time, she gave the HI children presents, but none to the other students. On Valentine's Day, only the HI students received candy hearts. The teacher of the HI class assured her privately that she knew it was "easy to do," but it wasn't fair to the other students. Following their talk, the cafeteria manager put any surprises in a bag and discreetly gave them to the teaching assistant.

The preschool class moved to a new building the next year. Because the selection of a new site was made just before classes started, their teacher was faced with inservice needs after being in the building for a short period of time. Administrators at Oswego BOCES were concerned about the degree of cooperation that would be available to her. However, before the HI class teacher could make plans for inservice, the principal approached her to ask about her needs and to offer his support. Three primary teachers asked for presentations in their classrooms and an opportunity to learn signing. The HI class teacher scheduled workshops and prepared basic sign booklets for each class, the cafeteria workers, bus drivers, and the principal.

While inservice remains an important component for effective integrated programming, the parameters of its implementation are extremely diverse and challenging. However, the end results are usually rewarding and productive.

## Classroom Management

Primary responsibility for disciplining the HI students rested with the HI teachers. However, when the students became older and when HI students with emotional difficulties entered the program, the issue became less clear.

One teacher had two HI students with severe emotional problems. One of the students had a mild hearing loss, used his hearing well, but required services primarily as an emotionally disturbed (ED) student. He was eventually transferred to an ED classroom, but the teacher of the HI class had discipline conflicts prior to his transfer. Oswego BOCES was located 30 miles from Bradford, a distance that prohibited intervention within a reasonable time period. The principal's philosophy was to let all his teachers handle discipline in the classroom and only bring students to him if classroom intervention failed. The problems of these two students were beyond his ability. He also felt strongly that BOCES administrators should be handling the main responsibility under these circumstances. For the HI teacher, the source of support in these situations remained uncertain. On the other hand, at the junior high level, the teacher of the HI class was told at the start that the HI students would be expected to follow the same rules as the other students and similar disciplinary actions should be expected.

Another HI class teacher also encountered a situation where her assistant required clarification on the importance of consistent discipline in a regular classroom where HI students were placed. This teacher's first assistant moved in midyear and was replaced. The assistant who replaced her had a different style of discipline than the mainstreamed teacher and was more likely to overlook behavior problems. The teacher felt it wasn't her responsibility to deal with this mismatch and asked the HI class teacher to handle it. Although this mainstreamed teacher assumed responsibility for discipline in her classroom, she felt the difference in styles between her and the assistant would be detrimental.

Another facet of discipline related to the role of the interpreter in mainstreamed classes. In many cases, the teacher anticipated that the interpreter would discipline the HI students. Inservice on the role and functions of the interpreter clarified this question, and proposed district guidelines on mainstreaming were written so to avoid future confusion.

## Administration

A broad spectrum of services, needs, and policies within the HI program required administration. But just as responsibility for discipline was fragmented and uncertain, the administrative structure was unclear. A group of competent, energetic, and self-motivated teachers had been recruited to staff the HI program. As individuals, they coped well with a wide range of demands, yet still felt the need for a hierarchical network of authority.

The director of special education at Oswego BOCES was ultimately responsible for the program. Day-to-day management, however, fell to individual principals in most cases. When problems arose of sufficient magnitude, the director would visit the program to discuss or alleviate problems. The distance between Oswego BOCES and its satellite programs made regular administration and supervision difficult, if not impossible. HI teachers also felt a great need for administrative leadership combined with a sound knowledge of deafness and its implications. They lobbied for a supervisor to handle their curricular, material, and audiological needs as well as to offer guidance on a regular basis. Teacher evaluations required someone with expertise in the field to accurately assess their skills and offer appropriate suggestions for continued improvement.

## GROWTH OVER TIME

### Curricular and Extracurricular Activities

Due to the increased focus on mainstreaming, HI teachers typically followed the district curricula and state recommendations as much as possible. Specialized curricula for deaf students were replaced in most instances by existing curricula used by normally hearing peers. At the preschool and early primary levels, there was greater use of specialized materials, but such usage decreased, in most cases, up through the junior high level.

Obtaining district curricula and textbooks was not always possible, particularly at Bradford, where the curriculum coordinator felt that BOCES should purchase their own copies. At the junior high, the teacher of the HI class received enormous support in all subject areas. In social studies, a new curriculum was being developed and teachers worked from various sources. The HI class teacher presented corresponding units to her students to maintain their level of background.

At the junior high, clubs were common for organizing participation in areas of interest, so the HI class teacher initiated a Sign Club. More than 20 hearing students joined, along with a few teachers and a secretary. Extensive options were made available to the HI students, who were provided with interpreters by BOCES in any situation they requested. One problem that arose for the teacher of the HI class was a delay in receiving notices about clubs and activities. Because she did not have a homeroom per se, notices were not automatically delivered and her students missed the first and sometimes second meeting of a particular group. One HI student joined the Track Club, but because it was the third meeting, the distance required to be run was three miles. Although he was able to complete the distance with effort, he became very frustrated and decided not to join. Another HI student decided to join the Newspaper Club and initially hoped not to use an interpreter. He soon recognized his need for an interpreter and continued his membership with support services.

Parents found after-school sports to be an area of difficulty, since the families lived quite a distance from the school and scheduled games. Most preferred to have their child participate in their home school district, because as one mother said, "If he's going to be in it, I want to be there for support whether they win or not."

## Increasing Student Responsibility

As the HI students became older, it was crucial that they effectively and independently utilized the support services made available to them in mainstreamed classes. In order to increase the level of student responsibility and enhance successful mainstreaming, HI teachers instituted a contingency policy for participation in mainstreamed classes through consultation with the school psychologist. Students had to meet two requirements: (i) use the interpreter correctly as needed, and (ii) demonstrate appropriate study skills. Students had developed the habit of taking the interpreter's presence for granted or expecting her to assume responsibility in place of their own. They were required to ask for clarification in the mainstreamed class and for assistance in the resource room as needed. The students also had to be prepared for class, keep organized notes, and participate in class discussions. If requirements weren't met by any HI student, he or she returned to the resource room for primary instruction until the intent to maximize the privilege of supportive mainstreaming was demonstrated.

## Interpreters vs. Assistants

The salary schedule and title for assistants in the HI program were the same ones assigned to all BOCES teacher assistants, even though their role as interpreters required specialized training, usually at their own expense. One interpreter who had been with the program since 1978, had completed all available local training and wished to take advantage of the specialized training available at the National Technical Institute for the Deaf in Rochester, New York. The assistant superindendent of BOCES agreed to support her tuition and other costs in return for a commitment by this interpreter to return to the HI program. Based on a series of meetings with the interpreter following her training, the assistant superintendent agreed to consider a change in the pay scale to provide compensation for additional training in signing. The director of special education supported this request as an aid to his recruitment efforts for skilled interpreters.

The interpreter felt her training and required code of ethics deserved recognition. She encountered a problem in upholding confidentiality in the teachers room when she was questioned about various students' functioning. These inquiries were particularly awkward because the teachers asking the questions usually didn't have the particular student in class. She resolved the problem by changing the subject or suggesting that the individual ask the HI teacher. Despite this avoidance, she recalled, "I really resented it, because as teachers I know they have their code of ethics and shouldn't put me on the spot."

As teachers became more familiar with the individual interpreters, they sometimes used the time to converse, have her watch the class, or have her correct papers. It became necessary for each interpreter to inservice the teacher by defining their role in the classroom. These efforts, carried out early in the school year, paved the way for more successful mainstreaming.

## Demographic Changes

Increased population growth in Bradford resulted in a need for an additional kindergarten following the second year of the HI program. The principal had to move the HI program to two smaller rooms, but feared they might lose the program altogether. The director of special education met with the parents and the HI classroom teacher to discuss the move. Given the success of the program at Bradford, everyone was willing to trade smaller space for the chance to stay at Bradford. The principal made concessions and was able to accommodate the program.

HI staff changes occurred over the eight-year period, requiring new adjustments on everyone's part. In addition, more HI students were added to the program, making a move to new quarters for some classes mandatory. Two HI classroom teachers were relocated to two other schools, and thus the HI program operated in three separate schools. Expansion of the original class of five students to four classes totaling more than 20 students was a noteworthy accomplishment.

The five HI students who formed the original class completed the 7th grade in June, 1985. Two of the students were mainstreamed for all content areas and ranked in the top 10% of their class. Their personal achievements seem likely to continue. The other three original students were mainstreamed for more than 50% of their content areas and expectations are that this level will be increased.

## Program Assessment and Evaluation

There was general agreement on the part of all teachers that a formal review of the program and its components would be highly beneficial. To date, a formal review has not taken place, although informal meetings have been held with the director of special education to encourage an objective, external evaluation in areas identified by the teachers.

One teacher cited areas of need not being addressed because of the director's broader responsibilities. She advocated appointing a "team leader" knowledgeable about deafness to oversee operations. Another teacher had concerns about duplication of orders and the lack of a person available to keep records on purchases made and on program needs. Management of auditory equipment required greater supervision, and even the director admitted, "Staying equipped appropriately is very difficult and costly." All HI classroom teachers recognized the need for assessment of program goals, but conceded that unless major problems arose, BOCES was not compelled to go further in analyzing progress attained. Further efforts by the HI staff to obtain evaluation continue.

Teacher evaluations are completed by the director of special education, who advises teachers to evaluate the performance of their assistants. There is a recognition by teachers and administrators that these evaluations may be inadequate.

## FUTURE DIRECTIONS

### Move to the Senior High School

Future plans focus on the original five students and their entrance into senior high school. The assistant superintendent emphasized the intent to make this transition within the same school district if at all possible. Consistent curriculum, administration, and busing arrangements are some reasons cited for this preference. However, the final decision will depend on the attitude of staff and administrators at the senior high toward the program. He indicated that future success of the program is dependent on strong administrative support.

The other three classes added between 1979 and 1985 were mainstreamed earlier and are benefiting from the experiences of the original class. Administrators and teachers exposed to the program have gained a personal understanding of deafness. Areas of conflict, uncertainty, and disagreement remain a challenge to the teachers and administrators, who are continually working to maximize their successes. The model presented at Bradford has much room for growth and improvement, yet it has gotten many strong recommendations and had its share of successes.

### Deaf Infant Program

The youngest component of the HI program in Oswego County was added in 1983. The teacher who initiated the program in 1977, returned to the county to speak to the director of special education concerning the growing need for services to HI infants from birth to 3 years of age. She knew of two families who traveled more than 35 miles into Onondaga County with their young children in order to obtain assistance. The director agreed to her proposal and the Deaf Infant Program began service to these two families in March, 1983.

As additional infants and toddlers are identified, early intervention is a reality in Oswego County where six infants (nine months to two years) are currently served. The program is heavily parent-oriented, with involvement by extended family members encouraged as well. Preacademic achievement for the two-year-olds is a goal shared by teacher and family. Formal school sessions are supplemented by home visits and a weekly parent group meeting. Dissemination of information on the availability of program services in Oswego County is necessary. The teacher of the Deaf Infant Program has prepared and distributed an information flyer to pediatricians, clinics, and other agencies throughout Oswego County to enlist their aid in identifying hearing loss in young children as soon as possible. These efforts will help eliminate the kind of advice given to one mother about her two-year-old HI son. When she originally requested assistance for her deaf son, a professional told her, "We'll cross that bridge when we come to it." For parents of HI children in Oswego County, the bridge is built.

## SUMMARY

Examination of the Bradford model of service to HI children has encompassed an eight-year overview and a discussion of key program elements. We began with a look to the recent past, where educational placement for HI students meant a primarily segregated setting in a residential facility. National, state, and local factors associated with increased integration were identified and led to the development of the Bradford model in upstate New York. The situation in Oswego County is representative of many areas of the country, because of the small numbers of HI children residing in suburban or rural communities whose families want them educated in as integrated a setting as possible.

The growth and subsequent success of the Bradford model was followed through an examination of elements necessary for program initiation, implementation, and expansion. Conflict management at each growth phase was highlighted, for conflict is likely in other integrated programs and settings. While resolution strategies will necessarily differ from program to program, the ultimate goal of providing quality-based integration will not.

---

REFERENCES

Brill, R.G. (1978). *Mainstreaming the prelingually deaf child.* Washington, DC: Gallaudet College Press.

Craig, W. (1979). Residential centers for the hearing-impaired and the community. In L.J. Bradford and W.G. Hardy (Eds.), *Hearing and hearing impairment* (pp. 275-286). New York Grune & Stratton.

Davis, J. (1977). *Our forgotten children.* Minneapolis, MN: Bureau of the Education of the Handicapped, National Support Systems Project.

Hehir, R.G. (1973). Integrating deaf students in career education. *Exceptional Children, 40,* 611-618.

Hesseltine, M.K. (1980). *BOCES and the education of deaf children in New York State.* Unpublished master's thesis, California State University at Northridge.

Munson, H.L., & Miller, J.K. (1979). *Mainstreaming secondary level deaf students in occupational education programs.* Rochester, NY: University of Rochester.

Ross, M., & Nober, L. (Eds.). (1981). *Special education in transition: Educating hard-of-hearing children.* Washington, DC: Alexander Graham Bell Association for the Deaf/Council for Exceptional Children.

# Chapter 9

# Mainstreaming Orthopedically Handicapped Students in a Regular Public School

*Judy K. Montgomery*

Since 1972, the Fountain Valley School District has been operating a fully integrated public school program for orthopedically handicapped students in a suburban area of Orange County, California. The students, aged two to fourteen years, are transported from four other school districts in the area to attend school with nonhandicapped children from kindergarten through eighth grade. Each student has a complete range of academic and therapeutic services outlined on an Individualized Educational Plan (IEP). This plan is formulated with the help of teachers, parents, medical treatment unit personnel, and community services. Gradations of age-appropriate integration are provided, ranging from a self-contained classroom with reverse mainstreaming to a regular classroom with periodic support services as needed.

## THE HISTORY AND DEVELOPMENT OF PLAVAN SCHOOL

The Fountain Valley School District in 1971 was a middle class "bedroom community" of 50,000 residents who commuted to jobs in the Los Angeles vicinity. It remains today a moderately populated area of four square miles—about six miles from the Pacific Ocean and thirty miles south of Los Angeles. Fountain Valley's Plavan School was built in 1971-72, long before PL 94-142 legally outlined the parameters of education and mainstreaming for the special education student. Five school districts in the immediate geographic area, serving approximately 75,000 students, had identified a need for a multiservice site for students with physically disabling conditions. Up to this time, severely handicapped students were placed in a few separate sites for handicapped students (usually considerable distances from their homes) or were educated by home tutors provided by the school district. Both solutions left much to be desired with respect to the students' social, academic, and emotional growth. For example, it was not unusual for severely physically handicapped students to spent 3 1/2 hours a day on the bus going to and from their special schools. Classes were begun after everyone arrived (9:30 to 10:00 A.M.) and dismissed early in the afternoon (1:30 or 2:00 P.M.) to allow for the long bus ride and heavy traffic conditions. Students who needed intensive instruction under the best conditions were in school for the shortest amount of time—time preceded and followed by fatiguing transportation. Further, normal afterschool social activities with classmates or friends were impossible, since students lived so far apart and had contact only during school hours.

The state of California was seeking a site to pilot a fully integrated school for physically handicapped students. The State Education Department held preliminary meetings with many school districts in Orange County, since needs here were already identified. The department was looking for a cost effective program that would reduce transportation overlaps, reallocate instructional funds, and meet the needs of education-conscious parents in the area. Possibly due to its current success in fully integrating both learning disabled and mentally handicapped youngsters, Fountain Valley School District was selected to build and administer the new school. The district was a high growth area with the potential to attract large numbers of both regular education students and those with special needs. Due to a series of highly successful state and federal grants in the late 1960's, Fountain Valley had developed a first-of-its-kind special education program. A cadre of young, enthusiastic, innovative educators were attracted to the district to develop a school-by-school decentralized curriculum, a team-teaching concept for all grade levels, and the concept of "support personnel" to assist all children attend regular classes.

The first superintendent, Dr. Edward Beaubier, had a sky-is-the-limit leadership style that fit the era perfectly—the Orange County building boom, the new industrialization, and the corresponding emphasis on education. He established a "learning coordinator" position in each school that facilitated a master-teacher coordination of all instructional services. The learning coordinator orchestrated highly individualized instruction for each student, reorganized groups of students in the central area of each school, monitored paraprofessionals, and brought teachers into contact with each other. Special education became a logical extension of this idea. Resource teachers "pulled" students with special needs from the classroom periodically for intensive work, but basically every student "belonged" in a regular class. Thus, disabled students received a wide range of services from specialists, all of whom worked within the concept of supporting the classroom teacher.

The early discussions about the school lasted for approximately one year. Careful architectural plans were made that utilized ongoing input from school administrators, health personnel, university and higher education program instructors and researchers, educators at separate sites for physically handicapped children, and state and county physical and occupational therapy services personnel. A rereading of this planning process revealed that agreement was reached very early on the concept of full integration, the physical arrangement of classes and common areas, and the students it would serve. In recent interviews with five of the original fifteen people who took part in this stage, all five remarked that the time "seemed right" to integrate. It is noteworthy that the greatest support came from families in the community. Letters were sent to the school board urging the planning committee to develop a totally new and fully integrated model for the school. Real estate agents in the immediate area of Plavan actually toured the school during the construction phase and printed flyers hailing the educational opportunities for potential home buyers. Two of the early planners recalled that the community was so supportive that it took a court decision six years later to *remove* eighty nondisabled students from this integrated environment because their parents felt it was so educationally beneficial for their children. Plavan took an additional year to build, with only minor delays in construction.

## PHYSICAL PLANT PLANNING

Completed in September, 1972, Plavan was named for Urbain Plavan, the head of a bean-farming family in the immediate area who donated the land to the city specifically for a school. The round shape of the building was unconventional. (See Figure 9-1.) It allowed students to see each other throughout the school day by placing a cluster of classrooms around a central library/ assembly area all on one level. The central area housed the stage, music area, physical and occupational therapy program, all the supplemental services such as speech therapy and reading labs, and the school library. As in many other southern California schools, the lunch "room" was a group of picnic benches outside at the edge of the playground. The playground completely surrounded the school and was accessible from each classroom and from the central media center. All of these school facilities were open to all students— handicapped and nonhandicapped—throughout the school day.

All the internal doors were sliding doors or collapsible walls so that rooms could be further opened into one another. The outside doors were extra wide for wheelchairs and for moving equipment. Both carpeting and hard flooring were installed in every room, so that while common activity noise was muffled, wheelchairs and canes could still be maneuvered easily. The same tables and desks were used throughout the school so that it would be perceived as one school, not two schools in the same building. Many physically impaired students used their own wheelchairs, while others used

**Figure 9-1** Plavan School Plan

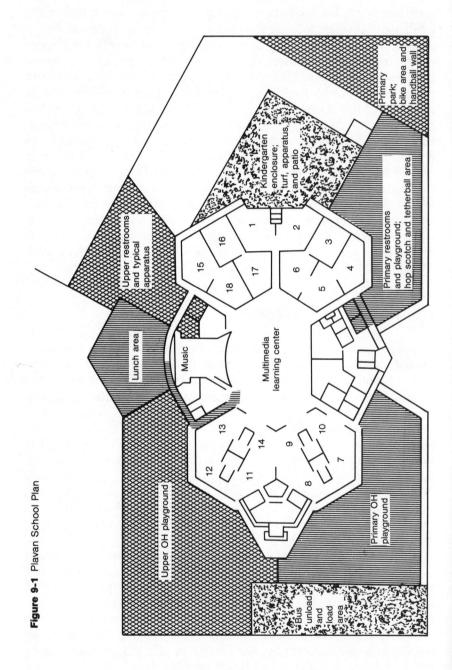

equipment provided by the school or California Children's Services (Department of Health Services). Special chairs with ski-like runners to prevent tipping were purchased for the younger children; and some of the special chairs looked like normal chairs—except they had seat belts!

While Plavan School was intentionally constructed to exhibit many positive accessibility features, we have learned through experience that many potential problems were not properly addressed in the school's initial construction. Restrooms, for example, were not fully accessible. Support bars and extra wide access doors were placed in only three sets of student restrooms. These rooms, however, could not be entered from the playground and were a long distance from the opposite side of the large central learning area. Orthopedically handicapped students who were mainstreamed with nondisabled classmates all day actually had to return to special classrooms to use the restrooms with support bars. Furthermore, the faculty restrooms were not equipped for adults with special physical needs—an oversight that continues to plague the staff and community to this day. All of the outside doors are large wooden doors with which even the typical students struggle. These were impossible for the wheelchair user to manipulate. Children with canes or walkers could get right up to the door but not have the strength or leverage to pull it open away from their body. Electric eye doors that sense a person approaching and open automatically were installed five years ago.

## THE STUDENTS AND THEIR SERVICE OPTIONS

The students who have attended Plaven represent a wide range of physically and mentally handicapping conditions. The largest number are youngsters with cerebral palsy from prenatal or perinatal causes. They range from having mild orthopedic involvement of one limb to spastic or athetoid quadriplegia (paralysis of all four limbs). Other students experience muscular dystrophy, head trauma, hydrocephaly, Spina Bifida, post polio, cerebral vascular accident, effects of near drowning, and genetic or endocrine disorders that result in neurological, skeletal, or muscular impairments. Some of the disabilities are temporary in nature, such as Legg Perthes, where the child might spend all of his elementary school years in full leg casts and then be able to walk when the hip bones or sockets mature. Some students have conditions which respond to short-term rehabilitation and have less academic ramifications, such as those learning to use prostheses for amputated limbs.

In addition to their special physical needs, most of the children had multiple emotional and social needs requiring counseling, speech and language therapy, adaptive physical education, and medications administered at school.

About 40% of the students had severe mental as well as physical limitations and needed instruction in basic self-help skills. Each year, the staff faced the highly sensitive issue of terminal illness. Students with muscular dystrophy became more difficult to encourage as their bodies became weaker and they questioned the point of memorizing the multiplication tables or conquering algebra. At one time, there were also students at Plavan who were undergoing cancer treatments. Most of these students now remain in their home schools with support services provided there. Plavan has also served an increasing number of children who have survived traumatic births or have developed serious heart ailments. This wide range of physically handicapping conditions makes it impossible to characterize the student population with any one set of criteria. The best description is that they are atypical and respond best to an individually modified, fully integrated school program with age-appropriate peers.

Plavan utilizes the California state formula for determining percentage of integration. Students who receive special services more than 49% of the school day are considered special day class students. Students in a regular class 51% or more of the day receive special education support services. Students who receive support services from several specialists (e.g., speech and language pathologist, adaptive physical education specialist, mobility specialist) can do so for only 49% of the time they are in school each day. This formula aided the Plavan staff to place students in the least restrictive environment.

There were ten classrooms for kindergarten to eighth grade typical students. There were eight classrooms available for preschool to eighth grade handicapped students. These students were in one or more classrooms, each of five basic types. Briefly, these types were:

1. a self-contained class of atypical students with reverse mainstreaming
2. a self-contained class with a brief time each day with typical students
3. a self-contained class with almost half the day spent with typical peers
4. a typical class with daily support from specialists
5. a typical class with support provided only periodically (e.g., occupational therapy consultation services, adaptive physical education)

There were some students served for the whole day in self-contained classrooms with 15 or less children with physically handicapping conditions. In these rooms, typical students came to the class for cross-age tutoring, science labs, art, music, assembly programs, and similar reverse mainstreaming experiences.

Other students reported to self-contained special education classrooms for their morning assignments and to typical classrooms for appropriate subject area studies. They were also seen by the resource specialist teacher if they continued to have lags in achievement or needed more time or special equipment to complete assigned work. Some students spent four hours in the typical classroom, while others began this integration process with only half an hour in a typical class with 30 other children. At times, students would be accompanied by an aide or volunteer.

In other situations, orthopedically handicapped students waited in their class lines with typical peers to enter typical classrooms for all-day programs in rooms with adapted equipment such as electric typewriters or mobile arm supports on a pulley frame. These students usually left the classroom only for physical and occupational therapy, which was provided during the school day on site. In some cases, therapy was provided in the classroom. In the original conception of the building, large therapy areas were included in the self-contained classrooms. Students could take part in discussions or listen to instructions while they received routine physical management, such as range of motion exercises.

The level of noise and commotion in the classroom was not conducive to the therapy. Conversely, the activity and interesting materials used in therapy were sometimes distracting to the other students. Consequently, these therapy areas came to be used less frequently. From Figure 9-1, one can see that the area designated for therapy is large and open in the middle of the school. It was decided that it was important for all students to see each other's therapy programs and activities and not make them so highly individual as to appear secretive. In a typical classroom, physical and occupational therapists monitor their students, adjust equipment, train peer coaches and assist students in ways which affect the educational program minimally or not at all. Plavan staff strived for a balance that ensured students were with their peers without intruding upon the attention of the class. Achieving this balance has required great flexibility and patience on all sides.

The gradations of mainstreaming have made it possible for students to experience typical peer interactions at all levels but still receive the maximum appropriate instruction in the most conducive setting. Although there were no hard and fast rules about what level of mainstreaming was initially appropriate, IEP teams usually suggested that the starting point be based on the child's previous experience, age, and academic needs. The team usually placed students at a level that required them to challenge themselves a little to be successful rather than at a comfortable level. We learned that "striving to make it" became a learning habit for many children. After a year of successful full integration, the atypical child could begin the process of returning to his or her home school with physical or academic support.

## A Philosophy of Integrated Curriculum and Language

While the Fountain Valley School District provided a significant amount of specialized adaptive equipment for the school, the most important pieces of the original equipment were certain items packed in boxes sent from other schools in the district. These boxes contained the school's textbooks. All Fountain Valley students were to use the same district and school selected textbooks. There weren't any "special" books for handicapped students. There wasn't a different curriculum for the children who arrived with wheelchairs, braces, and more fragile medical equipment. The expectancy for self-paced predictable academic growth was the same for all. The instructional strategies and intermediate steps, however, would be different for some of the students.

The decision to use the same curriculum, but to modify the instructional strategies, was consciously made by staff and parents. It had worked for many years with mainstreamed learning disabled and mentally handicapped children in the Fountain Valley district. By using the same list and sequence of skills for all children, it was possible for teachers to effectively plan for the inclusion of the mainstreamed child in their classroom curriculum. Specialists and regular education teachers could discuss a student's needs in terms of expectations for that class or grade level. It was not unusual for significantly delayed students (2–4 years below their peers academically) to use books for much younger children so they could participate in a group, or to use non-text materials such as workbooks or study papers that dealt with their areas of need. The staff felt it was more important for the children to have group interaction than to be concerned about the span of ages in each group. If students were adversely affected by using the same books as younger children, alternatives were used. Students were graded at their appropriate academic level. In some cases, textbooks were not the best medium for orthopedically handicapped children, since they could not turn the pages, read the print size, or handle that much material at one time. Other methods, including manipulatives and less cognitively demanding concepts, were taught or incorporated into therapy sessions.

Implementing a normalized curriculum required careful planning by teachers. The district had for each subject area a curriculum outline developed by a committee of teachers. The teachers organized all of the skills taught in each subject into a grade level scope and sequence. This served as the framework for the Plavan staff. The district curriculum was matched to the standardized tests, proficiency tests, and placement tests used each year by every teacher. Students who were mainstreamed into the regular program were placed into the academic sequence outlined by this document.

Another tool the staff used to guide all students toward the same educational goals was designed more recently. Known as the Essential Skills Curriculum, this listing of skills included only the ones necessary for a student to move to the next grade level. Teachers following the district curriculum and the Essential Skills Curriculum could teach the same material, in the same books, and gauge their atypical students' ability level by the same bench marks as typical students. The process of integrating a student into a regular class for even a portion of the day was greatly facilitated by all teachers using the same skill continuums. These documents also helped parents to recognize how many essential steps were necessary before a child was working at age or grade level. Summer tutor agencies or outside educational services used by parents asked to review the district curriculum to help prepare Plavan students for a vertical, rather than horizontal, move when they returned after vacation. Although instructional strategies varied from teacher to teacher and student to student, curriculum was kept constant for the typical and atypical students.

Perhaps an equally important aspect of Plavan School was the terminology used by the staff members in the characterizations of students. They referred to the nonhandicapped students as *typical*, not *regular* or *normal* or other names that suggested the special students were irregular or abnormal. Students who were enrolled at Plavan because they had serious physically handicapping conditions were called *atypical*. This simple use of a specific, yet nonjudgmental, term had far-reaching positive consequences for students, staff, and the community. The principal consciously modeled this language at all times. Staff quickly followed suit. Students were always introduced as Johnny Jones, a typical student in Mrs. Kelley's kindergarten, or Mary Smith, an atypical student in Mr. Markel's seventh grade. Over the years, all Plavan educators have come to adopt this mindset about the ways in which they talk about students. It is always interesting to watch the yearly batch of new student teachers acclimate to the new words and then proceed to use them adroitly while their college supervisors stumble with the unfamiliar jargon. Students who have graduated from Plavan often sent notes or letters to their teachers from their next school or activity. A favorite came from a former student to tell me he had become an Eagle scout. It began, "Dear Mrs. Montgomery, I don't know if you remember me. I was a typical kid named Marc E. in your language group on Tuesdays."

## THE STAFF

Staff members for Plavan are chosen carefully to assure the continuation of mainstreaming students at all different levels and in all situations. The largest proportion of staff members are regular and special education classroom teachers. Teachers interested in a teaching position at Plavan must have the same qualifications as other schools require, with the added stipulation that they accept that all students—typical and atypical—benefit when they are educated together. Selected teachers must be highly flexible educators who are willing to take the extra time to meet with a large team of professionals and parents to determine students' individual needs. Student teachers are placed at Plavan by the local university programs after a discussion with the principal and a visit to the school. As a result, they are usually skilled and dedicated people with a sense of what is different at Plavan and why it works so well. Any staff positions that became available during the school's first seven years were filled exclusively by former student teachers who had been grounded in Plavan's integrated philosophy and practice. As the district's early enrollment increases stabilized and new positions no longer added, openings have been filled by transfers within the district. Selection of the teacher has been handled by the principal, who looks for a person who is self-motivated, knowledgeable in current special education instructional strategies, skillful with a broad range of ages and abilities, sensitive to differences but with high expectancies for all students, and flexible with respect to change and reorganization whenever necessary.

Instructional aides are placed in special education classrooms to assist with small group instruction, supervision, and personal care tasks like toileting and feeding students. They play a major role in the transition to greater independence for the handicapped student. They are particularly helpful when students are ready to spend time in the regular classroom but need some physical assistance. It is often the physical process of getting from one location to another that stands in the way of the handicapped child being fully mainstreamed. For example, when Greg D. began to do the same work in math as his fifth grade peers, it was necessary for him to be grouped with six other students for math in the typical classroom. This was discussed with the regular education teacher, who agreed that she was teaching the same concepts and would be glad to include Greg each day in the math group. The instructional aide was included in this transition since Greg needed three types of support to be successful—physical, academic, and emotional. The aide and the teachers worked together so that Greg would be slightly ahead of the other boys in the group before he was mainstreamed, giving him some time to get adjusted in his new learning situation. The aide was responsible for setting up his mobile arm supports so he could hold a pencil during the math group. She also sat with him in the group every day for the first week, then every third day, and finally only if he requested it. If Greg had any difficulty with the assigned homework, he was to check with the typical teacher first. If he needed additional instruction or support, the aide would provide it during his study period after lunch. In this way, Greg was successful within a month and the typical teacher did not feel overburdened. The instructional aide was critical for the actual physical transition.

Plavan is also served by support staff who are specialists from a variety of fields and who provide the individualized services that severely handicapped children require. The physical and occupational therapists at Plavan work under a physician's orders and are employees of the California Children's Services, which is in the Health Department rather than the Department of Education. They serve both Plavan students and outpatient students from other schools who are assigned to Plavan during nonschool hours. An adaptive physical education specialist, speech and language pathologist, school psychologist, resource specialist, and nurse are the other school support staff. Vocal and instrumental music teachers serve Plavan, providing chorus and band for typical and atypical students together.

There are two major groups of staff members who meet to decide on the needs of all Plavan students. The first group is the physical and occupational therapy staff who conduct monthly "clinics" under the auspices of a pediatrician and orthopedist. Teachers, support staff, and the principal also attend these meetings, which focus on the needs of a particular handicapped child. Teachers, parents, and specialists report on the progress of the child and make suggestions for possible medical interventions. Discussion topics often include medications, appropriate behavior, height and weight, and results of surgery. Before state and federal laws brought about the advent of the IEP meeting, this clinic provided the opportunity for the full team to discuss a child's educational progress. With the IEP meeting now assuming a major role in educational planning, the clinics have primarily come to serve as a vehicle for the school educational and therapeutic team to interface with the physicians who are treating the child and counseling the parents. At times, the physicians will request a report on the child's academic skills or the effects of mainstreaming upon emotional and social growth. The medical personnel have been supportive of, though perhaps sometimes amazed at, Plavan's dedication to the mainstreaming of all physically handicapped children.

The second group is the Guidance Team, which is composed of the parents, support staff, therapists, and teachers for the particular child under discussion. The Guidance Team serves the entire school and determines interventions for any student with academic, social, or emotional needs. The team meets once a year for each child, or more often if necessary. The yearly update alerts all staff members to the student's growth and to possible changes in program. Any member of the team can call a meeting of the group at any time. These meetings are typically lengthy—at least an hour—since information is shared from many sources. At particularly important steps in the child's mainstreaming sequence, meetings have lasted two or three hours. One cause of long Guidance Team meetings is when parents are asked to support the transition of their child from a more restrictive classroom option where the child's progress has been good to a less restrictive atypical option. Parents often feel comfortable with a familiar arrangement and dislike disturbing it, even when the next step could be a very positive one. It has been helpful to have parents of successfully mainstreamed students there to talk about the difficulties that may lie ahead.

A critical factor in Plavan's staff coordination was contributed by the first principal. He arranged the extraduty and recess schedules for teachers so that all educators spent time in parts of the building to which they were not routinely assigned. For example, regular education teachers had yard duty on the playground that special education preschool children used. With one common schedule, it became possible for all staff members to experience the different programs for students at Plavan. Lunch duty, when all the children ate together, was also commonly shared. In a large, round, one-floor building with open classrooms and a learning center shared with medical therapy, the library, and adaptive physical education, it was almost impossible for staff to remain isolated from one another!

Another innovation of Plavan's first principal was the use of all-school staff meetings. All teachers were expected to follow all the policies of the district—even if their students were atypical, couldn't talk, or needed to be fed lunch. While this wasn't always perceived as positive by all of the teaching staff, the "one staff" orientation served as a great cohesive force. This orientation led to sending home the same style of report cards for all children and to structuring parent conferences so that all of them—regardless of whether they were about typical or atypical students—operated from the same parameters.

California State regulations allowing for year-round education were used by Plavan administrators to foster still another unifying innovation. During the vacation periods of the school's year-round schedule, severely handicapped students have the opportunity to receive continuous instruction from regular education classroom teachers. These teachers are able to teach special classes for less than 20 days without the special education credential. In this way, they are able to gain first-hand experiences that enhance their mainstreaming efforts for the remainder of the year. Using hindsight, it has sometimes been the result of these subtle structure changes, such as in staff meeting formats or teaching schedules, that have caused the greatest changes in attitude.

Inservice programs are provided for all teachers of typical and atypical classes. For example, all Plavan teachers took part in the presentations on math curriculum, science curriculum, the new reading adoption, Recognizing

Child Abuse, the Guaranteed Guidance Program, Computer Literacy, Computer Software for Problem Solving/Critical Thinking, and the Identification Program for Gifted and Talented children. Other programs have been targeted to specific groups of teachers (e.g., Turners Syndrome, Use of the Adaptive Firmware Card for the Apple Computer, Creative Dramatics, Interpreting the K–ABC Test, and Water Color Painting for the Physically Handicapped Person). Over three-fourths of the inservice programs have been attended by the entire staff, and this continues to be the district's philosophy. The director of special education conducts a needs assessment each year for potential inservice presentations for general and specific staff groups. These presentations are provided by local university educators, other school districts, state and local agencies, and Fountain Valley staff members.

## The Administration

The administration of Plavan School was designed to be identical with that of all other schools in Fountain Valley. The principal was responsible for all programs and activities on campus and was required to follow all of the policies and procedures established by the Board of Trustees and district level administration. The board and central office administration have strongly supported the concept of full mainstreaming of students at Plavan. This was true when the concept was first presented in 1970, and their support has not wavered, despite three major changes among board members and six among superintendents.

An example of the board's commitment to Plavan was demonstrated in the original teacher-student ratio. The ratio of teachers to students was not to exceed 1:30 district-wide; however, to facilitate mainstreaming at Plavan, it was held at 1:27. This was a district policy until it became a negotiated item between teachers and management in 1978. Additional time was allotted for nursing and psychological services at this school to accommodate the increased time spent with parents and community members. Other than these changes, Plavan was provided the same level of resources, supplies, personnel, and support as any other school in Fountain Valley.

In 1979, five school districts formed a special education service delivery unit called the West Orange County Consortium for Special Education. Each district agreed to pool its funds for special education from the state and serve all individuals with exceptional needs. Each of the districts offered fully integrated programs for its learning disabled and communicatively handicapped children. Each also offered to provide one low-incidence disability program, such as for the blind, deaf, or severely orthopedically handicapped child. Plavan is one of the many schools to which this unit refers children with special needs. Placement at Plavan requires the family to live within the boundaries of the consortium and to take part in the assessment of and educational planning for their child. A goal of Plavan staff is to serve children from other districts for the shortest possible amount of time and then to begin the process of transitioning them back to their home school or district. One method of fostering this transition has been by offering medically-related services after school so that students in their home schools can return to Plavan for occupational and physical therapy. Dual enrollments at Plavan and the student's home school is another transition method. This permits the student to slowly adapt to the change in environment. Teachers from the two schools meet often to plan the move, and parents are actively involved. Another common approach utilizes a trial period without support in the typical program at Plavan. Finally, instructional aides or therapy personnel sometimes visit the new school on request.

The California State Department of Education now strongly discourages all separate site placements for low-incidence handicapped children. The state will no longer permit the building of schools or the initiation of programs that place more than the normal proportion of special education students at one school site. For low-incidence disabilities, any grouping of similarly handicapped children would be out of proportion with the normal distribution of school-age children. Ironically, Plavan—the first fully integrated site for physically handicapped children in the state—now serves 66 atypical children and 270 typical children. This exceeds the percentage acceptable to the State for low-incidence programs and will necessitate new program planning efforts.

## THE COMMUNITY

The school district Board of Trustees was very supportive of the new program and helped to conduct informational meetings for parents and other community members. Parents of typical children living in the Plavan attendance area were included in many evening discussion groups and meetings about the new school before it was opened. The school psychologist, director of special education, and school principal offered classes for the parents to learn about the medical conditions of students who would be coming from various parts of Fountain Valley and surrounding cities. Parents learned the causes of common handicapping conditions and were encouraged to ask questions about cerebral palsy, dwarfism, genetic disorders, and muscular dystrophy. The newly formed parent teacher organization (PTO) held informal gatherings in homes to assist parents to share any possible anxieties about the school.

Many of these sessions included the parents of handicapped children as well. Fears about contagion, safety, and reduction of attention to students were dealt with on a direct parent-to-parent or parent-to-staff basis. From this arose an important group—a parent teacher organization for all of Plavan School. It was crucial that there not be one PTO for neighborhood parents and another for parents whose children were bused to Plavan. Parents from the local area handled much of the organization because of their greater proximity. Thirteen years later, the same PTO organization still continues representing the needs of all students at Plavan. Each year, fundraising activities such as a school carnival, paper drive, and book fair are carefully planned by the PTO so that all children can fully participate in the events as well as benefit from the financial contributions to the school.

Another spinoff of this early parent information campaign was the establishment of a very active volunteer program. About 30% of the parents in the Plavan community volunteer time to the school each year. Volunteers of all ages assisted in the classrooms, library, playground, and afterschool activities. Boy and Girl Scout programs organized by parent leaders for all interested children at Plavan have continued today. Grandparents, senior citizens, and local volunteers help with field trips, assembly programs, and playground activities. Students from five local universities use Plavan to do their observations of both regular and special education programming. Interns in occupational and physical therapy are assigned to Plavan yearly, as are school psychologists doing field work and educational administration trainees.

The community remains highly supportive of Plavan School and believes that the fully integrated school arrangement provides as much or more special attention to able-bodied children as to the orthopedically handicapped children. The relatively small size of the school compared to others in the area also tends to create a closer, more family-like feeling. Parents are welcome in the classrooms and feel at home in any part of the school. Large numbers of parents turn out for evening school programs, IEP meetings, School Improvement Council meetings, and curriculum modification meetings. School board members have had their typical children placed in Plavan School since it opened, sometimes by special request.

## EXPANDING THE PROGRAM BOUNDARIES

As mentioned earlier, Plavan has a year-round calendar. Students go to school for nine weeks and are off for "intersession" for three or four weeks. They attend school for 180 days a year in four quarter sessions. The severely handicapped children also have the option of attending 20–30 days of self-contained instruction during any of the intersessions to prevent possible loss of skills during a noninstructional time. Since typical students do not attend at this time, full integration is not possible. Approximately 50% of the handicapped students attend at least one intersession and 20% attend all of them. Informal studies of the success rate of the students who attend intersession vs. those who do not has shown no difference in skill level or rate of progress. It appears that students who attend all intersessions do so because there is no alternative care provider at home.

A class for preschool students from ages two to five was added to Plavan as the need for even earlier intervention was recognized. Classes were recombined to permit one class to handle only preschoolers. Without a typical preschool at the site, these students have had to be mainstreamed with kindergarteners or spend the afternoons in typical day-care settings with age-appropriate peers. This was difficult to work out initially, and still presents problems. Some students need the preschool academic level, but also should be spending social time with age-appropriate peers who are at school different or longer hours of the day.

Three classes for the severely communicatively handicapped children were added to the school in 1981. Again, classes for the physically handicapped were reorganized as students with less severe physical disabilities were referred to Plavan. This was also made possible as successful support systems for orthopedically handicapped students were established at their own schools. Plavan was able to return many students to their home schools. A new arrangement for mainstreaming was developed. Since the language handicapped students do not have physical disabilities, the physically handicapped children were integrated with less disabled age-appropriate peers. Because these communicatively handicapped students also begin school at age three, a gradation of integrated options is now possible for Plavan's preschoolers.

The impact of Plavan has also extended to the creation of appropriate programming for high school students with orthopedic disabilities. The high schools in the Fountain Valley area are organized as a separate school district serving five small cities. These five high schools all receive students from Plavan. The articulation process to the high school program from the elementary district was particularly important for physically handicapped children and their parents. One high school began by observing Plavan's program in 1974 and added a few of the Plavan graduates each successive year in a closely monitored program. The next year, several Plavan teachers were hired by the high school district to set up an extension of the program on one of the four-year high school campuses. Each spring, teachers from both schools meet to develop programs for graduating Plavan students entering high school the next fall.

IEP's are rewritten to accommodate the departmentalized high school program. The move to a high school program allows the atypical student several levels of integration with typical peers. For example, students attend football games, pep rallies, and other all-school events that are age appropriate. They can also take elective classes, go to the vocational counselor, and even work in the school office, gym, or cafeteria—common activities for able-bodied students.

Plavan staff have assisted the high school staff to make a variety of modifications to assist the atypical students. Additional aide support, for example, is provided to get students from class to class quickly or to take lecture notes. Another modification involves training several students to use microcomputers. Some nonverbal, severely physically handicapped students who are capable of doing grade level or above work use these personal computers for all of their communication needs. Proficiency testing for the high school classes is also administered to the mainstreamed students with whatever modifications are necessary to accommodate their physical limitations. For example, students who cannot write an essay due to poor hand coordination can dictate their English proficiency test on a tape recorder for transcription and grading. And finally, great emphasis is placed upon full school-community integration, with atypical students attending sports events and participating in clubs, school elections, and other social events. Five years ago, the Homecoming King at Fountain Valley High School was a graduate of the special education program at Plavan School. This same emphasis has led to the development of appropriate off-campus work placements and career or vocational opportunities.

Several state and federal grant programs have been housed at Plavan over the years. The unique integration of able-bodied and physically and mentally handicapped children had made several innovative programs possible. A Title III Early Integration Program for High Risk Preschoolers established a parent education program and a diagnostic preschool in 1973. Children were referred for a full diagnostic work-up and placement in a program to determine the extent of their learning disabilities. Most of these children had multiple physical problems and were followed closely by the project staff after placement in schools and regional agencies. At least 40% of those children remained at Plavan for educational and therapeutic intervention.

In 1977, a Title IV-C Grant established a Non Oral Communication Center for severely handicapped students who could not speak and used instead augmentative communication systems. In place for six years, the project documented the use of augmentative aids in school settings for children who were considered untestable due to their complete lack of vocal communication skills and of the physical dexterity to use signs or point to language boards. Seven satellite centers to replicate this project were set up in schools in California from 1980 to 1984. The services for all students using augmentative aids have been continued by the existing staff members at Plavan, even though the grant money has been expended. Augmentative systems are used in the classrooms, therapy sessions, on the bus, and at home. The high school has a companion program for nonspeaking students.

At the present time, Plavan has a new grant program called *Speaking From Experience,* which teaches nonhandicapped children about their peers with handicapping conditions. This project represents the first time children with special needs will train their typical peers to understand mental and physical disabilities. The grant began with a pilot program at Plavan that has spread to every other school in the District. The consultant to the project is severely physically disabled himself, uses an electric wheelchair, and discusses his struggle to be educated along with his fellow students. Special needs children tell about their own experiences, lead discussions, and introduce hands-on activities. The effect is powerful, and students love it!

Grant money has had a continuing positive effect on the staff and services at Plavan school. New ideas were generated by staff members skilled at pointing out unmet needs. Solving problems in new ways has become a part of the Plavan tradition. Seeking out support—either financial or moral—was encouraged by the administration. The eager leaders spoken of earlier were behind each of these grants and helped to disseminate the new ideas throughout the school. Even if Plavan had not procured outside grant dollars, it is highly likely that staff commitment to improvement through problem solving would have brought about many innovations.

## THE MANY IMPACTS OF PLAVAN SCHOOL

The impact of the fully integrated program for physically and severely handicapped children at Plavan School can be measured in several ways. The school was designed for full integration 13 yeas ago and continues to provide educational services to typical students and their handicapped peers in a neighborhood school setting. It is important to note that two similar schools in California designed at the same time as Plavan have reverted to separate sites for handicapped children only. Recent interviews with each site administrator revealed that both schools could not keep staff members willing to allocate the extra time necessary to mainstream children.

Student achievement testing is conducted at Plavan just as it is at every other school in the Fountain Valley School District. All students who are mainstreamed take the state and district standardized tests of achievement on a year-by-year basis. Overall, the school has maintained achievement test scores consistent with the rest of the district. Students who are not fully mainstreamed have the option of taking, at parental discretion, the standardized tests or being evaluated by their progress in reaching their IEP goals and objectives.

Fourteen years later, neighborhood students continue to walk to Plavan School for kindergarten to eighth grade classes. Many have made close friendships with their handicapped peers who come to school on a bus from other areas. A birthday party story told by one of the parents of a typical kindergartener at a PTO meeting puts this in perspective. This parent's six-year-old daughter had been planning her first "real birthday party with school friends" for several weeks. She talked about her upcoming "special day" for several weeks, naming and renaming all the little girls from school who would be there. Her mother was anxious to meet all these new friends and asked her daughter to describe each one so she could recognize them when they arrived at the house. Her daughter was highly verbal and enjoyed this game of describing her friends in every detail. When the day came, her mother was able to recognize many of them from her daughter's descriptions. However, she was quite surprised when Lisa, one of the playmates, arrived. She was wearing leg braces and used a walker. After the party, she asked her daughter why she hadn't mentioned Lisa's leg braces when she had described this friend. Her response shows the value of mainstreaming. She said, "I guess I must have forgotten about them."

Greater percentages of severely involved children are seen at Plavan now than when it was first opened, because mildly physically handicapped children are now able to begin at their home school in a regular classroom with itinerant special assistance. At one time, all physically handicapped children began school at Plavan first. They would stay a year or two until parents and staff were convinced that the same level of support could be provided at the home school. Plavan still serves many disabled children for a short period of time to help them get used to the pace of a regular classroom, and it provides the greatest support possible with physical and occupational therapy on the same site. The same high degree of medical and educational interaction is not necessary once a student's condition has stabilized or support systems are working maximally in the school setting.

Several surrounding cities have special needs students who once attended Plavan and are now able to return to their home school with modifications in the curriculum or with special equipment. The built-in steps of gradual mainstreaming found at Plavan facilitates a return to the home school as soon as the student is ready for a typical classroom. Administrators and teachers from other consortium schools are encouraged to observe students at Plavan who are about to return to home schools to see the physical modifications (e.g., wheelchair ramps, desk equipment, mobility aides) that may be necessary to support these children's programs in the home school. Sometimes staff members from Plavan will visit the home school and help the staff there to "trouble-shoot" architectural barriers, personal care needs, safe recess activities, and academic support. Technical assistance is provided by teachers released from their usual assignments for a portion of the day to meet with staff members from other schools.

The Sergio Duran Award was established many years ago at Plavan in remembrance of a student who overcame great personal obstacles to realize his potential. Each year, an eighth grade graduate in special education at Plavan who personifies this combination of effort and enthusiasm is presented this award. Students from all classes—regular and special education— look forward to the conferring of this special honor. It is an indication of the closeness that develops when they spend so much time together.

The criteria that Tom Bellamy and Barbara Wilcox (1981) use in measuring the effectiveness of integrated programming for moderately and severely involved students are roughly as follows:

1. a range of integration possibilities
2. an age-appropriate effective curriculum
3. a community-referenced future orientation
4. parent involvement in the school decisions

Although these were meant to apply specifically to secondary education settings, they also apply to the elementary and middle school model that Plavan is based upon.

Reviewing these criteria with respect to Plavan points up its successfulness. The extent and depth of the integration varies for the students at Plavan and is determined by their IEPs. There is a wide range of integration options, which are even more varied at the high school level. Plavan has an age-appropriate curriculum because it is determined by the grade level curriculum for the entire school district. Students are evaluated on their ability to meet individual goals based upon the expectancies for students their age and ability in typical school programs. Great efforts are made by staff members, students, and administrators to work with the community to assure success for all of the Plavan pupils. It has been crucial that the staff has a problem-solving orientation, because almost all special needs children have required a different type of program. Each time a decision is made, for example, regarding peer interaction, level of physical or academic support, or length of school day, the future ramifications are taken into account. Finally, all parents—through a single parent teacher organization—are involved in program planning, integration decisions, methods of instruction, and transition to high school or to their home school.

Beyond these critera are other measures of program success. Parents have remained very active throughout the years that Plavan has been operating.

Achievement test scores for typical and atypical children have remained at the district average. Each year, intellectually gifted students are identified from among both types of children. The children receive intensive instruction to expand their academic skills horizontally, instead of just vertically. Staff satisfaction is evident in the yearly school climate evaluations completed by the staff. They have a great sense of pride in their school and in their students. Almost 90% of the staff have taught one or more intersessions, exchanged roles with a colleague, experienced a special day class or a fully integrated typical class. The first principal remained at the school for 13 years, and staff turnover at Plavan is less than any other school in the district.

In addition to such tangible measures of success, there are many intangibles that only a person who deeply believed in the concept of full integration of students with physical disabilities could fully appreciate. Working at Plavan School for nine years was an outstanding personal and professional experience for me. I relished both the initial frustration and the ultimate satisfaction of successfully scheduling students with so many varied needs. I enjoyed the challenge of writing meaningful IEPs for children who needed to accomplish so much in such a short time. I liked the openness with which parents and teachers shared their concerns about how much we could pack into one school day—and still physically manage the equipment, paraprofessionals, and cross-age tutors. I liked the feeling of adventure we all experienced as educators, specialists, and administrators doing something new without known boundaries or limitations. If something didn't work the first time, we put our heads together and came up with another answer. But most of all, I thrived on the sense of wonder and satisfaction when a full integration program worked well, as it did much more often than not.

## REFERENCES

Bellamy, G.T., & Wilcox, B. (1981). *Secondary education for severely handicapped children: Guidlines for quality services.* Eugene, OR: University of Oregon.

Fountain Valley School District, Superintendent's Office. (1984). *Fountain Valley School District philosophy statement.* Fountain Valley, CA: author.

Fountain Valley School District, Superintendent's Office. (1985). *Fountain Valley School District strategic goals 1985-1986.* Fountain Valley, CA: Author.

Mahnken, J. (1985). Personal communication. Fountain Valley, CA.

McGookin, R. (1985). *Speaking from experience grant.* Sacramento, CA: State Department of Education (grant AB-2841).

Meyers, Sheila. (1985). Personal communication. Fountain Valley, CA.

Price, Waldo. (1985). Personal communication. Fountain Valley, CA.

# Chapter 10

# Seriously Behaviorally Disabled Children in the Mainstream

*Stillman Wood, Michael MacDonald,* and *Linda Siegelman*

The intent of law, policy, rules, and regulations for the past decade has been to facilitate the provision of compensatory and special programs for children in the nation's schools. They have inadvertently, however, provided support for a "deficit model of educational intervention" establishing several "categorical programs." Such programs were designed to provide separate services and instruction, replacing or supplanting general education instruction in basic skills for those students possessing specified eligibility characteristics.

The impact of these programs (e.g., Chapter 1, special education) has been focused upon students at the lower end of an achievement continuum. Criteria established for program eligibility has not always clearly differentiated between the needs of these students. As a result, considerable debate has occurred over questions of which students should be served in each of the categorical programs, i.e., which students are disadvantaged and which students are handicapped. These discussions led to the identification of a group of students who were not eligible for either program but who required additional service.

The Washington State Legislature addressed these needs when they enacted bills in 1981 and 1984 to assist districts with the development of programs for these students who were felt to be neither disadvantaged nor handicapped. Programs sponsored under this legislation for students who were considered "at risk" for academic achievement were described as remedial assistance programs (RAP). The intended purpose of RAP was to provide "supplemental remedial services in basic skills" for children who scored below the 50th percentile on a standardized achievement test and who did not receive similar services from existing special education or Chapter 1 programs.

While writers most frequently have concerned themselves with an adverse impact upon a student's social development when directed into categorical programs (Johnson and Johnson, 1981, 1983), the impact upon academic programs has been regarded neutral at best, and quite possibly negative (Carlberg and Kavale, 1980; Kavale and Glass, 1981, 1982; Wang and Birch, 1984). Further, the very assumptions underlying the categorical distinctions among the categorical programs and among the students being served appear to be false (Epps, Ysseldyke, and McGue, 1981; Ysseldyke, Algozzine, and Allen, 1982; Ysseldyke, Algozzine, Shinn, and McGue, 1979; Ysseldyke and Thurlow, 1983), suggesting that the traditional separation of students into "homogeneous" groupings may no longer be justifiable.

Other problems inherent in categorical service delivery have included (i) the label stigma, (ii) the lack of agreed upon classification criteria for certain handicapping categories such as specific learning disabilities (SLD) and serious behavior disorders (SBD), (iii) inappropriate degrees of emphasis upon causal factors, and (iv) overlap and duplication of services. Utilizing such findings, researchers have begun to suggest that it is time for reintegration of categorical and special programs with regular education (Lilly, in press; Stainback and Stainback, 1984). This position, while reflected in special education literature, is not easily discernible in federal, state, or local policies and practices.

In the 1980-81 school year, the Olympia School District undertook a study of its special needs programs within the district to determine ways in which special education and remedial education programs could be fully integrated. An initial response to the study was the reorganization of administrative responsibilities for special and remedial programs (assignment to a single administrator) and the development of a teacher consultation model to be based upon identified student instructional needs. The current Olympia model was designed to address the instructional and behavioral needs of SLD and SBD students through adherence to a process which focuses upon student needs rather than upon a student classification system. The prerequisite of classification systems for state and federal funding has provided a challenge for those who have worked to develop and implement the Olympia model.

The primary focus of this chapter is the development and implementation of the Olympia model as it relates to SBD students, although it should be emphasized that SBD students are considered together with other students as *special needs students*. Discussion will include a description of (i) system parameters affecting delivery of appropriate service, (ii) implementation of the first Olympia consulting model (1981), (iii) the current Olympia model—Project Merge, (iv) the intervention program for students with behavioral difficulties, (v) the leveling process towards integration, (vi) staff development and instructional support models for teachers, and (vii) an illustrative case history. Concluding remarks will include an evaluation of the current service delivery model.

## SYSTEMIC PARAMETERS

As the remaining portion of this chapter will focus upon the integrated service delivery model as it is utilized with SBD students, a review of the criteria for the classification of SBD students is appropriate. This classification is influenced by both social and political factors. Firmly established belief systems that SBD students can best be served in self-contained special education classes are reinforced when programs are available which encourage classroom teachers to refer to "specialists" children whom they do not consider to be performing to standards. The lack of firmly delineated criteria has contributed to the confusion and inconsistency in addressing the needs of such referred students.

### Identification of SBD Students

The state of Washington has attempted to link its classification system for SBD students to classroom behaviors through a definition which requires that identification procedures focus upon observable behaviors in multiple settings. This definition of SBD students is detailed in the Washington Administrative Code (WAC 392-171-386). Students who are served as SBD in Washington must exhibit one or more of the following characteristics over a long period of time and to a marked degree that adversely affect their educational performance (p. 18):

1. an inability to learn that cannot be explained by intellectual, sensory, or health factors
2. an inability to build or maintain satisfactory interpersonal relationships with peers and teachers
3. inappropriate types of behavior or feelings under normal circumstances
4. a general pervasive mood of unhappiness or depression
5. a tendency to develop physical symptoms or fears associated with personal or school problems

Judicious application of this definition has resulted in the identification of some 35 students as SBD within a total handicapped student population of approximately 900 students. The SBD component represents a total of 3.9%

of the handicapped enrollment. Additional demographic information adds perspective to the small proportion of SBD students.

## Demographics: Olympia School District

The Olympia School District is a small urban school district located in the capital city of Washington. The district has a total enrollment of 6,900 students in kindergarten through 12th grade. In addition, the Olympia School District serves as the host district for the Thurston County Cooperative Special Services (TCCSS) which contracts to provide all special education and related services for handicapped children identified within the member districts. The student population of the TCCSS member districts totals approximately 14,600 students at 32 individual school buildings. The Olympia School District is strongly committed to the neighborhood school concept, utilizing 10 elementary school buildings to serve approximately 1900 elementary students. The secondary age students attend three middle schools and two high schools.

## Additional Problems in Defining and Servicing SBD Students

Students served within the Olympia School District's special education program as SBD students meet the state criteria for SBD as outlined above. Although few students have been classified as SBD, classroom teachers have identified additional students who present significant disruptive behaviors within the classroom (e.g, disregard for classroom rules, verbal and physical aggression toward  peers, disruption of classroom activities). Even with a known rigorous eligibility definition of SBD coupled with an educational philosophy oriented toward student academic success, teachers have continued to refer these students for "behavioral" reasons. This led the special education staff to conclude that in many cases it was not possible for them to discriminate between SBD students and others who were presenting classroom management problems.

Communication to classroom teachers as to whether or not an individual child is eligible as SBD by definition did little to assist either the teacher or student with the management of behavioral problems. Moreover, an emphasis upon causal factors detracted from the programming requirements at hand, i.e., parents and educators expected improved behavior and learning from the students. The desired role of the classroom teachers was to deliver instruction, not to provide "therapy based interventions." These factors led to an instructionally based approach for one group of students—special needs students—and to the development of a continuum of interventions that might be used within the regular classroom for all students presenting performance problems.

## THE INITIAL STAGES

Traditionally, the Olympia School District's special education program served low-achieving and behavior-problem students within special education classrooms. Although specific programs structured and identified for SBD students had never been provided, existing special education programs delivered instruction and support services separate from the services and programs of regular education. Moreover, the numbers of students referred for these services were increasing for two primary reasons: (i) the services were available and (ii) classification of students as SBD bore a direct relationship to state and Federal funding models for special education. Thus, the expectations among district teachers were that any child who experienced learning or behavioral difficulties could be made a "focus of concern" in order to qualify for "specially designed instruction" within a special education setting.

The need for the adoption of a service delivery model through which regular educators would take responsibility for students who evidenced performance problems was apparent. For the reasons delineated above, a consultation model was viewed favorably by the special education administration. However, funding patterns prohibited formal adoption of the model and consultation was left to individual teachers—who did or did not consult depending upon what they saw their role as special educators to be. Events which made the consultation model a possibility for the Olympia School District occurred in the early 1980's.

### Changing the Conceptual Framework

An interim funding model for the 1981-82 school year, described as a *block grant* approach, did much to remove the barriers to integrated service delivery programming. As noted earlier, funding for programs had been dependent upon the classification of students. Models which did not depend upon a categorical program structure and classification of students as a prerequisite to intervention were in direct conflict with policy level decisions at both the federal and state levels. The block grant approach enabled local districts to receive funding without direct dependence upon classifying students as handicapped (i.e., additional students identified as handicapped would not generate additional revenue). Basically, this approach to funding local districts was an allocation approach rather than a child-count approach. The approach enabled the district to develop and receive funds for an alternative service delivery model.

## Implementation of the First Consultation Model

The Olympia Consultation Model was developed initially as a teacher consultation model utilizing school psychologists and educational specialist personnel. Both personnel groups had formerly provided assessment and special education instructional support in a consultation role with classroom teachers. The intended purpose of this model was twofold: (i) to provide an alternative special education service delivery model with the potential to reduce referrals to special education by as much as 60% and (ii) to maintain increased numbers of handicapped and low-performing students in basic education classrooms. The model did not address particular classifications for students, but rather sought to design interventions around individual child or teacher needs, thus providing a service delivery alternative to referral.

Although the model was described locally as a *teacher consultation model,* it frequently was referenced as a *pre-referral model.* Central to the model were problem-solving processes and the design of individual classroom-based interventions. Its conceptualization as a pre-referral model, however, tended to reinforce expectations of the traditional student classification process rather than a classroom level service delivery plan. For example, following a prolonged series of activities described as the pre-referral process, the child would then be referred and eventually placed in special education—which was the traditional service delivery model.

Administratively, the consultation model was perceived as a service delivery model. Through it, classroom interventions could be developed and implemented within regular education classrooms as an alternative to referral and placement in special education. In fact, the implementation consequence of the model was a marked reduction in the numbers of referrals and placements in special education.

## The Early Consultation Model

In its broadest form, the Olympia Consultation Model focused on three major activities: (i) consulting individually with regular classroom teachers, (ii) conducting workshops and staff development sessions with groups of teachers (and/or teacher assistants) at the building or district level, and (iii) working cooperatively with regular education instructional personnel at the building level. Of these three activities, consultation with individual teachers was considered to be the most critical. Consequently, this process was detailed through a series of staff development sessions with school psy-

**Table 10-1** Descriptive Comparison of the Consultation Model and the Referral-Assessment Model

| Consultation Model | Referral-Assessment Model |
|---|---|
| 1. Request for consultation | 1. Focus of concern |
| 2. Classroom observation | 2. Parent notice of referral |
| 3. Curriculum referenced assessment | 3. Decision to assess |
| 4. Consultation/problem solving with teacher | 4. Parent notice/decision to assess |
| 5. Identification of resources | 5. Formal assessment/determination of eligibility |
| 6. Modification of the student's program in regular education | 6. Parent notice/student eligibility/ noneligibility |
| 7. Monitor student program | 7. IEP meeting |
| 8. Steps 1–8 of assessment model, if necessary | 8. Placement in program |
| | 9. Annual review |
| | 10. Three year reassessment |

chologists and educational specialists, who played the role of consultants. Table 10-1 above details the consulting process as an alternative service delivery model.

The procedural outline of the consultation model as detailed in Table 10-1 purposely was intended to contrast the more direct classroom-based interventions of the consultation model with the established referral-assessment model of special education. However, three additional points should be made about Table 10-1 and the consultation model.

First, while the above outlined steps of the consultation model are from the standpoint of intervention with an individual student, the consultation model itself was not that restricted. Regular classroom teacher concerns could relate either to individual students or to more general concerns such as curriculum issues, teaching techniques, or classroom management. Both types of concerns—individual or classroom issues—could be dealt with during implementation.

Second, Table 10-1 represents a very simplified scenario of the way that the consultation model would work if circumstances were optimal. That is, the consultation model portrayed is just that: a model. Actual implementation in the field is a matter of adaptation to meet the circumstances and exigencies encountered.

Finally, a conceptual understanding of the consultation model can be achieved by attending to the two models outlined in Table 10-1. For example, casual scrutiny of the two models could lead to the conclusion that the consultation model is instructional or behavioral strategy intensive in addition to student intensive. On the other hand, the assessment-referral model is diagnostically and procedurally intensive; instructional strategy planning is only possible after eligibility has been established.

Consultation, as utilized in this model, provided diverse forms of direct and indirect support services for developing effective instructional programs and managing problem behaviors within the regular classroom setting. Direct services entailed a consultant providing assistance to a teacher regarding a specific student or classroom management problem. Indirect services were provided through consultant involvement in planning and conducting staff development training for teachers, administrators, instructional assistants, peer tutors, and other concerned persons. The primary objective of both direct and indirect support service was to train and motivate teachers to attempt alternate management or instructional approaches for special needs students without regard to an assessment-classification model. The emphasis, therefore, shifted attention from special education classrooms to prevention of learning and behavior problems at the regular classroom level.

### Reviewing the Early Consultation Model: The Transition from Consultation to Active Building Staff Planning

The extent to which consultation services met the needs of classroom teachers was felt to be critical if the utilization by regular classroom teachers of the consultation model was to be established as a program option. Steps were taken to determine the problems identified by classroom teachers as of major concern. Information about such problems would provide the foundation for future adaptations of the model to the specific needs of the Olympia School District.

Program evaluation data on the consultation model (Hauser, 1982) indicated that concerns about classroom behavior were the most frequent among regular classroom teachers. Problems of this nature occurred among 33.6% of students for whom consultation services were provided. This finding, together with referrals for students being classified as SBD, prompted an administrative review by the Special Services Department. The intent of the review was to determine what types of support services could be provided to ensure that "behavior problem students" were not referred for classification and programming to special education classrooms as SBD.

The incidence of such referrals were particularly high at one school within the Olympia District, Roosevelt Elementary, where a total of eight students were referred for reasons of behavior and ultimately classified as SBD students. In part, the emphasis upon behavioral problems at this school related to the demographic characteristics of the school itself. The school had a high student mobility rate (21% of a student body of 360 either moved in or out of the school during the year), approximately 40% of the student population was receiving special or remedial education services (Chapter 1, RAP, and special education programs were all established within the building), and 31.2% of the student population was considered disadvantaged (as indicated by eligibility for free and reduced price lunches). Moreover, the building teachers continued to express concerns, through the consultation process, about students who were not classified as SBD, but were judged to be disruptive or troublesome within their classrooms.

A special services review of the factors identified above prompted a decision to seek assistance and consultation from instructional staff assigned to Roosevelt. The central question to be posed to the staff was,"How can the special needs of the student population best be met?" The assumption was relayed that additional financial resources (through the categorical programs of Chapter 1, RAP, and special education) would not be allocated to the building. However, alternative ways to utilize existing personnel possibly could be identified.

The building principal began this process at a building faculty meeting with the assistance of the educational specialist assigned to his building. The initial meeting provided the staff with an opportunity to identify and prioritize the special needs of their students and to articulate additional and related concerns. Within this initial discussion, the staff quickly identified the special learning and classroom management needs posed by students judged to have behavioral problems.

Programming for students with behavioral problems was quickly established as the most important issue for the teachers. Ensuing discussion focused upon additional programming concerns, such as decisions to remove students from regular classrooms for Chapter 1 instruction (available in reading), RAP (available in mathematics), and special education (available in all basic skills). These concerns were widely felt to be significant barriers to the staff's ability to teach effectively.

As an outcome of the first meeting, the building principal determined that the discussion would be more productive if it were continued with a smaller but still representative group. Subsequently, a steering committee was appointed to meet for continued discussion. Membership of this committee included a primary grade teacher, an intermediate grade teacher, the Chapter 1 teacher, a special education teacher, and the building educational specialist. A total of two days of release time was provided for the steering committee, with a command to report back to the entire faculty within a three week time period.

Initially, the steering committee identified two major building problems that served to structure their discussions. The two problems identified for resolution were (i) the continuing difficulties of classroom management and instruction that teachers encountered with students they viewed as having significant social and behavioral problems, and (ii) the continuing classroom management difficulties presented when students left the classroom for instruction within categorical programs. Subsequent discussion focused upon strategies to help students deal with their social and behavioral problems within regular education classrooms. Only one restriction was administratively placed on any solutions—that funding of any alternative services or programs would be limited to current budget expenditure levels.

A thorough review of the consultation model was held during these discussions. This review raised concerns that the model was regarded as a pre-referral model, with the implication that students would eventually be referred and placed in special education. A second concern was also raised: that the consultation model focused more directly upon academic rather than behavioral needs. In response to these concerns, two recommendations were formulated: (i) that one of the two special education teachers assigned to the building be replaced with a staff member (identified as a social worker or school psychologist) who would be expected to focus upon the behavioral and social needs of students rather than their academic needs, and (ii) that provision be made for "teachers helping teachers" as opposed to special itinerant special education staff assuming consultation responsibilities.

## PROJECT MERGE

Although the recommendations of the steering committee were clear and straightforward, considerable administrative review of the recommendations occurred among the special education staff and administrators, building principals, and central office administrators. These discussions focused upon specific strategies for implementing both recommendations as well as upon restraints in place through categorical programs. Also discussed was the need for expanded staff development activities through implementation of a service delivery model capable of meeting both academic and behavioral needs of students through direct teacher involvement within a consultation process. Moreover, it was recognized that the expressed needs identified through faculty planning at Roosevelt School (and perhaps evidenced there to a greater degree than other schools) were also shared in other elementary schools throughout the district.

For these reasons, it was determined that additional short-term funds might be required to address the staff development needs for teachers working in a revised service delivery model. However, additional staff would not be employed. This distinction was considered crucial to the successful implementation of strategies and services to address the building recommendations—so that success would not depend on short-term external sources of funding.

During this period, applications for competitive grants were sought by the Office of the Superintendent of Public Instruction (OSPI), Division of Instructional Programs and Services for the "development of refinements in the current educational delivery system for students with mild learning problems who are experiencing difficulties in the regular classroom." It was the stated intent of the request for proposals (RFP) "to encourage school districts to develop enhanced pre-referral instructional strategies for students within regular classroom settings if effective instructional options were available." The Olympia School District successfully competed for these funds with a grant entitled Project MERGE (Maximizing Educational Remediation within General Education).

## Goals of Project MERGE

The central proposal of Project MERGE is to address a variety of major concerns found in most traditional service delivery models within special education. This includes the frequent lack of direct involvement of regular education staff in developing programs for SBD students. Another problem Project MERGE seeks to address is one found in most models: that a teacher who is experiencing difficulty with a student can only obtain assistance through a referral or a categorical program, a situation found even in many consultative approaches. It also seeks to solve the problem that such referrals most often terminate in student labeling and placement in special education, resulting in an overidentification of students as handicapped (Ysseldyke et al., 1982).

Project MERGE has three primary objectives: (i) to restructure services to students with mild handicaps and students considered at risk for being referred and labeled as handicapped, (ii) to restructure student selection procedures for categorical programs, and (iii) to conduct a formal evaluation of in-classroom assistance for purposes of program implementation guidelines. All three project objectives support two assumptions. The first is that children will not be labeled as a prerequisite to classroom interventions. The second is that the majority of interventions will take place directly within regular education classrooms.

Previous experience with the teacher consultation model had demonstrated the importance of eliminating reliance on handicapping labels for program development for referral and classification of mildly handicapped students (including those with SBD) and students at risk. Increased referrals and classification for SBD students resulted when the consultation model was perceived by classroom teachers as more responsive or appropriate for students with academic needs (learning disabled and mildly mentally retarded students with developmental disabilities rather than SBD). This was felt to be the outcome of a service delivery model (i.e., the consultation model) that was not responsive to teacher concerns about student behavior. When it did respond, the model frequently relied upon classification and placement in special education resource classrooms. Again, regular classroom teachers were then expected to deal with SBD students for a portion of the day (usually as much as three hours daily), without either direct or indirect support services.

Clearly, teachers were requesting assistance within their classrooms in meeting the needs of students presenting behavioral problems—whether those students had earlier been labeled as SBD or were being considered for referral. A total approach to intervention without student handicapping labels was judged as having the potential for effecting positive contributions to general education programs (through staff development activities and other strategies focused upon classroom assistance and support). A further positive effect was the possible reduction on the dependence upon labels for service delivery and student descriptions. Thus, Project MERGE goals were implemented without reference to handicapping conditions and built around the assumption that all students who enter the public school system in regular education programs could be served within these programs.

## Restructuring Existing Services for Mildly Handicapped Students

The restructuring of existing services for mildly handicapped students was guided by several procedures that have demonstrated their effectiveness in linking regular education and support services. These included teacher assistance teams (Chalfant, Pysh, and Moultrie, 1979), curriculum-based assessment (Elliott and Piersel, 1982; Gicklins and Havertape, 1981), teacher consultation (Hauser, 1982), peer tutoring (Jenkins and Jenkins, 1981, 1982), classroom organization (Good and Brophy, 1978), direct instruction (Rosenshine, 1982), social skills (Walker et al., 1983), and study skills. Although these procedures were known to be effective, it was still necessary to organize resources, programs, and personnel for successful implementation. This was particularly evident with reference to SBD students.

The need for organization of personnel was particularly evident at the building level. Personnel assigned to categorical programs within buildings were not in a position to expend either the time or energy for implementation of any new services or programs. The primary reason was that all available staff time (categorical teachers and their instructional assistants) was utilized to provide direct instructional service on a pull-out basis in categorical programs. A solution to the pull-out problem identified earlier by regular teachers appeared likely to help solve the problem of available staff time.

A building master schedule was developed through buildingwide planning which provided that all pull-out services for skill instruction would be significantly restricted through scheduling. Minimal pull-out would be provided during the first one and one half hours of each school day. (Exceptions for SBD students requiring interim pull-out for crisis management would be provided as needed.) The master schedule then allowed grade teachers to work with their entire classes, including handicapped students, for the majority of the day. Simultaneously, the schedule enabled categorical program personnel to work directly in regular classrooms throughout the school day delivering services in an in-classroom model for students formerly seen in a pull-out model. The availability of categorical staff to regular education classrooms had the immediate effect of (i) providing a lower student to staff ratio for provision of instruction, (ii) establishing a functional teamship between categorical and regular education teachers, (iii) facilitating the delivery of instruction in small group settings with groupings based on student need rather than on program eligibility standards, and (iv) establishing a pattern of consistency in instruction, curriculum, and management strategies for special needs students.

A second restructuring strategy, intended specifically for both SBD students and other behavioral problem students, involved a change in categorical personnel. This was accomplished through replacing one special education teacher with a school psychologist for purposes of providing consultation support, specialized instruction in socialization and study skills, and direct intervention services. Prior to this change, the special education teacher who was replaced team-taught with another special education teacher using a pull-out model. One special education teacher served multicategorical primary (K-2) children. The other teacher served the intermediate group. Both classes included SLD, SBD, and mildly delayed (MMR) children. The regular classroom teachers had recommended this change in personnel so that they might receive the support and classroom assistance by the school psychologist when they took responsibility for the SBD students (and other identified handicapped students) for the majority of the day. This structural change from pull-out to consulting model provided a buildingwide emphasis upon the social and behavioral needs of all students. This emphasis enabled teachers to more successfully manage and provide instruction within their classrooms.

Obviously, restructuring personnel assignments involved staff assigned to all three of the categorical programs, necessitating a coordinated approach. The assignment of all categorical programs to one administrator facilitated this process. However, a major barrier to programming was the utilization of categorical program funds in patterns that would not conflict with program compliance standards defined by funding sources.

The funding dilemma was compounded by the numbers of funding sources that each had separate compliance standards. The school psychologist was jointly funded by Chapter 1 funds (adhering to the social services model requirements of Chapter 1) and special education (utilizing a caseload of eight SBD students.). Funding patterns for the Chapter 1 teacher and a Chapter 1 instructional assistant were not changed, although the service delivery model was changed from limited pull-out to in-classroom, again as specified in Chapter 1 program standards. Personnel in the RAP program (instructional assistants only) were also assigned to an in-classroom model, with assignment to the curricular area of mathematics only.

### Restructuring Student Eligibility Procedures

Program adherence to categorical eligibility procedures required three separate sets of eligibility standards that were judged to be assessment intensive in nature. Both Chapter 1 and RAP required administration of student selection instruments (a standardized academic achievement test) and administration of pre-post instruments (an objective academic achievement test different from the selection instruments) for student progress and program evaluation. In addition to these tests, special education required a Multi-Disciplinary Team Assessment (MDT) inclusive of academic measures, and adherence to one of the sets of requirements for assigning a handicapping label. All three sets of requirements were intensively reviewed and a single set of student eligibility standards was developed.

Although detailed procedures were established for staff utilization, the revised student selection procedures were designed to make maximum utilization of common measures, establish a common cutoff score for further review of student needs, and maximally utilize data from the district testing program. These student eligibility criteria are organized to meet categorical program standards currently required by the Office of the Superintendent of Public Instruction. Essentially, eligibility in the various curricular areas is established through a common National Curve Equivalent (NCE) score. Possible referrals to special education are also screened through the utilization of this score. Though they save time, the common student selection approaches contribute little to the need to develop services centered around individual child needs.

### Developing an Educational Support Team

The development, organization, and utilization of an educational support team (EST) was intended to achieve two major objectives: (i) to determine an individual student's high-risk status and (ii) to help teachers establish successful instructional or behavioral programs for children with learning or behavioral problems within regular education classrooms. Although the EST is tailored to the individual school, the approach employed by the Olympia district is based upon the teacher assistance team concept (Chalfant, Pysh, and Moultrie, 1979). The building faculty selected members of the EST through an election process. Three members were selected by open ballot. One member was elected by the K-2 teachers from their ranks. Similarly, one was elected from grades 3-5. The third member was elected at large and could be any certificated staff member assigned to the school.

As utilized up until now, one primary purpose of the EST has been to determine the nature of learning, behavior, and social problems that teachers experience with children. A second purpose has been to help teachers establish successful programs for students with learning or behavior problems within the framework of the regular classroom. The EST receives teacher requests for assistance through several sources. The EST may be alerted to a high-risk student by (i) the Kindergarten Information Delivery System (KIDS—a curriculum-based assessment screening program utilized for all kindergarten students within the district), (ii) the results of regular standardized achievement testing, or (iii) through a teacher request for assistance.

After having been alerted that the teacher is in need of assistance with a student, the EST will convene to accomplish the following (Chalfant et al., 1979):

1. clarify with the teacher requesting assistance the nature and extent of the problem through team discussion and review of relevant data
2. identify, with the referring teacher, a few objectives which are appropriate expectations for the student
3. generate alternatives to accomplish the identified objectives
4. identify and select instructional or management strategies and techniques the referring teacher may elect to try
5. delegate the responsibility for carrying out recommendations
6. establish a follow-up plan for monitoring student progress, providing assistance to the classroom teacher, or re-evaluation if necessary
7. when appropriate, refer students for consideration to an MDT

In addition, the EST may engage in such tasks as (i) screening and monitoring high-risk learners, (ii) sharing resources and materials, (iii) participating in promotion or retention decisions, (iv) acting as an instructional resource to grade teachers, and (v) working with building discipline and study skills committees to establish staff development activities.

## Other Service Activities

Immediate classroom assistance to the teacher, rather than comprehensive child assessment reports, have been provided through restructuring existing services, establishing common student eligibility standards, and developing an EST. In addition, adaptation of the regular curricula, instruction, and classroom environments has allowed for the integration of categorical programs with regular education programs. Thus, pull-out time has been significantly reduced and a closer contact and communication among all teachers responsible for an individual child's program has been maintained. Finally, the utilization of supplemental or alternative materials (i.e., Reading Mastery Programs, Study Skills Curriculum, and Social Skills Curriculum) has occurred in regular education classrooms. New curricular materials in social and study skills have also contributed directly to the development of a buildingwide discipline plan. Consistent and positive buildingwide statements of expected behavior from behaviorally troubled students were also developed and implemented.

## INTERVENTION FOR STUDENTS WITH BEHAVIORAL DIFFICULTIES

While the majority of Project MERGE interventions are oriented towards all special needs students, some interventions are particularly effective for children with behavior problems. Among the behavior problems addressed by interventions through Project MERGE are: classroom disruptions, disrespectful verbalization towards adults, general noncompliance, aggression towards peers, unrestrained anger, outbursts, tantruming, poor peer relationships, and avoidance of accepting personal responsibility. These behaviors may range from relatively isolated incidents to pervasive behavioral patterns. The intervention approach taken depends on the degree of severity and the length of time over which the problem is exhibited. These factors help determine which children are brought to the attention of the EST. The team then determines the need for team consultation or whether management by the classroom teacher with individual consultation and assistance from the school psychologist is more appropriate.

### Specific Intervention Strategies

Interventions are not based upon whether a child has had a previous SBD label. Rather, emphasis is placed upon perceived student or teacher needs. Following are some of the major building interventions implemented for students who have behavior problems (regardless of whether or not the child has been classified as SBD) and have been placed in regular education classrooms.

## Social Skills Training

The absence of functional skills (i.e., those accepted within the school environment) is sometimes the explanation for problems such as disruption, verbal aggression, noncompliance, and poor peer relationships. Selected students with a history of such problems receive small group instruction in the regular classroom or elsewhere. This instruction is focused on teaching appropriate skills intended to mitigate the problem behaviors.

The major curriculum used for this instruction in the Olympia district is the Walker Social Skills Curriculum: the Accepts Program (Walker et al., 1983). Twenty-nine social skills required by students to succeed, in addition to social skills generally required within a regular classroom, are taught through a direct instruction approach. Each skill is taught through a four-step process involving direct instruction, modeling of a specific skill, guided practice for skill acquisition, and independent application and generalization in school environments.

## Individual One-to-One Counseling Intervention

This intervention is only infrequently utilized because of a philosophical belief that group approaches can effect greater generalization within school environments. However, its structured approach to problem solving for specific problems related to behaviors makes it appealing. Counseling sessions are directed to problems encountered within the school setting (as contrasted to home, family, etc.), and they include modeling, feedback, and reinforcement strategies.

## Small Group Counseling

Similar approaches to those in individual counseling sessions are utilized with students who experience some common problems. In addition, peers may assist with modeling or provide support as new skills are developed. Since small group counseling sessions assume an instructional focus, they are usually conducted within the regular classrooms.

## Whole Classroom Lessons Focused on Social Skills

Upon individual classroom teacher requests, the school psychologist may provide whole classroom instruction. Such instruction is designed to be short-term and to focus upon specific social skills considered important to student success within that classroom. The classroom teacher participates and prepares to maintain the focus, reinforcing positive social and interactional skills.

## Behavior Contracts

Individual student behavioral contracts involve significant others (the teacher, a peer, the school psychologist, parents) in the identification of specific behaviors coupled with resolution strategies. The development of a behavioral contract followed a sequential problem-solving sequence that involves identifying the problem, reviewing possible solutions, selecting a trial solution, developing strategies for trying the solution, and reviewing the problem development and its relationship to the selected solution.

## Classroom Management Systems

Grade teachers, in consultation with the school psychologist, have developed individual classroom management systems. These provide the opportunity for students to practice positive and functional behaviors. Expectations within these systems, in the form of rules, are posted in positive format and may involve whole group instruction on given components, e.g., maintaining objectivity toward rules. Since the rules are posted, expectations are known and consistent, possibly resulting in an increase in positive interactional opportunities between the teacher and individual students. Emphasis is placed upon providing students a chance to be recognized in a positive manner.

## Out-of-Classroom Management Systems

Similar approaches are utilized for out-of-classroom settings (playground, lining up to return to class, etc.), where direct instruction is provided for students to enable them to achieve success with posted rules. Bonus tickets, together with positive verbal comments, are awarded randomly to students as reinforcers. The tickets then gain entry for the child to a classroom staffed by parents during the noon hour where students can socialize, play table games, etc.

## Study Skills Curriculum

Project SUPPORT (Ryder, Bennett-Forman, and Shipley, 1983-84) is a study skills curriculum utilized by the Olympia District which includes training in six skill areas: self-management, seatwork, group discussion, direction following, textbook reading skills, research, and test taking.

## Parent Home Involvement

By invitation, parents are provided the opportunity (on scheduled evenings) for participation in a parent study group. Specific emphasis within these groups is placed upon positive skills for interaction with the child in home settings. The focus of these skills is their application to school work and reinforcement of skills and behaviors addressed in school programs.

*Systematic Use of Regular Education Peers as Appropriate Role Models*

The utilization of peers is easily facilitated through activities that involve small groups or students or that involve an emphasis upon appropriate school behaviors. In addition, all rules in the building apply to all children and instruction for rule observance is continuously provided. Removal from classrooms occurs only infrequently, thus maintaining full contact with peers who provide positive role models.

## The Leveling Process Towards Integration

When interventions for behaviorally troubled children (labeled as SBD or not) are necessary beyond those detailed above, more intensive procedures have been established. These procedures involve the loss of personal freedoms within the school environment, removal from the assigned grade classroom, and placement in a self-contained setting. Removal strategies use a leveling process (a series of levels) intended to place maximum responsibility upon the individual student for "earning" the right to return to the grade classroom. Moreover, the strategies are predicated upon the belief that behaviorally troubled children are motivated to participate in the regular classroom environment as much as possible. It is held that their achievement in such a placement will be superior to their achievement in a self-contained program.

The steps involved in the Olympia leveling process at Roosevelt Elementary School can be conceptualized as a continuum of restrictiveness. The least restrictive level is that of full-time placement in the regular classroom. An SBD child maintains his placement in the appropriate regular education class with the support of the building special education teacher, the school psychologist, or the instructional assistants working within the regular classroom. Support services provided may include, but not be limited to, the interventions described in the above section dealing with SBD interventions. As long as the student does not create major disruptions to the learning environment or pose a threat to self or others, he or she will remain in the least restrictive option. Emphasis is placed upon the fact that all classroom management procedures in effect for that classroom also apply to the individual SBD student.

The breaking of a classroom rule by any student, including an SBD student, will trigger an initial step toward more restrictive management, such as having to take a seat in the rear of the room until readiness to return to the group is indicated. The student retains the responsibility for determining such readiness, and indicates it by a raised hand. Permission must be obtained from the classroom teacher to return to the group. All work missed because of the time away from the group is completed during the student's private free time. Refusal to comply with the specified procedures at this step results in lost free time (i.e., by detention during time blocks free to the students). A continued refusal results in the second level in the restrictiveness continuum. A student at this level might be removed from the regular classroom and placed in a self-contained setting for the remainder of the day.

Repeated violations result in an in-house suspension. Such a suspension involves a supervised period of time in a self-contained setting and a complete loss of privileges associated with independence (e.g., going to the bathroom unescorted). In addition, a parent conference is arranged at this level with the purpose of affecting home reinforcers and contingencies. Other specified examples of behaviors leading to an in-house suspension include physical or verbal aggression toward other students, verbal disrespect toward adults, refusal to comply with teacher directions when classroom rules are enforced (open defiance), acts which endanger the safety of self or others, and destruction of property.

An SBD student who demonstrates the above behaviors is placed full-time in a special education setting with total supervision throughout the day. For such children, this means an isolated, self-contained special class until they earn back the privileges of the less restrictive placements. Reinstatement of privileges and return to regular classrooms may occur over a period of days through consistent demonstration of appropriate behavior in all activities. Failure to generalize the appropriate behavior within the classroom to which the student returns will effect the self-contained placement again, starting a new cycle.

Though these procedures have been established for utilization for all students with behavioral problems, only SBD children have experienced the more restrictive level, i.e., temporary placement in a self-contained special class. All of the above leveling situations occurred during the 1984-85 school year. During the first half of the 1985-86 school year, no child was removed from the regular classroom for more than the remainder of a single day. This phenomenon can be explained by two major factors. First, the range of buildingwide interventions (as discussed in the interventions section) that focused upon the development and maintenance of appropriate and positive behaviors were not in place during the 1984-85 school year. Second, the undesirability of the self-contained placement acts as a deterrent.

Removal from a grade classroom to the self-contained setting occurs immediately following display of problem behaviors and upon teacher request.

The student is then escorted from the classroom to the self-contained setting. This classroom is a standard classroom without any special architectural features. Upon entry, the behavioral patterns are briefly reviewed and explanations provided concerning the restrictions of the self-contained program. Program restrictions include supervised independent academic work, eating lunch within the classroom, having an escort for bathroom privileges, etc.

Individual student standards are also established with the student, together with procedures for earning entry back into the regular classroom. The order in which privileges are earned (or returned) is dependent upon the child's interest and ability to make a rapid return to the regular classroom. For example, prior to a return to the regular classroom, a child may earn recess with peers, admittance into music or art activities, library time with the regular class, or physical education time. Moreover, the intent behind the self-contained placement is that such placement will be short-term.

Interventions using in-classroom assistance and support as outlined above firmly establish the goal of placement of all students (including SBD students) in regular education classrooms—a fulfillment of the least restrictive concept of federal special education law. Utilizing these approaches, appropriate staff development activities can be designed in support of in-classroom interventions, putting the focus upon acquisition of instructional and management skills as opposed to student eligibility characteristics.

## Staff Development and Instructional Support Models for Teachers

The Olympia district utilizes a staff development model that provides that each teacher will be paid their established daily rate for an annual total of up to 15 hours of staff development programs. At least nine of the 15 hours are districtwide, reflecting district level planning. The remaining six hours are developed from building level goals. Building level staff development activities developed from these goals may be considered as supportive of district level staff development or may instead more directly reflect the needs of an individual building.

All building staff development activities must be planned through a building steering committee, be delivered in a workshop format of no less than three hours duration, and relate directly to a programmatic need. Identification of programmatic need is made either through achievement data or staff review of programs and building needs. For Project MERGE, additional staff development time was subsidized through the district's special services office.

Staff development began in August, 1985. The entire instructional staff (of both basic education and categorical programs) met for a total of six hours in a two day period. Activities considered essential to the successful implementation of the project goals were planned during that time. Over the course of the year, other workshops included presentations in handling disruptive behavior, current research and review of special education, instruction in study skills, and problem solving as a team. Speakers on the various topics included some from university settings (such as Drs. Randy Sprick, Steve Lilly, James Chalfant, and Margaret Psyh) and some in-district personnel (such as Ms. Bonnie Cuddie, special education teacher, and Gus Denzler, building psychologist).

A total of 25 hours of staff development time in formal settings at the district level and an additional six hours at the state level have been utilized for the project's implementation. Of specific interest is that these workshops were all directly related to the concerns and needs identified by the staff and stated in goal format within the project. Finally, building utilization of the material presented immediately followed the workshops.

## AN ILLUSTRATIVE CASE HISTORY

For purposes of illustrating the impact of the above described programs and services upon an individual student, the following case history is provided. A student is tracked through the developing and changing phases of service delivery at Roosevelt School, providing a description of the sequence of available programs as they were utilized.

### Case History

*Name:* Tommy Randal (not real name)
*Birthdate:* April, 1977
*Sex:* Male

Tommy was an eight-year-old boy who qualified for special education as a seriously behaviorally disabled child in June, 1984, during the final quarter of the first grade at Roosevelt Elementary School (grades K-5) in Olympia, Washington. While not unique to the program, what makes Tommy's case most interesting is his exposure to all phases of the leveling process. The fact that he progressed through increasing degrees of restrictiveness up to and including nearly full time placement in a multicategorical special education classroom indicates lack of success at less restrictive levels. We do not consider this an indictment of the program but rather a discriminating factor between SBD children and the nonhandicapped behavior problem child.

The reader should keep in mind that in Olympia documented efforts at less intrusive levels help determine referral for special education. In the case of Tommy (and others designated SBD), long-term, significant behavioral difficulties are documented through a history of teacher requests for assistance and consultation. For most children, these less intrusive interventions affect behavior positively and referral does not become necessary. Tommy offers the opportunity to view Olympia School District's program offerings, evolution, and the efforts of staff to help the more difficult children.

Tommy was 4 years 10 months when he was originally referred to the Olympia School District by the Headstart coordinator. He was attending a local preschool and participating in the Headstart program. Concerns were speech, vision, activity level, manageability, and direction following. A thorough preschool assessment was conducted. Though Tommy had delays in expressive language, fine and gross motor skills, and cognition, the delays were less than the 25% cited in Washington State special education preschool eligibility criteria and did not warrant special education at that time. It was noted on the report that "it was difficult to determine if the delays were this great or due to behavioral interference." The recommendation was for continued placement in the preschool and Headstart with a review upon entry into the kindergarten program in the fall of 1982.

In September, 1982, Tommy was placed in the regular kindergarten class. His progress was monitored, and consultation services and support were provided through the building Student Review Committee. The committee included an itinerant educational psychologist, the building resource teacher, the Chapter 1 teacher, the school nurse, and the classroom teacher.

Tommy began receiving Chapter 1 services in October through the Parent Involvement Program. This consisted of home visits conducted by a trained instructional assistant to coordinate school goals with the home environment and to provide support for the parent. The program also provided aide time in the regular classroom to support the regular teacher's efforts with low-performing students.

In February, 1983, the kindergarten teacher requested the assistance of the Student Review Committee in dealing with escalating problems. Concerns were low academics, impulsive and uncooperative behavior, refusal to comply, and "naughty" behavior toward peers. Intervention included a DISTAR I reading group in the regular kindergarten classroom lead by the remedial reading specialist and behavioral management procedures set up by the school psychologist and carried out by the classroom teacher. Results of these interventions were at least partially positive. It appeared as though the highly structured small group direct instruction provided by the DISTAR curriculum had a positive effect on Tommy and that he also responded to a highly structured behavioral management program with frequent adult reinforcement. However, problems continued to escalate in unstructured settings and when the behavioral plan wasn't strictly followed. In addition, there seemed to be little generalization from one setting to another or from one adult to another.

Tommy entered first grade the following school year, with the team recommendation that the parts of the plan which met with at least limited success should be continued. His teachers would also monitor his progress and modify the plan as necessary. He was immediately placed in a DISTAR reading group through the Chapter 1 program and given additional adult attention for academics. A behavior plan also was established using a simple point system with stickers, adult attention, and recesses contingent upon appropriate classroom behavior and work completion. Up to this point, all interventions had been based within the regular classroom. The only exception now was the Chapter 1 reading group which was done in a resource room setting as a limited pull-out model.

Tommy exhibited inconsistent behavior at best. His inability to attend to tasks, follow adult directions, comply with classroom rules, or relate to peers resulted in frequent classroom and school disruptions and greater teacher concern. By this time his inappropriate behavior included running from adults, leaving the school grounds or hiding from adults, aggressive behavior toward peers, and verbal disrespect ranging from direct refusal and obscenities to refusal to respond. He also appeared frequently upset and would whine and cry when expectations were made known to him. His mother (a single parent) and grandmother (the day care provider) reported similar difficulties at home.

In April, 1984, the team decided to refer Tommy for assessment to determine eligibility for special education as a seriously behaviorally disabled student. Tommy's intellectual assessment was well within the average range, his reading and written language scores were approximately a half year behind, and math was at grade level. His mother reported that his self-help skills were above age level, while his social skills were a deficit area. Observation and previously documented behavioral difficulties clearly demonstrated Tommy's need for the special programs offered through special education. Eligibility was established and he was signed into special education as an SBD student in June, 1984.

Tommy was placed in a multicategorical resource room at his home school, with the goal of mainstreaming up to three hours a day. Initially, he was mainstreamed for an opening activity, a story/sharing time, physical education, and a weekly art activity for a maximum of one and a half hours a day. He was described by the mainstream teacher as "highly emotional," with behaviors similar to those previously mentioned and, in addition, destructiveness of property, noise making, and stealing. When those behaviors occurred, he was directed to return to the resource room, but on several occasions help was necessary to remove him.

Because of the experiences with Tommy and similar difficulties with other mainstreamed SBD children, the mainstreaming component of the plan for all SBD children was modified. Participation in any activities in the mainstream would be allowed, though contingent upon appropriate behavior and work completion in the resource room. Continuance of participation in mainstream activities was dependent upon complete compliance with all classroom rules. Those children who lost the privilege of attending the regular classroom were placed in the special education classroom 100% of their day without recess or breaks, staying in the room for lunch and being accompanied to the restroom. The student could begin earning a return to the mainstream after a full day of compliance with the rules and cooperation with teachers and peers. The activities earned were determined by the child's interest. The application of this intervention was based upon the belief that, given opportunities to succeed, all children want to spend time in the regular classroom.

Under this plan, Tommy's behavior became noticeably different in the resource room, where he was still spending most of his school day. The academic programs were generally small group, direct (teacher-led) instruction, with a high degree of structure and very clear expectations. Behavioral expectations were clearly posted and taught to all children, reinforcement was frequent, and consequences and contingencies were applied consistently. To facilitate the mainstreaming process, social skills training was implemented using the Project Accepts Social Skills Curriculum (Walker et al., 1983), which uses direct instruction to teach how to get teacher attention, how to sit quietly and attend, organizational skills, neatness, and appropriate questioning strategies. The support teacher responsible for teaching social skills also provided assistance in the regular classroom during initial mainstreaming activities to model programs for the teacher and to provide additional reinforcement to Tommy for meeting classroom expectations. Tommy was successfully mainstreamed for up to three hours a day by the end of the second grade through replicating these plans and programs in the regular classroom, providing in-class support, and using the resource setting as a consequence for inappropriate behavior. His progress was further enhanced when Roosevelt School became a site for the Project MERGE refinements at the end of the 1984-85 school year.

Tommy is now in the third grade and mainstreamed for all but a one hour block of time, which is spent in a reading group in a separate location. Removel of that group was due to a lack of space available for an additional group in the regular classroom at that time. In addition to the reading group, Tommy receives in-class support from instructional assistants during spelling and math. During the first semester, he received daily from the school psychologist thirty minutes of social skills training in a small group setting.

Within the regular education environment, contingencies for removal from the regular class are still in effect, but the need to remove Tommy for an extended time occurred only three times the entire school year, all three during a two-week period early in the fall. Social skills and behavioral support for Tommy and the third grade class, which has two other SBD children, is now in the form of consultation to the regular education teacher and occasional "crisis intervention," which takes the form of reviewing previously taught behavior and social skills, problem solving, and conflict resolution. Moreover, these services are available for all classrooms and for all children. A consistent simplified behavior plan with clear expectations is in effect for the whole school in all locations and is systematically taught to all children.

Transition times are most critical and are structured as though they are part of the classroom lesson. When this structure is adhered to, classroom behavior, including that of the SBD children, is appropriate much of the time. Tommy's continuing problems in unstructured settings was evident in his placement on a special education bus. The change from the regular to the special education bus was necessitated by his inappropriate behavior and verbal disrespect toward the regular bus driver. Staff efforts to involve the bus driver in a plan designed to maintain Tommy on the regular bus were not received positively by the driver.

A past and current administration of the Project Accepts Social Skills Curriculum Placement Test resulted in data indicating Tommy's gains. A teacher questionnaire was completed on October 26, 1984, by Tommy's second grade teacher and another on January 19, 1986, by his regular third grade teacher. Table 10-2 shows Tommy's scores on a variety of social skills. Possible scores range from 1 (not descriptive of this child) to 5 (very descriptive of this child).

Table 10-3 shows the total points possible in the five areas rated and the number of points given to Tommy in both administrations.

## EVALUATION AND FUTURE OF PROJECT MERGE

The program development described within this chapter addresses current issues within the field of special education with alternative strategies. Issues addressed within service delivery included pre-referral systems, classification of children as a prerequisite to service provision, reliance upon pull-out services for providing supplementary instruction, and, perhaps most importantly, the lack of participatory planning among teachers and building administrators. The evaluation of these efforts can be addressed primarily

**Table 10-2** Social Skills Scores

| Item | Oct. 1984 | Jan. 1986 |
|---|---|---|
| *Classroom Skills* | | |
| 1. Sits quietly and attends | 1 | 3 |
| 2. Follows teacher directions | 2 | 3 |
| 3. Does work of acceptable quality | 2 | 3 |
| 4. Follows classroom rules | 1 | 3 |
| *Interaction Skills* | | |
| 1. Engages in eye contact | 2 | 3 |
| 2. Uses moderate tone of voice | 1 | 3 |
| 3. Pays attention | 1 | 4 |
| 4. Responds appropriately | 2 | 3 |
| 5. Converses relevantly about topic | 2 | 3 |
| *Getting Along Skills* | | |
| 1. Is polite | 1 | 3 |
| 2. Follows rules of games | 2 | 1* |
| 3. Helps others | 2 | 3 |
| *Making Friends Skills* | | |
| 1. Initiates making friends | 2 | 2 |
| *Coping Skills*** | | |
| 1. Responds appropriately to rejection | 2 | 1 |
| 2. Expresses anger appropriately | 2 | 1 |
| 3. Ignores teasing | 2 | 1 |
| 4. Avoids fights initiated by others | 1 | 1 |
| 5. Responds appropriately to frustration | 1 | 2 |
| 6. Tries another way when frustrated | 2 | 2 |

*Unstructured settings.    **Coping skills is the only area which had yet to show significant improvement as judged by the regular classroom teacher at the time of the second assessment. It should be noted that this may have been, in part, due to increased expectations because of increased time in the mainstream.

**Table 10-3** Point Ratings

| Area | Total Possible | Oct. 1984 | Jan. 1986 |
|---|---|---|---|
| Classroom skills | 20 | 6 | 12 |
| Interaction skills | 45 | 20 | 29 |
| Getting along | 25 | 10 | 12 |
| Making friends | 20 | 11 | 16 |
| Coping skills | 30 | 10 | 8 |

through two major sets of data: (i) teacher attitude and acceptance of revised service delivery models such as Project MERGE, and (ii) student achievement outcome data. Both sets of data are currently being analyzed by evaluation staff from the University of Washington.

### Teacher Attitudes Toward Behaviorally Difficult Children in the Mainstream

A preliminary study was developed because teacher attitude was identified during the participatory planning stages as a potential barrier within the district. In order to determine their attitudes toward behaviorally difficult children in the mainstream, teachers from Roosevelt Elementary and a comparable elementary building within the district were asked to agree or disagree with the following statements:

1. Children labeled seriously behaviorally disabled and those with significant behavior problems should be educated in classrooms separate from regular education.
2. The level of support services in this building for behaviorally difficult children is sufficient.
3. A mainstreamed service delivery model with support services provided in the regular classroom is superior to pull-out and self contained models traditionally used for SBD children.
4. When a behavior problem that requires additional assistance occurs in a classroom, that assistance is available to the classroom teacher.
5. Regular classroom teachers generally have the skills to deal with behavior problem children.
6. Staff development designed to increase a teacher's ability to deal with behavior problems in the classroom is an effective strategy for maintaining difficult children in regular education.
7. Children with behavior problems are too disruptive to educate in the regular classroom.

Figure 10-1 summarizes the data from both schools. Although not fully conclusive, since a preproject survey was not available from Roosevelt Elementary School, the difference in the attitudes of the teachers of the two schools was dramatic. Of course, the Roosevelt teachers might have been more accepting of the integration of behaviorally difficult children at the outset. Surveys taken at the second school after a year's participation in Project MERGE will most likely provide more dependable information.

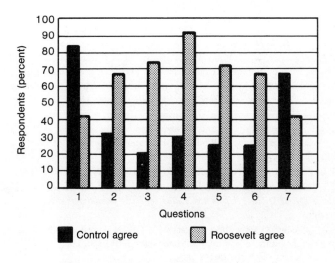

**Figure 10-1** Results of Teacher Attitude Poll

## CONCLUSION

Educational services and programs for special needs students (including SBD students) who evidence problems of behavior and learning can be provided through a supportive relationship between regular and special educators. Such relationships, when carefully developed, can facilitate the provision of clear and consistent behavioral plans for SBD children—a primary requirement of effective programs for this group of students.

The development of such programs does require a commitment to planning, communication, and adaptation of educational strategies and systems for student and staff success. With such commitment, adherence to the least restrictive environment becomes a reality for special needs students, with educational efforts focused directly upon intervention and support rather than upon the maintenance of classification-based systems. Further investment in these areas can continue to contribute toward an educational system that provides services to students and their teachers, minimizing the deficit child model so prevalent in special education today.

## REFERENCES

Carlberg, C., & Kavale, K. (1980). The efficacy of special versus regular class placement for exceptional children: A meta-analysis. *The Journal of Special Education, 14,* 295-309.

Chalfant, J.C., Pysh, M.V., & Moultrie, R. (1979). Teacher assistance teams: A model for within building problem solving. *Learning Disability Quarterly, 2,* 85-96.

Dunn, L. (1968). Special education for the mildly retarded—is much of it justifiable? *Exceptional Children, 35,* 5-22.

Elliott, S.N., & Piersel, W.C. (1982). Direct assessment of reading skills: An approach which links assessment to intervention. *School Psychology Review, 11,* 267-280.

Epps, S., Ysseldyke, J.E., & McGue, M. (1981). *Differentiating LD and non-LD students: "I know one when I see one."* (Research Rep. No. 52). Minneapolis: University of Minnesota, Institute for Research on Learning Disabilities.

Gicklins, E.E., & Havertape, J. (1981). Curriculum based assessment (CBA). In J. Tucker (Ed.), *Non test-based assessment* (R1-R36). Minneapolis: University of Minnesota, National School of Psychology Inservice Training Network.

Good, T.L., & Brophy, J.E. (1978). *Looking in the classroom.* New York: Harper & Row.

Hauser, C. (1982). *Integrating remedial education in Olympia Public Schools and Thurston County Cooperative Special Services: A formative evaluation of the consulting model year 1.* Unpublished manuscript.

Hunter, D., & Wood, S.W. (1985). Project MERGE: Maximizing educational remediation within general education. Washington State Grant 32014 (pp. 1-25). Olympia, WA: Office of Superintendent of Public Instruction.

Johnson, R.T., & Johnson, D.W. (1981). Building friendships between handicapped and non-handicapped students: Effects of cooperative and individualistic instruction. *American Education Research Journal, 18,* 415-423.

Johnson, R.T., & Johnson, D.W. (1983). Effects of cooperative, competitive, and individualistic learning experiences on social development. *Exceptional Children, 49,* 323-329.

Kavale, K.A., & Glass, G.V. (1981) Meta-analysis and the integration of research in special education. *Journal of Learning Disabilities, 14* 531-538.

Kavale, K.A., & Glass, G.V. (1982). The efficacy of special education interventions and practices: A compendium of meta-analysis findings. *Focus on Exceptional Children, 15*(4), 1-14.

Lilly, M.S. (in press). Divestiture in special education: An alternative model for resource and support services. *The Educational Forum.*

Ryder, R., Bennett-Forman, P., & Shipley, S. (1983–84). *Project support study skills curriculum.* Poulsbo, WA: North Kitsap School District.

Rosenshine, B. (1982). *Teaching functions in instructional programs.* Paper presented at Research on Teaching: Implications for Practice, The National Institute of Education, Teaching and Instruction, Washington, DC.

Stainback, W., & Stainback, S. (1984). A rationale for the merger of special and regular education. *Exceptional Children, 51,* 102–111.

Walker, H., McConnell, C., Holmes, D., Todis, B., Walker, J., & Golden, N. (1983). *The Walker Social Skills Curriculum: The Accepts Program.* Austin, TX: Pro-Ed.

Wang, M.C., & Birch, J. W. (1984). Comparisons of a full-time mainstreaming program and a resource room approach. *Exceptional Children, 51,* 33–40.

Ysseldyke, J. E., Algozzine, B., & Allen, D. (1982). Participation of regular education teachers in special education team decision making. *Exceptional Children, 48,* 365–366.

Ysseldyke, J. E., Algozzine, B., Shinn, M., & McGue, M. (1979). *Similarities and differences between underachievers and students labeled learning disabled: Identical twins with different mothers.*

(Research Rep. No. 13). Minneapolis: University of Minnesota, Institute for Research on Learning Disabilities.

Ysseldyke, J. E., & Thurlow, M. (1983). *Identification/classification research: An integrative summary of findings.* (Research Rep. No. 142). Minneapolis: University of Minnesota, Institute for Research on Learning Disabilities.

# Chapter 11

# From Accident to Design: A Dual Program Approach to the Integration of Preschool Children

*Christy L. Ground* and *Beth Yeager*

Approaches to providing integrated education in the least restrictive setting for minimally and severely handicapped preschoolers may take a variety of forms. While systematic planning from conception to implementation of integrated programs is always desired, there are often circumstances beyond the control of those directly responsible for students that create opportunities for mainstreaming where few previously existed. It then becomes the responsibility of the staff to take advantage of these opportunities and to turn an accidental juxtaposition into a fully developed design for integrated education. The programs discussed in this chapter provide a model for turning accident into design, while at the same time demonstrating that without ongoing advocacy and efforts to achieve change, even accidents may not evolve.

## DUAL PROGRAM APPROACH: WHO IS INVOLVED?

The dual program approach to integration in Santa Barbara, California involves two administratively and fiscally separate preschools located in close proximity on the same campus. The proximity provides opportunities for the commingling and integration of children. The first program includes the Santa Barbara State Preschool (State Preschool), funded by the California State Department of Education, Child Development Division and administered by the City of Santa Barbara School and High School District. The second program includes the Santa Barbara County Special Education Preschool (Special Preschool), funded by state and federal monies and administered by the office of the County Superintendent of Schools.

The California State Preschool Program serves families with four-year-old children who meet low income eligibility requirements. The Santa Barbara State Preschool serves 140 children, 85% of whom are of Hispanic or

Mexican-American background and 60% of whom are Spanish-speaking. The program is comprehensive and emphasizes cognitive, physical, social, and emotional development as well as health and social services for the children and their parents. The State Preschool, like the Special Preschool, emphasizes parent involvement and education. It offers two three-hour sessions, with 80 children served in the morning and 60 children in the afternoon. Each class has 20 children enrolled with one teacher, one assistant, and volunteers as needed. Five classes are taught bilingually.

The Special Preschool serves children who meet California State eligibility criteria for placement in a special day class program. Students in this preschool range in age from 3.0 to 4.9 years. Children leave the program in September of the year in which they reach kindergarten age unless appropriate placements are found earlier. If, at the time the child reaches elementary school age, appropriate placement is not available at the district level and other special circumstances and considerations exist, the child may remain in the program an additional year.

Children who meet criteria for placement in the preschool are those who demonstrate a significant delay in one or more areas of development. The developmental areas most frequently identified include speech and language, fine motor, gross motor, social-emotional, self-help, and cognition. The program and its services are free to children who qualify under these exceptionality descriptions: speech impaired, orthopedically handicapped, mentally retarded, other health impaired, multihandicapped, severely emotionally disturbed, hard of hearing, visually handicapped, specific learning disabilities, deaf, and deaf and blind.

The Special Preschool provides a 3½-hour morning session for one class of children with no maximum class size. One teacher, one instructional assistant, and a bilingual instructional assistant are assigned to the class. In addition, a speech and language specialist, an adaptive physical education therapist, a visually handicapped therapist, and a hearing specialist provide itinerant instructional services.

## EVOLUTION OF THE MODEL

Until 1983, the preschool programs existed on separate campuses. When the Special Preschool was moved onto the same site as the State Preschool, a system of integrated education was not a priority for the Santa Barbara School District and its State Preschool. The philosophical basis for mainstreaming, however, existed long before the move.

In theory, the State Preschool supported the mainstreaming of developmentally delayed/handicapped youngsters in "appropriate" situations.

Guidelines provided by the state indicate priority enrollment may be given to a handicapped child when two or more eligible families have the same income. The child's handicap must first be documented in order for the child to receive such a priority. In practice, while the State Preschool has enrolled children with some degree of impairment, it has often been difficult to find students who meet both the income guidelines as well as the *documented* handicap guidelines and who are not already being served. There was a need for increased search and serve efforts (referred to in some states as *childfind*) in order to find children who met both sets of guidelines and for whom placement in the State Preschool was most appropriate. While status quo referral levels were maintained by the State Preschool, the Special Preschool had been actively involved in search efforts to locate handicapped preschoolers in the area. Due to this thorough search process, it became evident that those children meeting both the handicapped and income guidelines who were not referred to the State Preschool were probably being served elsewhere in the county.

In addition, the State Preschool staff had initial reservations about its capabilities in meeting the needs of severely handicapped children, particularly in view of the fast-paced nature of the program. Group times, for example, are somewhat longer than might be appropriate for some special needs children who lack age-appropriate play skills or sustained attention-to-task skills. During the free time portion of the day as well, a large number of children move independently through two classrooms and an extensive outdoor area with several activities in which they may choose to engage. The combination of the numbers of children and activities and the extensive use of space provides for much stimulation (although there are many areas for quiet play) and contributes to the fast pace.

The attitudes of staff are vital to the success of any approach to integration and it becomes critical to address any reservations. State Preschool staff members were receptive to change, however, and, as a result, increased awareness, training, and support from colleagues later became key elements in the success of the program that was to evolve.

Earlier efforts at dual program integration had occurred at two other elementary school campuses containing similar preschool programs. In each instance, the arrangement was less than optimum. While programs were housed reasonably near to each other, they lacked cohesive interprogram leadership. Once the facilities were obtained, the administration became less directly involved. The staffs had not been brought together to create a common philosophy or commitment.

On one campus, during these early efforts, the regular education preschool was receptive and pursued mainstreaming opportunities. The special education teachers were faced with a variety of problems, such as instability of staff and lack of adequate planning and preparation time, and so did not make the integration of special needs preschoolers a high priority. It was enough to get through each day and provide a quality program for the special education youngsters themselves.

In the second attempt to create a dual program model, the special preschool staff was ready for integration and their counterparts on the same campus were not. The move onto the elementary campus was done with such immediacy that a joint program philosophy was never developed. Self-preservation attitudes prevailed and integration priorities were preempted by the basic needs of each program. In this and similar efforts, individual teachers in the regular programs were receptive to the idea of integrated education, but there were few invitations to expand, plan, and develop the existing regular program to meet the needs of the special education program. Therefore little bonding took place between children and staff. The regular classroom programs viewed their interactions as accommodating to the special needs children but not necessarily as beneficial to their own students. Integration, therefore, never developed into meaningful mainstreaming.

Staff attitude, along with space considerations, were key elements in the dissolution of these integration efforts. When space was no longer available to house either preschool on these elementary campuses, the programs were relocated.

The Santa Barbara School District follows policy as stated in PL 94–142 regarding the placement of children in the least restrictive environment. While the school district was not opposed to mainstreaming, the integration of the state preschool program—particularly the integration with children from another program—was not a priority.

Special education administrators within the Office of the County Superintendent of Schools were, on the other hand, committed philosophically to the concept of integration for special needs preschoolers. The county also recognized, however, that the least restrictive environment for the special needs children they were actually going to serve—the severely handicapped—might be a self-contained classroom with optimum opportunities for integration and mainstreaming. Those opportunities could best be provided, when space was available, by placement of the classroom adjacent to a regular preschool. In addition, at the program's inception as a pilot program in the state, it was easier to utilize funds to serve children in a centralized location in order to consolidate use of staff, materials, and other services.

When originally piloted under PL 94–142, numerous attempts were made to negotiate for a facility adjacent to existing public preschool programs. The county philosphically was not pursuing an isolated classroom approach. Instead, it adopted a policy of building local school district awareness and interdistrict cooperation, in the hope that longer range goals for affordable and economical classroom space would be made available and that future integration program developed would transpire,

The teachers and administration believed that given opportunity for normal peer interaction, modeling would take place, thereby fostering social competence, awareness, and understanding between regular education and special needs students. The staff also believed that this social structure would benefit the special needs students significantly in the area of self-image.

Classroom space was offered to each of the special preschool programs—now consolidated—on a regular elementary school campus with the promise of kindergarten integration opportunities. This offer was less than optimum, but better than complete isolation. The classrooms were not adjacent. When on the playground together, children tried to initiate conversation with special needs children and tried to include them in symbolic play activities. When the special needs children failed to respond, the kindergarten children then ignored them. The novelty of their presence soon wore off. The kindergarten children were also involved in their own social structures and peer relationships and, despite facilitation efforts by staff, the special needs youngsters were simply chronologically and developmentally too young to become effectively involved in those relationships. The age and developmental gap of the students, then, played a substantial role in undermining the effectiveness of and opportunities for the integration experience.

When the Special Preschool was again asked to move the following year because of city school district classroom needs, the county's priority was again finding space for this class. It continued to give strong consideration to its philosophical goal of placement adjacent to another preschool program. Additionally, parents of children attending the special preschool became more actively involved in advocating for placement with opportunities for integration. As participants the Individualized Educational Program (IEP) meetings, parents were educated regarding their rights and their role as advocates. Parents whose children were city school district residents and would eventually graduate into the public school system felt strongly that their children deserved to be placed on those public school sites. The county administration invited the most involved parents to assist by viewing the prospective relocation sites and writing letters of support.

One of the sites considered by the county was a campus no longer used as an elementary school and on which the State Preschool was located. The city school district administration viewed the rental of some of the space used by the State Preschool as a potential source of additional revenue, easing that program's financial burden. It became evident that financial benefits were initially as important as integration philosophy in setting priorities.

Head teachers were asked to observe each other's program. The State Preschool head teacher was to determine whether rental of the space was feasible. Would the Special Preschool need its own classroom? Would the State Preschool be able to provide full services, including a parent education program, and share its available space with the Special Preschool? Following the observations of the programs, the staffs had to deal with some very basic considerations. The developmental age level of the Special Preschool children was very low. Did that preclude their effective integration with the State Preschool students? Given the nature of the State Preschool program and its maximum class size of 20, the head teachers felt that the full-time integration of all Special Preschool students on a daily basis within the classrooms and during group time would not be an effective educational practice. The Special Preschool would need its own classroom for a part of each day. Given the wide individual differences among students with exceptional needs, it was decided that the least restrictive, most appropriate environment, necessitated part-time use of a special classroom. Minimum and maximum length of integration opportunities would depend on each student's readiness and ability to function within an integrated program.

Head teachers explored the use of the staff/parent room of the State Preschool as a part-time Special Preschool classroom, but found that it was used on a regular basis for State Preschool parent education and support services. Initially, there was insufficient space available on the same campus and adjacent to the State Preschool for the Special Preschool. The desire was there, but the means for implementation were not.

The current county special education teacher and parents continued to advocate for placement on a campus with age-appropriate peers. Having come so close to a prospective move with the potential for optimum quality integration—brought about by strong advocacy and philosophical commitment from teachers, administrators, and parents—integration was becoming more than just a stated policy. The county special education administrator was feeling increasing pressure to provide such a setting. As part of the advocacy process, parents indicated that they might exercise their due process rights to ask for payment for private preschool placement in a less restrictive setting because the county lacked appropriate integration opportunities. The county was motivated to go beyond philosophical considerations and deal with the financial implications of precedents that would be set by the parents' actions. The county increased its efforts to establish an integrated site.

These advocacy efforts by staff and parents were successful during the summer of 1983 when additional space became available on the campus where the State Preschool was located. Although teachers from both programs were unaware of what was occurring, the county and the city school district quietly negotiated an agreement for the rental of the space. The Special Preschool teacher learned of the move to the McKinley Elementary

School campus upon her return from summer vacation. The State Preschool staff became aware as school was about to open and they saw their colleagues unpacking equipment. Although staff members from both programs had desired such a transition, the actual planning for the integrated program came after an almost accidental placement of the preschool programs on the same campus and adjacent to one another.

Whether or not the placement was actually accidental in terms of efforts to integrate children depends upon the perceptions of each district's attitudes. From the county's point of view, the move was seen as the successful outcome of concerted efforts to find age-appropriate peers for the special needs students. Its actions were seen as part of careful planning and design. The city school district's perspective was framed by its space needs along with the needs of the entire elementary district. The opportunity for integration became—for the city school district—less a planned outcome than a fringe benefit. It appeared, in this situation, that philosphical commitment was not enough. The dynamic interaction of administrative support with staff and parental advocacy was necessary for the implementation of that philosophy and of this integration effort. It was left to each preschool staff to take advantage of the opportunities created by the placement and to design a program for mainstreaming children.

## DESIGN OF A PROGRAM

It became very important for the members of each staff to know and become comfortable with each other. A step-by-step approach to program planning and design was adopted. Programming had to be designed that would be effective and safe for all children. Each part of the daily schedule had to be examined and a determination made as to when, where, and how to facilitate successful integration. (See Table 11-1.) These determinations were made easier because both preschools utilized individualized instruction, small and large group instruction, and a large block of open structured time providing for free choice of activities. Additionally, the state preschoolers were free to move from indoor to outdoor space and back. The major and potential obstacles of those early days included staff attitudes, safety, and appropriate supervision.

It became apparent that not all State Preschool staff members were prepared to work closely with some of the special needs children enrolled in the Special Preschool and that it would be necessary to foster a sense of open communication very early in the planning process. All of the instructional assistants in the State Preschool are former parents in the program. At least two have been with the program since its inception. Parents are asked to

**Table 11-1** Teacher Schedules

| STATE PRESCHOOL TEACHER | SPECIAL PRESCHOOL TEACHER |
|---|---|
| A.M. SESSION | A.M. SESSION |
| 8:30—Children arrive | 8:45—Arrival |
| Group time | 9:00—Free play—large toys |
| (self-contained classes— | 9:20—Clean up/toileting |
| Planned large and small | |
| group and/or individualized | |
| activities) | 9:30—Open structure—Integrated |
| 9:30—Open structure—Team free | free choice |
| choice of activities | MW             TTh |
| (staff—supervise play/ | Rotating groups |
| monitor) | 10:30—Language     Table toys |
| 10:30—Rest | Sensory motor  Art |
| Group time | Library        Group games |
| 11:00—Lunch, closing | |
| 11:30—Home | F |
| | Cognition |
| | Cooking |
| | Special projects |
| | 11:45—Lunch |
| | 12:05—Clean up and toileting |
| | 12:15—Dismissal |

volunteer actively in the program and when an opening on the staff occurs those parents are encouraged to apply. Like Head Start, the California State preschool program is encouraged to provide a "career ladder" for parents. The experience of working with multihandicapped children and with their specially designed equipment was new for these assistants as well as for the teachers. The initial reaction on the part of many staff members was fear, primarily from the anticipation that a special needs child would be hurt and that the staff would not know how to handle the situation. There was a tendency to treat the children with kid gloves and, on occasion, withdraw to let the "experts" handle the children. If a child wore a helmet and was subject to seizures, should he or she climb on gross motor structures? Did the student need to be closely monitored and protected? Wasn't it necessary for trained and certificated professionals to work with these vulnerable students most of the day?

Knowledge builds confidence. The county special education teacher initiated the communication process by attending State Preschool weekly staff meetings. No formal inservice sessions were held. The weekly staff meetings, with the explanations of the special education teacher, served as an open format for discussions and discoveries. Special Preschool staff discussed each child with the State Preschool staff and emphasized both the child's limitations and strengths. The intent was to help teachers and assistants find effective and successful ways for working with the students. Because the special needs students were younger chronologically, younger in developmental capability, sometimes physically smaller, and often seemingly frail or medically fragile, it was important that staff confidence in their ability to work with such children be fostered as much as possible.

When State Preschool staff expressed an unfamiliarity with dealing with varying kinds of disabilities, the special education teacher explained those disabilities at early staff meetings. It was important to proceed at a pace that was comfortable for all concerned (both State and Special Preschool staffs) and planning timelines reflected that need. It was decided to begin at a simple level of integration and to proceed to other levels of mainstreaming at a natural and comfortable pace that was agreeable to all staff.

Both staffs also shared concerns about their ability to provide adequate supervision and safety for children within the large perimeters of the school. The Special Preschool staff was quick to assure State Preschool staff of its willingness to follow children, to help in particularly difficult areas, and ultimately to be the responsible party for all special needs students, particularly in the area of liability. This was especially important given the fact that the two programs were administered by different sponsoring agencies.

The shared outdoor setting—a large space with wide boundaries—was a particular challenge. If staff was truly to operate on the belief that handicapped children are more like than unlike normal children, then it would be necessary to plan for the problems, reactions, strengths, and weaknesses of each student within that normalized setting. Rather than attempting to provide the special needs students with an artificial environment free of all hazards, staff would attempt to teach children how to safely approach the realistic obstacles and hazards of mainstreamed school culture.

Initially both staffs were somewhat overprotective. Slowly, staff allowed students more freedom. In many ways, the children themselves demonstrated to the staff how simple it could be. The child with the helmet gravitated to the bikes and was able to ride without falling off. The nonambulatory child crawled freely on the mats without being stepped on. The child who had no orientation to boundaries learned to stay near friends and activity centers. Their experiences were contagious!

Another challenge was meeting the gross motor needs of the nonambulatory population of the special day class (Special Preschool). Several solutions were designed to accommodate their special needs. Rather than purchasing adaptive equipment which could be used only by special education students, gymnastic mats were placed on the playground and sensory motor equipment was provided during free time for all students to utilize (the matted section became known as the "purple area"). The mats encouraged low-playing positions for all. Nonambulatory students placed on the mats could easily establish eye contact with other students during gross motor activities. Additional materials which reinforced certain indoor activities were also included in this area. Special equipment was designed and constructed by a senior citizen volunteer working with the State Preschool program. This economical and individualized equipment allowed nonambulatory students access to numerous activities.

Initially the Special Preschool students explored only the outdoor space during the free time period. They were given purple name tags to correspond with their classroom color, and each State Preschool class was known by a color as well (red, yellow, orange, or blue class). Children outside moved from the purple area to large motor playground activities, to bike, sand, or water play, to carpentry, or to art. Indoor activities included blocks and dramatic play (orange room) and cognitive skill activities (red room). The State Preschool staff regularly assigned someone to work in the sensory motor area (the purple area, which is adjacent to the purple class). While Special Preschool staff continued to follow its students into other areas, there was a distinct change in both staffs, most noticeably a decrease of anxiety and fear, particularly among those who had been unfamiliar with disabilities.

In order to foster sensitivity and awareness among students, numerous techniques were and continue to be used. At the time of enrollment in the State Preschool, the staff informs prospective parents about the purple class (Special Preschool) and its special needs population. Parents of the special needs students are informed of the integration potential at placement meetings and encouraged to make visitations. Books about special needs children are read during school to the regular education students. Mini-demonstrations are conducted in each State Preschool classroom regarding special equipment. The children have an opportunity to see the equipment used with stuffed animals and then are given opportunities to use the equipment themselves. State Preschool classes visit the purple classroom at the beginning of the school year, because that room is not used during the free choice activity time (the purple area is located outside in front of the bungalow).

Efforts are made to expose all students to sign language as a means of communication whenever appropriate. The Special Preschool utilizes SEE (Signed Exact English) sign language to augment language acquisition and development. Few of the special needs students demonstrate spontaneous use of sign language. The introduction of sign language to all children is viewed as an awareness activity to build sensitivity and understanding of how others feel and what others experience. Through gestures, children are encouraged to "read expressions," whether signs accompany the body language or not. At group activities and assemblies for all children, signs reflective of the particular theme are often demonstrated, such as the "Exit Cheer" taught to children during their fire safety study. The use of SEE signs provides a strong visual and tactile reinforcement of concepts all the children (special needs and regular) are learning.

The programs have placed a strong emphasis on respect, safety, and on the similarities rather than the differences among children.

## EXPANSION OF PROGRAM DESIGN FOR STUDENTS

As handicapped youngsters grew in their abilities, staff implemented a new design in which small groups of these children visited the indoor free time area (wearing another name tag with the color of that area in addition to their purple name tags) accompanied by a special education staff person. The color tag served as a quick visual cue to supervising adults that special needs students had been guided into the activity room and were facilitated by special education staff.

More developmentally ready students who are able to adjust to the space are allowed to move freely from outdoors to indoors along with the State Preschool students. Others continue to visit areas with a staff person. Activities are designed to include all children. All children participate in special assemblies (e.g., Grandparents' Day, when grandparents visit the school). Staff makes an effort to plan together for integrated field trips (e.g., to the pumpkin patch) and other experiences in the community.

Special education children participate in many of the same theme curriculum activities (e.g., dental health, fire safety, and sexual abuse prevention) as do the regular education students. The existing and available curriculum requires some adaptation to the needs of the special education students. Certain curriculum units are introduced to all children through the use of outside resources. Following this introduction, special needs students practice unit skills. The instructional content is divided into smaller task components and thus made appropriate for student skill and comprehension levels.

Some students in the Special Preschool have demonstrated readiness skills that have brought some additional integration opportunities. These include dual A.M./P.M. enrollment for students meeting both programs' criteria. Michael, for example, benefited from six months of special education preschool. He still lagged behind in most areas of development but demonstrated consistent developmental gains and a readiness for new social experiences. At the beginning of the 1983-84 school year, Michael attended the Special Preschool class for the A.M. session. In addition, Michael attended a

State Preschool P.M. session class from the beginning in January. The special education teacher helped Michael to make the transition and communicated regularly with the afternoon teacher. The following school year, Michael deferred his entrance to a school-age program and completed another year of preschool. At this time, he completed the transition from Special Preschool to State Preschool. He attended the State Preschool program and was provided with itinerant support services from county special education. He is now enrolled in a regular elementary kindergarten class.

Students have also joined State Preschool (A.M. session) for short periods of actual classroom instruction or circle time. These students maintain full enrollment in the Special Preschool. They demonstrated independence skills and the ability to follow familiar and unfamiliar directions, with an attention span ranging from 15 to 25 minutes for large and small group settings. Marsha and Karen, for example, had demonstrated these skills to their special education teacher. Both students could select and participate in a variety of instructional-oriented activities. Both demonstrated the ability to generalize from their classroom routine to following other routines in progress on campus (in free choice times, in the red or orange rooms). Both students demonstrated safety awareness and orientation to the localities of school rooms and boundaries. Both demonstrated social interest and success on the playground. Marsha and Karen participate in the second group (or circle time) of a particular State Preschool classroom. They come and go independently or with the help of a friend from the regular program. The children's readiness skills enabled the special education teacher to facilitate and expand on their mainstreaming opportunities, while not decreasing teacher time or supervision within the special education classroom.

Further overlapping of services occurs when county resources are utilized by the State Preschool. Referrals are made for regular preschool students with delayed skills in areas where services are available through the county (e.g., adaptive PE, supplemental instruction) in addition to those provided by the city school district. Additionally, the Special Preschool utilizes the city school district lunch program services.

The Special Preschool benefits from the parent services provided by the State Preschool as well. All families are invited to participate in those parent involvement and education activities coordinated by the State Preschool. Open House is a joint activity. A representative from the Special Preschool serves on the Parent Advisory Committee for the State Preschool. Regular parent education meetings are designed to include Special Preschool parents as well as State Preschool families. As a result of this close contact, regular State Preschool parents are more inclined to include reference to the purple class when discussing planned State Preschool activities. Special Preschool parents have been advocates for the State Preschool program with the city school Board of Education when the school faced budget reductions. Most parents accept the two programs as one and tend to speak of them in that way.

In addition to parent communication, a primary emphasis is placed on on-going staff communication and support. If there is a problem, staff members discuss it openly. Teachers and aides discuss children from both programs at the weekly State Preschool staff meetings. The Special Preschool teacher attends and reports back to the staff. Without the give and take of communication between program staffs, the dual program model could not function.

Communication between staffs becomes doubly necessary when constraints or obstacles are placed in the way of long-term planning. A tentative program such as this is always dependent on the attitudes and priorities of the involved school districts, as well as on more pragmatic concerns such as available space. Difficulties increase in proportion to the number of programs and administrations involved. It becomes important to ensure that all program participants—parents, teachers, administrators, and significant community members—are kept informed of the program's successes and needs. That can only be done through ongoing systematic communication.

## EVALUATION: IS THE PROGRAM WORTH FIGHTING FOR?

When developing innovative integration models, it is important that program staff address both short- and long-term successes. No formal assessment of this program has been done. Informal assessment, though, such as qualitative observations by staff and parents, discussion groups with children, comments from staff, parents, and children, indicates that children have become more accepting of each other and interactive in their play. State Preschool children appear extremely receptive to and matter-of-fact about the needs and differences of special education students. The major problem the latter face has perhaps been that some of the smaller children have been "mothered" excessively (which has also happened to small regular preschoolers) and others have been the cause of disputes about who gets to help the most (e.g., who gets to push Chris' wheelchair).

Special needs children demonstrate an increase in self-initiation and selection of ongoing activities, in symbolic play skills, and in more appropriate social behavior. Both programs are rich in language stimulation, but it is an added benefit for special needs children to have age-appropriate language models in a more natural environment. These areas of growth are evaluated on the basis of each child's IEP at the time of evaluation.

Program staff see the future assimilation and acceptance of special needs students within the school and larger community as an important long-term goal that has its foundation in these early experiences of all the children. It is this early experience in integrated education that will lead to social competence, acceptance, and a positive self-image for both handicapped and nonhandicapped youngsters.

If a program model is worth fighting for, it becomes increasingly necessary to develop strategies for maintaining it and for disseminating information about it to the respective administrative districts, to the community, and to other potential sites. Staff from both programs make regular efforts to be advocates for the model with appropriate district administrators. Special education administrators of both districts are supportive of integration and the dual model approach when space needs and other considerations can be met. A brochure describing the integration of both programs was developed by the head teachers. It was disseminated at a state conference of a professional early childhood organization, has been given to all Parent Advisory Committee members, to the city and county boards of education, and is further used to inform community members about the programs. College students, groups from outside agencies, prospective parents, and others interested in integration have observed the program.

Parent education is essential. Slides used as a regular part of Open House orientation emphasize the integration component of the program for parents. Letters to parents from the head teachers help to bring the families together. The more that parents are aware of the positive impact of integrated education for children, the more effectively they will be able to advocate for the program in the future. Mrs. Torres, a parent in the State Preschool program, says of her daughter's experience:

> I believe the program is important to the children. They need to see all walks of life. The children learn to play with one another. They learn that the "special" children are special and some need help to get from one place to another, but they are not different. The children will learn to appreciate them when the "special people" are older. (Cindy Torres, personal statement, 1986)

Special Preschool parents shared the following thoughts at a Santa Barbara School District Board of Education meeting:

> Special learning groups isolate handicapped children—they belong in the mainstream of education because that's where they come from (Luis Goena, personal statement, January 23, 1986)

As my grandson is learning and growing, it is extremely important that he associate with normal children. Now, while they are young, is the time for children to learn to live and work together. . . After twenty years of teaching experience, I know how difficult it is to find teachers who can work as a team. We have an excellent program at McKinley [the campus containing the two preschool programs] and a well-functioning teacher-team. We need to keep it! (Betty Cunningham, personal statement, January 23, 1986)

I feel privileged to be the mother of a special needs child. By being a part of the mainstreamed preschool program at McKinley I have come to further appreciate both programs as unique and relevant parts of our community. (Bonnie Rupert, personal statement, January 23, 1986)

Following these comments and the advocacy efforts of the staff and other parents, the city school district superintendent and the board of education indicated their commitment to the dual-program approach and to making every effort to maintain adjacent housing for both programs.

It is essential for the dual-program approach, dependent as it is upon the vagaries of available space and financing, to be held up to the community as an example of effective educational practice. Both staffs and parents must develop an intensive campaign to disseminate information to school districts and to the community at large.

## CONCLUSION

The integration of special needs and regular education preschoolers within a school should—to the maximum extent possible—be a step-by-step process based on a model for change and involving careful communication and planning. When two programs come together to participate in that process, each step takes on new importance. There is a vitality and excitement involved in the communication process that makes growth and change inevitable. The key to the success of this particular dual-program model has been its willingness to incorporate even accidental circumstances into a larger design. A second key has been its ability to seize opportunities wherever and whenever they occur to foster change. While the difficulties and constraints will always be there, so, too, will the possibilities.

# Chapter 12

# Community Partnerships:
# A Collaborative Approach for
# Developing Integrated
# Preschool Programs

*Sandra Mlinarcik*

More than 300 children between the ages of three and five years have access to a full-day preschool program in Jefferson County, Kentucky. The preschool program also offers extended hours before and after school for working parents. Jefferson County Public Schools houses this preschool program in 12 geographically scattered sites, which include ten elementary and two junior and senior high schools. This brief description may not reveal any striking differences between the preschool program in Jefferson County and other programs typically available in urban areas. What sets the Jefferson County program apart is that in each preschool classroom, young children with moderate and severe disabilities participate in all aspects of the program with their nondisabled peers. This has been achieved through a linkage of community partnerships which spans the distance between public and private service delivery systems. Each phase in forming the linkage between Jefferson County Schools and Seven Counties Services, a nonprofit human services agency, demonstrates some of the ideological, fiscal, and programmatic issues that seem inherent in the process of integration. Subsequent sections of this chapter share strategies to address, resolve, and, in some instances, by-pass these recurring issues.

## THE PARTNERS

The Jefferson County Public Schools services a large district, one which ranks among the 20 largest districts in the country in terms of pupil population. Current assessment and placement practices categorize approximately 11% of the school population as disabled. Jefferson County provides special education services in a variety of instructional environments, including full-time mainstreamed placements in regular classrooms, self-contained special classes in regular schools, and two segregated schools. In accord with a Ken-

239

tucky State mandate, Jefferson County offers kindergarten to children who turn five years of age before October. Kindergarten-age children with disabilities qualify for free appropriate educational services in the public schools.

Obviously, a critical time gap exists in Kentucky between probable identification of a child's disabilities during the early childhood years and the provision of a public school program. Rather than mandating preschool programs, the state Cabinet for Human Resources allocates state and federal funds to serve preschool-age children with disabilities through a system of regional comprehensive care centers. Seven Counties Services, Inc., a private nonprofit agency, is one of the 14 regional comprehensive care centers in Kentucky. The state licenses Seven Counties to plan and provide mental health, developmental disability, and chemical dependency services to a metropolitan area with over 900,000 residents.

The Mental Retardation and Developmental Disabilities Office (MRDDO) of Seven Counties channels state and federal funds into community agencies for the provision of services. The MRDDO forms affiliate relationships with local agencies on a contractual, fee-for-service basis. In addition to a dollar amount, contracts specify both the nature of the services being purchased and a process to monitor the quality of service delivery. Through an affiliate agreement, a contractor commits to providing services in accordance with the mission and philosophy of Seven Counties Services, which states that services are best provided in the "least restrictive, most normative settings possible."

In regards to young children with disabilities, the MRDDO takes the philosophy of Seven Counties one step farther. The MRDDO seeks to develop services which adhere to Biklen's (Biklen, 1985) category of "unconditional mainstreaming." According to Biklen (Biklen, 1985, p. 28), unconditional mainstreaming calls for the combined efforts of administrators, teachers, and parents "to create a consciously thought out and supported version of integration." A more detailed explanation of the MRDDO's overriding goals follows in a later section of this chapter. At this point, it is helpful to remember that, from the perspective of Seven Counties Services, quality education for young children with disabilities necessitates not only a partnership with Jefferson County Schools, but also an implementation of unconditional mainstreaming.

## A PATCHWORK APPROACH TO PRESCHOOL SERVICES

Prior to Seven Counties Services' development of comprehensive public preschool programming in September, 1984, parents of young disabled children faced a maze of private agencies which offered a variety of services. In addition to locating the services prescribed by doctors or multidisciplinary assessment teams, parents had to maneuver their way through eligibility criteria such as income restrictions, category or severity of disability, and geographic boundaries. To assist families in tackling the early intervention maze, many agencies, including Seven Counties, disseminated brochures describing available services or delegated staff as contacts for information and referrals. While this type of stopgap assistance may have been helpful, it gave no assurance that needed services would be obtained. Among other difficulties, interviews with parents of young disabled children served by Seven Counties and its affiliates detailed the following scenarios:

- Physical therapy was covered by the family's health insurance, but services at the local clinic were only offered during hours when both parents had to be at work.
- The family qualified for medical assistance and obtained services from a home and health agency, but services were disrupted whenever overtime wages were earned, thereby making the family "income ineligible."
- A parent had no way to transport her multiply handicapped child on a regular basis to a local clinic for prescribed therapies; therefore, the clinic reported the parent to child protective services for medical neglect.
- Home-based infant stimulation, physical therapy, and speech therapy were each provided to a family once a week, on three different days, by three professionals who worked for three separate agencies—agencies that had not been in contact with each other regarding the child's needs.
- A severely disabled three-year-old child had been in transition from one foster home to another for the past two years, and each change in residence had resulted in a change or discontinuation of services.

Each of these familiar situations portrays the inconsistency and lack of coordination endemic to the prior patchwork approach to preschool service delivery. Adminstrators of private agencies and school district personnel who plan preschool services without the structure and support of their agency or district counterparts are familiar with the patchwork approach, which forces them to piece together limited resources to provide programming on a child-by-child basis.

In addition to frustrating agency and district personnel, the patchwork approach also impacts upon parents, who frequently experience isolation from other families with young disabled children. Interaction, support, and sharing of resources happen by chance rather than by plan. Parents and their young disabled children also can find themselves isolated from community environments and the normal activities which fill the preschool years. These families experience the rigors of a diagnostic process that frequently emphasizes deviant rather than normal developmental characteristics, deficits rather than strengths, and treatment rather than functional behaviors and skills.

Families often feel the isolating influence of patchwork services following diagnosis of their child's disability when initial steps are taken to seek out recommended programming. For example, imagine two parents visiting a local agency that provides physical therapy and equipment to children who are orthopedically disabled. The parents choose to enroll their child for therapy services and frequently observe other families in the waiting room. Even after several years of participation in this out-patient model of service delivery, these same parents typically face a go-it-alone experience when their child enters public school. A new maze of educational jargon, categories of classroom placements, and school sites in unfamiliar neighborhoods now replaces the former maze of agencies and services. The confusion intensifies if a child has been served by multiple agencies, which may or may not agree on recommendations made to the public school district.

Four main consequences of a patchwork approach to service delivery inhibit effective programming and contribute to the segregation of young children with disabilities:

1. provision of services that are easily disrupted by changes in family income, residence, or work schedules
2. utilization of medical, outpatient models of service delivery that emphasize deviance rather than normal development characteristics
3. absence of well-established parent networks or organizations for support and training
4. lack of "ownership" and responsibility for the transition into public school and participation in preliminary placement proceedings

### Strategies to Collect and Utilize Patchwork Data

Gathering the data to formulate the scenarios and consequences discussed in the above section constituted the first phase in developing the community partnerships and integrated preschool program in Jefferson County. The service providers in the Seven Counties region recognized the deficiencies of their existing patchwork of services. However, the popular solution seemed to be to request more funds for existing services rather than to propose new models of service delivery. The transition from one form of service delivery to another usually requires a needs assessment to justify the change. This demand for justification heightens when change impacts upon an agency's funding sources. The qualitative research techniques explained by Bogdan and Taylor (1975) offered Seven Counties MRDDO staff a practical and effective alternative to the traditional form of needs assessment. According to Taylor and Bogdan (1977, p. 201), qualitative research "represents less a set of techniques than a mode of relating to people and their experiences," and "implies a certain empathy, a willingness to understand the world as it is experienced by others." School district and agency personnel have a rich source of qualitative data available in their day-to-day contacts with the community. Qualitative research techniques were chosen because they had potential both to reveal gaps in the patchwork system of services and to give direction to negotiations with a public school district. The experiences of Seven Counties Services' collaboration with Jefferson County Public Schools suggested the following types of sources for data collection:

- interviews with parents whose children have recently been identified as disabled
- interviews with parents whose disabled children have entered public school programs
- interviews with agency administrators, direct service personnel, and public school officials
- observations in community and home-based sites where services are being delivered
- reviews of waiting lists for ages and number of children in need of services, for disability categories and levels of severity, and for geographic locations of children referred
- reviews of staff notes which document delivery of services over an extended period of time

Tapping the above sources for qualitative data did not consume any more staff time or agency resources than the design, dissemination, and analysis of surveys and questionnaires. In many instances, data emerged from regularly scheduled MRDDO work activities between July and October, 1983. Yet, there were additional "payoffs" in the qualitative data collection process. Beyond check marks and circled items, the data collectors gained new contacts and interactions with clients and service providers, greater knowledge of how services are perceived and received, and a more concrete understanding of what key participants would desire from a partnership between community agencies and public schools.

Presentation of the information to the MRDDO Advisory Committee of Seven Counties, public school officials, and representatives of community agencies followed the data collection. Informal presentations, during January and February, 1984, of these firsthand accounts of the patchwork of services had a convincing ring of truth. In addition, visual presentations of need based on demographic information pinpointed more sites where preschool programs needed to be established. Data collectors, for example, marked zip code maps for the residences of children referred for MRDDO services. When clusters of referrals appeared, further study of neighborhoods surrounding each cluster revealed why services had not been available or consistently accessed.

The following program parameters emerged from the qualitative study of the Seven Counties Service region:

1. A concentrated need for services existed in several areas throughout the county, particularly the downtown area bordered by subsidized housing projects and neighborhoods near the county's borders where neither public transportation nor private preschool or daycare programs are plentiful.
2. Provision of transportation would be necessary for a large majority of families who are not currently able to participate in services.
3. Comprehensive preschool programming must include individual educational planning, developmental therapies or support services, parent support, and organized procedures for transition to public school.
4. Moderately and severely handicapped children must be integrated with their nondisabled peers, who provide modeling for language and behavior and an emphasis on normal developmental characteristics.

The commitment by the MRDDO to community-based integrated services pulled these program components together into a coherent model for the Jefferson County Schools.[1] Some major precedents set by Seven Counties and affiliate agencies in previous years accounted for the prominence of integration in the proposed program model:

• The MRDDO of Seven Counties utilized funding criteria for community agencies that require both maximum integration of disabled

---

[1] The Director of the Mental Retardation/Developmental Disabilities Program at Seven Counties Services, Dr. Jeff Strully, is strongly committed to using the resources of his department for developing integrated services throughout the region. Information regarding integrated residential, in-home support and other educational programs can be obtained by contacting Dr. Strully at Seven Counties Services, 101 West Muhammad Ali Blvd., Louisville, Kentucky, 40202.

citizens into age-appropriate settings and interaction with nondisabled peers.

- Private preschools and daycare centers had received ongoing training and technical assistance from Seven Counties staff and affiliates to support the inclusion and participation of young children with disabilities.

- Carriage House Preschool, an affiliate agency, had been operating a private integrated program and advocating mainstreamed placements for their students when they entered public schools.

- Increasing numbers of parents, who had their disabled children in integrated community services, pursued mainstreaming for their children when they entered public school, and such parents pointed to their children's successful preschool "track record" with integration.

- The local Council for Retarded Citizens had been offering a variety of active programs, operated by council staff and parents, to support and provide advocacy for disabled children and their families, including an education committee that maintains communication with the public schools through monitoring and planning activities.

The precedents outlined above facilitated the subsequent collaboration and planning of the pilot integrated preschool program. School district and agency personnel in regions where integrated preschool services are being considered may find it beneficial to study their community for successful precedents and use them as a jumping-off point for forming partnerships.

### Transition From Patchwork Services to a Pilot Preschool Program

While current legislative practices prohibit Jefferson County Public Schools from allocating state educational funds for preschool programs, local school officials believe in the benefits of early intervention. In the past, they demonstrated their support by making inservice training sessions open to both parents and community service providers. In addition, the school district had been awarded federal grant funds for the Down's Syndrome Preschool Program that operated between 1980 and 1983. Using local funds, the Exceptional Child Education Department of Jefferson County Schools included preschool disabled children on a limited basis in existing primary level special education classes with school-age children as enrollment allowed between 1975 and 1980.

Following the collection of data pertaining to developmental services, ongoing contacts between the MRDDO program director and the director of the Exceptional Child Education Department in the school district included informal discussion regarding re-establishing preschool programming in the public schools. The MRDDO director shared the interest and support held by Seven Counties, the Council for Retarded Citizens, and other community groups. In addition, the school district officials were informed of the MRDDO funds that Seven Counties had available to support preschool programming. A series of meetings were held between the school district's special education administrators and MRDDO staff during December, 1983, and January, 1984. The meetings focused on numerous issues, including the following:

- Seven Counties wanted to develop and support an integrated preschool program in three areas in Jefferson County where families with disabled children had difficulty getting to existing services.
- Seven Counties was committed to putting as much money as possible into direct services and desired to obtain in-kind contributions of space, furniture, audio-visual equipment, and transportation.
- Jefferson County Schools could improve building utilization by locating and donating vacant classrooms for the preschool program, and no additional cost would be incurred by Jefferson County Schools for providing transportation on existing bus routes.
- District administrators were asked to arrange a meeting with regional supervisors in an effort to select building principals who were both receptive to housing a preschool program and had demonstrated an openness to integration.
- The Exceptional Child Education administrators planned to submit the general preschool program model proposed by Seven Counties to the board of education for approval in March of 1984.

As the initial agreement between Jefferson County Schools and Seven Counties Services was being formed, MRDDO staff began studying the options for funding a pilot program. The lack of any new revenue to support the preschool project necessitated a redistribution of existing funds. Any funding mechanism chosen by the MRDDO for support of the preschool program would have set a ripple effect into motion among all the affiliates that received funding for the patchwork of services. Positive and negative consequences of funding upon any agency's staffing, enrollment, and intensity of services became unavoidable. To facilitate this redistribution, a proposal method of awarding funds was set up by the coordinator of preschool services at Seven Counties. Affiliate agencies currently receiving funds were informed of the new process. Proposals were awarded for the new preschool program and some existing services in March, 1984. While the request for proposal method did not fully diminish the ripple effect among community agencies, it provided all agencies with an opportunity to compete for funding.

As a result of the proposal process, the MRDDO contracted with Carriage House Preschool, an affiliate agency of Seven Counties, to implement and administer the pilot integrated preschool program. Carriage House preschool operates a private, integrated preschool program near downtown Louisville in Jefferson County.[2] Carriage House Preschool was formerly known as the Louisville School for Autistic Children. The current site housed a segregated program, which included school-age children. When special education units for children labelled autistic were allocated in Jefferson County Schools, the school-age population moved out. At that point, MRDDO staff from Seven Counties began working with the board and staff of the Louisville School for Autistic Children to restructure its model and services. The integrated preschool program has operated at Carriage House since 1981.

The proposal which Carriage House submitted to Seven Counties reflected its experience in adapting curriculum to facilitate integration, in developing training for staff and parents, and in transitioning children from Carriage House into integrated public school settings for kindergarten and first grade. The Carriage House proposal had in its favor not only the staff's firsthand experience with integration, but also their enthusiasm and confidence in the benefits of integrated education for all children.

## PLANNING THE PILOT PROGRAM

The dialogue initiated during the first phase of data collection and the second phase of transition activities now moved into the third phase of program planning. In order to open a program in September, 1984, it was necessary to initiate planning even though board of education approval was still pending, and state and federal funding allocations to Seven Counties for fiscal year 1985 had not yet been finalized. While bureaucratic procedures ran their course, participants in the new partnership continued plans for delegat-

---

[2] Carriage House Preschool/Louisville School for Autistic Children evolved from a fully segregated to a fully integrated school over the past four years under the leadership of Jayne Miller, its executive director, in cooperation with the MRDDO of Seven Counties Services. Program inquiries may be addressed to the school at 1320 South Fourth St., Louisville, Kentucky, 40208.

ing programmatic and fiscal responsibilities, identifying resources, and structuring community support for the pilot program.

Each participant in the partnership between Jefferson County Public Schools, Carriage House, and Seven Counties Services had specific, as well as overlapping, roles to fulfill. In the initial pilot year, the public schools could be described as the "host" of the integrated preschool program. In its role as host, Jefferson County extended hospitality by giving space and support to the program. Carriage House Preschool owned and operated the pilot program and assumed full responsibility for providing services, in part through using monetary and material resources from its downtown site. Seven Counties Services provided the bulk of the funding for the pilot program through its contract with Carriage House. No monies were exchanged between Seven Counties and Jefferson County Schools. In addition to funding the program, the MRDDO served as a liaison between Carriage House and the administrators at Jefferson County Schools.

Ongoing meetings and dialogue with the partnership participants replaced a comprehensive written working agreement. Major components of the program were put into place through endless phone contacts and many joint visits. At times, a conscious effect was made to avoid committing details to writing in favor of "leaving the door open" to continued problem solving. While a certain degree of risk is involved in this style of collaboration, there were attractive benefits; namely, flexibility and very few pre-established barriers to program development. A very detailed working agreement, for example, might have restricted the manner in which each preschool later worked out unique ways of relating to, and participating in, the activities of its host school. Table 12-1 summarizes the responsibilities of each participant in the community partnership.

Written agreements to fulfill the responsibilities listed in Table 12-1 reinforced each participant's role in the preschool program. Seven Counties signed a working agreement with Jefferson County, that was a revised version of the one the district had used with the local Headstart program. The agreement's format was familiar to the board of education, which accepted it with little question or comment. Carriage House Preschool signed the standard affiliate agreement with Seven Counties, which detailed requirements for documentation of service delivery, recordkeeping, protection of clients' rights, grievance procedures, etc.

While the written agreements were being drafted and signed, the MRDDO staff initiated efforts to build knowledge of, and support for, the pilot program. Once again, the qualitative data, which was collected earlier in the planning process, was helpful in highlighting the key figures whose support and enthusiasm would lend credibility to the new venture. The following key figures were among those who collaborated in these discussions:

**Table 12-1** Responsibilities of Members in the Community Partnership

| Participant | Responsibilities |
|---|---|
| Jefferson County Public Schools | —Procuring board of education approval for the program<br>—Contributing classrooms, utilities, and custodial services<br>—Contributing early childhood classroom furniture, teacher desks, and storage<br>—Providing transportation on existing bus routes<br>—Providing administrative support by building principals and special education personnel |
| Seven Counties Services | —Funding on contractual basis to Carriage House for personnel and operating expenses<br>—Funding to contractors for support services (i.e., physical, occupational, and speech therapies)<br>—Monitoring of contracts for compliance with funding regulations and overriding agency goals and philosophy<br>—Coordinating referrals for children with disabilities<br>—Allocating staff to serve as liaison between the public schools, Carriage House, and other contractors |
| Carriage House Preschool | —Hiring, training, and supervision of classroom staff<br>—Providing parent training and support<br>—Collecting data on student progress<br>—Recordkeeping to document provision of services funded by Seven Counties<br>—Fund raising to meet expenses which exceed contract amount<br>—Enrolling of nondisabled children |

- Agency Advisory Committee and Executive Board of Directors
- Middle level supervisors in the school district
- Building principals
- An Early Childhood Program Planning Committee formed by Jefferson County Schools
- Faculty in early childhood and special education at the University of Louisville and Jefferson Community College
- Council for Retarded Citizens, the local advocacy organization
- Parents active in creating options for their disabled children in the public schools

The ideological commitments of Seven Counties Services and its affiliate agencies established the foundation and direction of the pilot preschool program. The five general strategies discussed thus far in this chapter, however, can assist school district and agency personnel in any region to plan a school-based, integrated program for preschool children:

1. Identify existing resources available in the public schools, which may include space, furniture, equipment, transportation and administrative support.
2. Implement redistribution of existing funds if no new monies are available to support a pilot preschool program.
3. Delegate responsibilities for program implementation to each member in the partnership between public schools and community agencies.
4. Fortify the partnership with written agreements and contracts that are approved by each member's governing boards.
5. Structure support for the partnership and pilot program by maintaining dialogue with key participants at each level of involvement, including parents, school officials at building and regional levels, professionals in related fields, and advocacy groups.

## OVERVIEW OF THE PILOT PROGRAM

An overview of the pilot program, which operated between September, 1984, and June, 1985, illustrates some of the strengths and weaknesses of both the program model and the partnership between Seven Counties Services, Carriage House Preschool, and Jefferson County Public Schools. Table 12-2 identifies and describes each program component.

Several of the points listed in Table 12-2 need to be expanded upon in order to fully understand the operation of the program and community partnerships. The following elaborations provide additional details and illustrations of several program components.

### Administration and Supervision

While responsibility for administration and supervision of the pilot program was assumed by Carriage House staff, there were situations which challenged the proposed channels of communication or chain of command. At one preschool site, the building principal interpreted the program model

**Table 12-2** Identification and Description of the Preschool's Program Components

| Program Component | Description |
| --- | --- |
| Population | Four- and five-year-old disabled children functioning at least 50% below their chronological age in two or more developmental areas; nondisabled four- and five-year olds |
| Class size and ratio | Three classrooms with 15 to 20 children enrolled, and ratios of nondisabled to disabled ranging from 3:1 to 1:1 |
| Staffing | Teacher with special education experience and two full-time assistants per classroom; itinerant music and movement instructor serving all three school sites |
| Support services | Physical and occupational therapies provided in each site by therapists under contract to Seven Counties Services; speech and language therapy provided by a therapist on staff at Carriage House |
| Administration and supervision | Responsibility assumed by the executive and assistant directors of Carriage House, with support provided by Seven Counties staff, building principals, and regional supervisors in Jefferson County Schools |
| Coordination of IEPs and transition to public school | A multidisciplinary team of Carriage House administrators, support therapists, parents, and the classroom teacher; assistance in accessing additional services or adaptive equipment provided by Seven Counties staff |
| Training | Carriage House administrators, with support therapists, during the two weeks prior to school's opening; topics included assessment in natural environments, nonaversive behavior management, and adaptations of curriculum to meet the individual needs of disabled students |
| Program evaluation | Methods outlined in Carriage House's proposal to Seven Counties, including pre- and postadministration of developmental scales, parent reports, videotapes of classroom interactions, and data collection related to IEP review; periodic observations by Carriage House administrators, Seven Counties staff, and representatives of community agencies |
| Fiscal support | Funds provided by Seven Counties through a fee for service contract utilizing state and Federal funds for MRDDO services; tuition on a sliding scale collected by Carriage House; grants from local foundations and service organizations procured by Carriage House |

and its components quite literally. This particular principal's style depended upon specific instructions from the regional administrators. For example, the principal received a request from the preschool teacher to use one of the record players available from the school library. Since this item was not specified in any of the principal's communications with district administrators, the teacher's request was denied. Tension accumulated from many such instances until the executive director of Carriage House approached the principal on behalf of the preschool classroom staff. Attempts to clarify the situation with the principal were unsuccessful and tension grew between all parties. No standard operating procedure had been designed ahead of time for conflict resolution. All participants in the partnership relied on continued dialogue and problem solving. Therefore, a series of meetings followed which shared a common agenda, namely, find ways to alleviate the tension or move the classroom to another building. At one meeting, an MRDDO staff person met with the principal and a regional supervisor from the school district. At another meeting, the Seven Counties staff person, the executive director of Carriage House, the regional supervisor, and an administrator from the Exceptional Child Department met. The meetings continued over a period of many weeks until interactions between the building principal and the preschool staff improved enough for the classroom to continue to be housed in that school for the remainder of the school year.

## Training

During the two weeks prior to the school's opening, the executive and assistant directors of Carriage House conducted training for the classroom teachers and aides. All of the teachers had experience in special education settings. Therefore, most of the training focused on facilitating interaction between disabled and nondisabled students, ongoing assessment in natural environments, and adaptations of standard preschool curriculum activities. The support therapists joined portions of the training to demonstrate the use of adaptive equipment and alternative communication systems. While Carriage House administrators planned each day of training, it was apparent that the teaching staff was allowed to express their needs and questions, and that these concerns were given priority regardless of the day's training agenda. Each of the administrators and support therapists regularly visited each site to provide ongoing technical assistance. In addition, the staff from all three preschool sites met together on a monthly basis at Carriage House. These meetings provided excellent support to the teachers who were each working at blending their classes into the larger public school environments.

Home visits by the teaching staff, prior to the first day of school, provided an additional source of training and information. Parents were invited to an orientation which included an introduction to the principles of integration, normalization, and the developmental model. While receiving explanations of the extent and nature of the support therapies available for their children within the integrated preschool classrooms, parents also received the message that their children shared developmental characteristics with their nondisabled peers. Families of disabled and nondisabled children were invited to informal get-togethers in each preschool classroom prior to the first day of school.

The final segment in the training was made possible by a staggered opening of the preschool classrooms. One site at a time was scheduled to open over the first six weeks of school. The rationale behind this planning was that the least experienced staff members could learn from guided observation of more experienced staff and gain some hands-on experience in a nonthreatening, supported manner.

## An Anecdotal Account of One Child's Experience

In October, 1984, Seven Counties referred a four-year-old boy for placement in one of the preschool sites. The child had been living in a pediatric nursing facility in Louisville, and he was returning to reside full-time with his family. The child, called Sam for purposes of this discussion, functioned developmentally within the one to three month age range. Sam required total care and support in all self-help tasks. He needed to be properly handled and positioned to prevent further deformities from developing. Due to the physical limitations of one of Sam's parents, Seven Counties made arrangements with the Council for Retarded Citizens to provide an in-home attendant who would help get Sam ready for and transported to school.

Before Sam's first day at school, the executive director of Carriage House and the MRDDO staff person coordinating the preschool program met with Sam's parents in their home on several occasions. Sam's parents visited the preschool classroom, and a list was made of necessary equipment for Sam's use in the classroom. The adaptive equipment, as well as an appropriate travel chair, was ordered through Seven Counties Services. The next step in Sam's enrollment in the preschool classroom was taken by consulting with physical and occupational therapists, who formulated individual activities and daily routines to enhance Sam's growth and development. The occupational therapist designed a special feeding program to be implemented consistently at home and at school. Sam began his participation in an integrated preschool classroom on a part-time basis and gradually built up to full-time attendance.

In spite of the severity of Sam's disabilities, he became an integral member of the preschool classroom. His feeding program was implemented in the school cafeteria during normal lunch time. Sam's facial and physical deformities, in addition to his adaptive chair and his being fed by the preschool teacher, drew attention from other children in the school. The classroom staff and, in some cases, the nondisabled preschool children answered questions about Sam's disabilities. Over time, an older student from a neighboring table in the cafeteria developed a relationship with Sam which grew beyond mere interest or curiosity. This student held Sam's hand while he was being fed. When the boy was questioned by his classmates as to why he held Sam's hand, the boy replied, "I'm his friend, and Sam likes it when I do this." Sam's mother observed her son being kissed upon occasion by a classmate who happened to be passing by Sam's chair. Sam's parents became aware, during the course of the year, of the important role friendships had in Sam's life. At the end of the school year, Sam's parents rejected a self-contained special education class for severely and profoundly handicapped children as a placement for Sam in the fall. His parents insisted that Sam's individualized education plan include ample opportunities for interaction with nondisabled children in a regular kindergarten environment. The experiences of Sam and his family were similar to those of other children and their families who were part of the first year's programming. The overall satisfaction of parents with the quality of the program and their acceptance of an integrated approach to service delivery provided a positive testimonial of the first year of community partnership.

## EVALUATION OF THE PILOT PROGRAM

Wilcox and Bellamy (1982) suggest the following factors with respect to which integrated programs can be evaluated for effectiveness:

1. the extent or depth of integration
2. the age appropriateness of the curriculum
3. the degree to which the curriculum is normalized and referenced to the student's community
4. the future utility of the curriculum
5. the extent of parent involvement in program planning

### The Extent and Depth of Integration

The preschool model implemented cooperatively by Carriage House, Seven Counties, and Jefferson County Public Schools fully integrates disabled children with their nondisabled peers. The model has no restrictions with respect to the nature or severity of a child's disabilities. Integration occurs not only within the preschool classrooms but throughout the other areas of the school. The teaching staff and consultants devised ways for the disabled children to participate with their classmates in the gym, cafeteria, library, and playground. Whether it was something as simple as a child's wheelchair being pushed by his or her "line partner," or something more complex, like blending a child's food and implementing a specialized feeding program in a noisy cafeteria, the emphasis was on full inclusion of the disabled children.

## The Age Appropriateness of the Curriculum

In each preschool classroom, Carriage House staff carefully balance each child's developmental level of functioning with age-appropriate materials and activities. Teachers utilize adaptive switches, for example, to enable even the most severely disabled child to initiate play activities and operate battery-powered toys and equipment, which are equally appealing to their non-disabled classmates. The curriculum includes sensory activities which anyone can enjoy, regardless of age, disability, or functioning level. A favorite activity in one classroom was experimenting with the warm air that blasted out of the room's heat vent along the windowsill. All the children enjoyed playing with colorful balloons that bobbed along on the currents of air. Even a child whose only independent, voluntary movement is the visual tracking of an object can be in the midst of this activity, tracking a favorite colored balloon and expressing excitement nonverbally.

## Degree Curriculum is Normalized and Referenced to the Student's Community

Incorporation of this factor begins with the placement of disabled students in preschool sites that are as close as possible to their homes and neighborhood schools. Such placement facilitates relationships from school being carried over to outside of school. The provision of support services, such as physical therapy, within the classroom environment allows habilitative skill development to become part of daily routines and activities.

## The Future Utility of the Curriculum

The operation of an integrated preschool program within a regular school and near regular primary classrooms maximizes the potential for later generalization and application of acquired skills and behaviors. For all the children in the preschool program, the normal school environment, with its variation in stimulation, movement, and activity, provides constant practice for functional skills and coping abilities.

## The Extent of Parent Involvement in Program Planning

Each stage in planning and implementing the preschool program depends on parent involvement. The MRDDO of Seven Counties includes parents in its program and on advisory committees that authorize program plans and fund allocations. Parents in each preschool site participate in an orientation to the program and have opportunities to provide data for program monitoring and evaluation. Home visits by teaching staff prior to a child's entry into the program, observation days, periodic parent conferences, and parent meetings at each school site seek to involve parents in program planning.

The preschool program during the initial year of collaboration in Jefferson County measures favorably with respect to the factors for program effectiveness listed above. The preschool program seems to be a successful implementation of unconditional mainstreaming. A closer look at various program components also indicates some weaknesses which must be addressed by future development of the preschool program and the community partnerships:

- Since all of the children are eligible for public school within one year, there is a complete turnover in program population, which increases training and planning demands on the staff as well as creating discontinuities for the children and families.
- The very limited number of openings for disabled children leaves many children still in need of a comprehensive preschool program and tends to revive the old argument that a segregated program could serve a larger number of disabled children.
- Although the program is housed in Jefferson County Schools, the school district does not "own" the preschool program, and this in turn may allow the district to "disown" the integration component and refuse to claim integration as accepted district policy.

Perhaps the underlying weakness of the pilot preschool program is its unintended duplication of the former patchwork of services. Parents still risk facing a smaller version of the maze of services and agencies discussed in previous sections. If parents have a question regarding their child's physical therapy, for example, should they call the building principal, the director of Carriage House, or the MRDDO? Many situations arise which require problem solving and decision making, but the shifting of responsibility between members of the partnership can delay or prevent appropriate action being taken.

## EXPANSION AND REVISION OF THE PRESCHOOL PROGRAM

Some of the observable changes in the current program and the partnership stem from the evaluation of the first year's efforts, e.g., multi-age groupings that reduce turnover in population. The most significant changes stem from a series of developments within the public school district between the fall of 1983 and spring of 1985. First of all, the superintendent of Jefferson County Schools gave a public validation of the importance of quality preschool and early childhood programming. Further, he committed Jefferson County Schools to developing a model for the community that might be duplicated by business and industry as an employee benefit. Following this announcement, the early childhood specialist was directed to form a program committee, which was to include district personnel and representatives from community agencies. The program committee's task was to design a preschool model and submit a proposal to the board of education. Directives from the superintendent and the board of education stated that the pilot program must be self-supporting and include before and after school care.

Paralleling, but entirely separate from, the pilot integrated program resulting from the community partnership described throughout this chapter was a pilot preschool program for three- to five-year-olds. The district operated program was housed in three sites different from that of the pilot integrated program. Seven Counties' involvement in the district's pilot program was limited to being represented on the program committee by the MRDDO staff person responsible for coordinating the integrated preschool program. The key barrier between the two pilot programs—one integrated and the other predominantly for nondisabled children—appeared to be a programmatic division between the regular and special education departments within Jefferson County Schools. The integrated preschool program grew out of the collaboration between Seven Counties and the Exceptional Child Education Department in the district. There was no representation by this department in the development of the district's pilot program.

Midway through the first year of the two separate pilot programs, Jefferson County proposed an expansion of its preschool program, with an addition of 10 sites each year for the next five years if community interest warranted the increase in sites. Shortly after the proposed expansion, Jefferson County school officials suggested that the two pilot programs merge for the following 1985-86 school year. Much like the initial informal discussions between the MRDDO program director at Seven Counties and the district's director of the Exceptional Child Education Department, which forged the initial partnership, these administrators discussed the proposed merger. There were potential benefits to the school district that encouraged incorporation of the integration component into its expanding preschool program:

- The district's program could apply for special funding through the State Office of Exceptional Child Education, which had some discretionary funds available for model programs.
- If the district was going to compete with private preschool and daycare centers, it would have to demonstrate at least comparable expertise in providing services for young disabled children.
- Since the district did not offer a sliding scale and had no scholarships available, their program would not be accessible to children from low income and poverty level families; with the tuition subsidies for disabled children available from Seven Counties, the county's program would become more heterogeneous.
- The community would more easily understand one comprehensive preschool program.

As a result of these potential benefits, Jefferson County Public Schools now "owns" and operates the entire preschool program, which includes the integration of three- to five-year-old moderately and severely disabled children with their nondisabled peers.

In the merged, expanded program, the school district assumes all of the administrative and operational responsibilities, including fiscal support, hiring and supervision of staff, registration of students, and provision of materials and equipment. The public school district receives funding from Seven Counties Services as an affiliate agency to provide preschool services for three- to five-year-old disabled children. The funding from Seven Counties subsidizes the tuition for disabled children who have been referred by the MRDDO. On the average, there are 5 disabled children in each of the 20- to 29-children classrooms.

Instead of operating the pilot integrated program, Carriage House Preschool now provides ongoing consultation to the Jefferson County Preschool Program to support and enhance the participation of children with disabilities. The consultation services, purchased through a contract with Seven Counties, include technical assistance to the preschool teaching staff, coordination of support services, and management of the IEP procedures.

Seven Counties Services maintains much of its former role, which centers around planning, funding, and monitoring. In addition to holding contracts with both the school district and Carriage House, Seven Counties continues to contract with physical, occupational, and speech therapists to travel to the 12 preschool sites.

The expanded preschool program strengthens certain aspects of the original model. The larger program, for example, serves greater numbers of children and increases the likelihood that children are attending preschool closer to home, possibly even in their neighborhood school. The revised responsibilities in the partnership, with Jefferson County Schools assuming greater ownership and control, lends increased coherency to the model. The building principal, for example, now has less of a role as host to the preschool classroom and greater supervisory and administrative involvement.

While growth in size and structure is positive, revisions in the program model and partnership responsibilities pose a risk to the prominence of integration in the preschool services. The mission and philosophy of Seven Counties Services, shared by Carriage House Preschool, directed fiscal and programmatic planning toward achieving unconditional mainstreaming in the pilot program. Other priorities direct the fiscal and programmatic decisions in Jefferson County Schools, priorities that may result in decisions undermining the process of integration. Through the community partnership, some strategies to safeguard the integration component were put into practice:

- The contract between Seven Counties Services and Jefferson County Schools stipulated that Carriage House teaching staff in the pilot integrated programs would be hired by the school district's preschool program.
- Jefferson County Schools included representatives from Seven Counties and Carriage House on their hiring committees for the preschool staff and program coordinator.
- Mandatory preservice training was designed and provided by Carriage House administrators for the Jefferson County preschool staff.
- Seven Counties contracted with Carriage House Preschool for consultations on the Jefferson County preschool classrooms, including scheduled classroom visitations, coordination of support services, and modeling of adaptive instructional methods.

Situations have arisen during the first three months of the expanded preschool classroom which demand problem solving by each member in the partnership. Scrounging for funds to hire additional assistants, soliciting resources from the state government, daily phone calls to worried parents, heated discussions between members in the partnership, exerting effort and support beyond all contractual agreement—all of these have been necessary during the first three months of operation. During this formative stage of the integrated preschool program, each member of the partnership has dealt with uncertainties about the effectiveness, stability, and future of the program.

In the months ahead, program evaluation, projection of funding, and revisions in the model will continue to develop preschool services in Jefferson County. Two powerful precedents have been established to guarantee the quality of program development, namely, the commitment to unconditional mainstreaming and the community partnership between the private and public service systems.

REFERENCES

Biklen, D. (1985). *Achieving the complete school: Strategies for effective mainstreaming.* New York: Teachers College Press.

Bogdan, R., & Taylor, S. (1975). *Introduction to qualitative research methods: A phenomenological approach to the social sciences.* New York: Wiley.

Taylor, S., & Bogdan, R. (1977). A phenomenological approach to "mental retardation." In B. Blatt, D. Biklen, and R. Bogdan (Eds.), *An alternative textbook in special education* (pp. 193-203). Denver, CO: Love Publishing.

Wilcox, B., & Bellamy, G.T. (1982). *Design of high school programs for severely handicapped students.* Baltimore: Brookes.

# Chapter 13

# The Edward Smith School Program: An Integrated Public School Continuum for Autistic Children

*Valerie Fenwick*

The program highlighted in this chapter is an integrated continuum of services spanning kindergarten through sixth grade in the Syracuse City School District. It is a program comprised of seven classes, one at each grade level, in a school of approximately 800 children; each class consists of 26 to 34 children, 5 or 6 of whom are labeled autistic and in some rare cases multiply handicapped. Each class is organized and directed by two teachers, one certified in elementary education and one in special education, although often one of these teachers is dually certified. The class is staffed by a teaching team including the two teachers, several teacher assistants, and in some cases a graduate or undergraduate student in special education from a nearby university. Providing support for this program as well as for other special education programs in the building are a social worker, a school psychologist (assigned to other buildings as well), and a coordinator. The building principal and vice-principal provide support to all classes and programs at the school.

It is probably most informative to begin with a brief history and a description of important ingredients that constitute the Edward Smith program.

## HISTORY AND DEVELOPMENT OF THE PROGRAM

When change does occur in the public schools, it is usually influenced by many factors and individuals. This is the case with the complete mainstreaming program described in this chapter. Despite the unique nature of the Edward Smith program for students with autism, its roots can be traced to the early 1970s and the development of alternative schools and open education. During that time of ferment in American education, Syracuse was fortunate to have several alternative schools that believed in the potential of all children to learn and develop. One of those, Jowonio School, became the model that Edward Smith School would base its program upon (Knoblock and Lehr, 1986).

Programs are made up of people, and while it is important for our programs to be firmly rooted in philosophical and conceptual frameworks, it is the inspiration and hard work of concerned adults that turns an idea into a reality. That is what happened in 1975 as the Jowonio School staff demonstrated that young children with autism could learn, and that teaching them in classrooms with nondisabled peers could facilitate their acquisition of academic, social, and communication skills. Parents of the students with disabilities became outspoken proponents of mainstreaming, and despite the lack of any existing integration efforts within the Syracuse City School District, they began to lobby for the establishment of a program that would maintain their children in homogeneous groupings. Teachers, too, began thinking about positions in the public schools, and they joined parents in their effort to export a model into the public system.

In 1980, an integrated third and fourth grade was established at Edward Smith for students with autism who needed to move into public schools because of Jowonio School's cut-off age. Deciding that students must leave after the second grade was an important policy decision for Jowonio to make. It pushed the issue of public school placement into sharp focus for parents and school district representatives.

Recognizing the need to provide additional integrated public school classrooms for other Jowonio "graduates," a second classroom was begun in 1981 at Salem Hyde School. A joint effort between Jowonio and the Syracuse City School District, the program took on-site direction from the Salem Hyde principal, who had requested that the program be placed in his building. The program began with approximately 16 children, 5 of whom were children with special needs, 6 of whom were children transitioning from Jowonio, and 5 of whom were children from the Salem Hyde neighborhood whose parents had met with the principal and program teaching staff and given permission for their inclusion. In addition to providing a teacher and an assistant teacher, Jowonio provided speech/language and support personnel as well. The Syracuse City School District provided a teaching assistant and the physical space needed. Both Jowonio and the Syracuse City School District contributed materials for the program, with Salem Hyde itself providing curriculum materials for the typical children. A paid inservice for all staff, kindergarten through third grade, including special teachers and kitchen and custodial personnel, was given prior to the opening of school and the beginning of this new program.

Given the nature of this jointly created program, in which services and supplies were contributed by two different sources, some areas were ill-defined the first year. Although many details were not spelled out, the program worked—largely because of excellent administration from both locations and the commitment of the individuals involved.

The availability of education programs for students with autism at Jowonio School and Edward Smith School helped to focus attention on children with autism, and referrals increased. Staff members and parents from these settings, anticipating the need for additional grade levels in the public schools, began to plan for an expansion of the Edward Smith School programs. Parents, especially, were active in voicing their support for this effort.

Many factors contributed to the original decision to provide Edward Smith School with teaching positions and to support the principal's efforts to implement the program. The fact that a working model had been implemented successfully at Jowonio School tended to validate mainstreaming. In turn, developing one classroom at Edward Smith School encouraged everyone in the belief that further expansion into Salem Hyde was desirable. From the start, staff members (and parents) shared their expertise with each other to reduce anticipated problems. For example, a portion of the summer inservice program at Edward Smith School was devoted to discussing autism, describing the children (including showing pictures of them to reassure the school staff that they looked like other children), and describing the team teaching model that involved regular education and special education teachers. Teachers helping teachers was very much in evidence during that summer orientation; and teachers as change agents contributed to the success of the Salem Hyde program as well.

The program at Salem Hyde continued into 1982-83 with its original structure, and then in June, 1983, a decision was made by the Syracuse City School District to centralize all services for children with autism at the Edward Smith site. So in September, 1983, the Syracuse City School District took over the second grade program, placed it at Edward Smith School, where the fifth grade class was already in existence, and created first grade and third grade integrated classes as well. Teaching staff who had trained at Jowonio through Syracuse University's special education program in autism and emotional disturbance were hired to teach in two of the three classrooms. The following year, kindergarten and fourth grade mainstreamed classes would be added to complete a continuum of integrated classrooms spanning kindergarten through sixth grade.

## PROGRAM INGREDIENTS

### Description of the Model

For an integrated class, defining the model is a critical step. How the class is set up will impact upon how integration is perceived by others in the school environment, how the autistic children are perceived by peers, how adults are managed, and a myriad of other factors. If one's goal is to educate children in the least restrictive environment and to build acceptance of the children within the school and the community, then this decision can create barriers or overcome already existing ones, and it will determine how successfully the program eventually functions. It is important to note that model decisions are largely defined by the roles of the two team leaders: the regular education and special education teachers. Central to role definitions are the willingness and abilities of these two teachers to work with both disabled and nondisabled children and to direct other adults in doing the same. Although each class is staffed by a teaching team, the three different models that have been used to date are as follows.

*Model One.* Two teachers divide responsibilities for special and typical children, formulating a schedule wherein teachers and children alternate between two given rooms. Responsibilities are clearly defined for specific time periods, but include responsibility for all children all of the time. In this model, teachers planning an activity for the typical children would plan alternatively for any disabled child who could participate, even if at a lower level.

*Model Two.* Two teachers divide responsibilities for special and typical children, splitting the day into morning and afternoon sections. One teacher assumes the roles of the regular education teacher in the morning and special education teacher in the afternoon; the other teacher does the reverse. In this model, roles are defined for large blocks of time, with smaller assignments delineated within each large time block, and teachers are primarily responsible for their respective children. If this model is defined mainly for the purposes of organization, so that there exists within the model free exchange between team members and flexibility in scheduling, then it can foster as much integration as the first model. But if roles are defined too strictly, with minimal communication between teachers and little spontaneity possible, then a situation can result that mainstreams the disabled child physically but not maximally.

*Model Three.* Two teachers decide that the special education teacher will be responsible for programming related to the children with special needs, and for designing ways, with input from the regular education teacher, that the disabled children can positively participate next to their peers throughout the day; this also necessitates scheduling the assistants to work with particular children. The regular education teacher is then responsible for daily programming for nondisabled students. Within this model, the autistic children are usually less fully integrated for several reasons. The regular education teacher leading the activity for typical children neither plans for the inclusion of special needs children nor interacts with them very frequently. Since children focus on the teacher leading, they see less interaction between the teacher leading and the disabled children and thus less modeling of how to interact. It would seem that there could be a subtle message in this for typical children: that interaction is not encouraged. Furthermore, less interaction is likely to happen within this model, for children with special needs are accompanied by adults. Thus, fewer chances exist for typical children to interact on their own with their disabled peers or to offer spontaneous suggestions.

Much of how autistic children are perceived by peers depends upon how the children are introduced and valued, the attitudes and interventions of adults, the interactions which occur between special and typical children, and the friendships which result. If disabled children are pointed out as different and these differences are made much of, then the children themselves can be devalued, teased, ostracized, and at times even abused. If children never see similarities but only differences, then children with special needs can be responded to inhumanely. If common ground is never established on which both typical and special children can stand, share, enjoy, interact, and respect each other, then different worlds always exist and crossovers happen much too infrequently. With all three of these models, if the classroom is a safe place where all children can be themselves, feel valued and respected, and learn at their own pace, then the autistic children will be valued and respected for themselves and their rates of learning will be accepted.

In considering the three models and the ways in which autistic children are perceived by peers, the most pronounced differences seem to be in how the children see adults treating children with special needs and in how these disabled children function in groups. While Model One puts a greater emphasis on teach teaching and communication, both teachers are interacting with all children throughout the day, ostensibly in much the same way that they interact with typical children. A teacher might teach a reading group of typical children and in the next half hour teach a child with special needs according to an individualized reading program. Much give-and-take happens among teachers and assistants throughout the day, for example, congratulating a certain child for some accomplishment, maintaining consistency with respect to behavior management, informing each other about the feelings expressed by a particular youngster. The same can be true of Model Two if free exchange exists among team members, together with scheduling flexibility. However, Model Two can also become very regimented, if there is pressure to save time on communication and cross-planning. If this happens, then roles are taken literally and the special child loses, for he or she is then included only partially in a group by the teacher leading the group, or if fully included, not given tasks that are similar to the tasks of others. Another drawback of Model Two is that if typical children perceive that special children are planned for by someone besides the teacher leading an activity, then they see this as a way in which special children are left out by the leading teacher. This, in turn, can cause confusion or uncertainty about how valued such children are or about whether they fit within the classroom.

In Model Three, there is a greater likelihood that children with special needs will be seen as less capable or less valued. This has to do with the assignment of the regular education teacher to the regular children and of the special education teacher to the special children. The special education teacher has the auxiliary role of planning for the assistants, who in turn work with the special children. Not only does this then require that one special education teacher plan for and support all of the assistants, but also that he or she be in several places at one time. Unless a great deal of communication takes place between special education and regular education teachers, the autistic children can lose out in the same ways as under Model Two. In addition, typical children often take the adult who accompanies the special child as that child's teacher, which can imply that the regular education teacher is not the child's teacher, and also that the child cannot do any tasks or parts of tasks independently. Within the entire integrated program, independence is a major focus, regardless of the model; assistants are instructed to pull back as much as possible if a child can in any way participate autonomously. In Model Three, allowing the child independence is more difficult, because assistants infrequently work with typical children. In Model One, and to some degree in Model Two, assignments for assistants can more easily include integrated groups of typical and special children.

## Staffing

Working in teams is necessary to the functioning of the integrated classroom. Even in a situation where a smaller class, with fewer mainstreamed students, could be taught by a single teacher, teacher assistants would still be necessary in order to provide support for the children with special needs. Working daily together, the teacher and the assistants would follow a complex schedule, communicate about changes, plans, specific children, behaviors, expressions of feeling, and overall direction. In difficult situations, team members could brainstorm and problem solve together. With specific structured programs, discussion of consistency would need to take place. Without a doubt, if an integrated program is to function optimally, team members must work together and assist each other so as to benefit all of the children and to facilitate maximal growth for all students.

Teaming, however, can be very complex. Anytime that people want to or must work together, there is the possibility of personality conflicts, authority

struggles, ego problems, communication breakdowns, philosophical differences, and even lack of definition and clarity. Team teaching in an integrated program is really no different and can therefore be affected by any
of the above. Sharing the same space with several other people can also be
difficult, even with everyone being careful to respect each other's roles and
space needs.

One of the foremost concerns facing the integrated programs at Edward
Smith is the initial forming of the teams. There are at the school many
qualified special education teachers commited to making the program work.
By and large these people have gone through Syracuse University's graduate
program in emotional disturbance and autism, have trained at Jowonio, a
private mainstreamed school now operating at a preschool level, or have had
experience with other people who have done one or both of these two. It
seems that attracting regular education teachers to the available positions is
more difficult, given the complexity of the schedule, the close teamwork involving several other adults, and the additional afterschool meeting time required to talk, share, problem solve, plan, and program with other team
members. Certainly some teachers express curiosity, interest, and respect,
but few are willing to take on the job in its entirety. This can mean that
teachers are interviewed who are unfamiliar with the program in action and
who therefore cannot really understand what teaching in the program entails.
This can result in hiring teachers who soon feel overwhelmed. At times,
teachers are interviewed who are new to the district and have varying
amounts of experience. When new or inexperienced teachers are hired, they
sometimes have little to offer the program. This is definitely a problem
which needs immediate attention.

On the topic of hiring teachers with some experience, there is much more
to be said. Given the amount of planning that each of the two teachers
assigned to every integrated class must do, it is imperative that each have
knowledge of special education or regular education curriculum. Given that
several models are possible, strong experience with one might be sufficient,
but strong experience with both is preferable. When a teacher is hired with
minimal practical experience in either, or with experience at a much higher
or lower grade level, it is more likely that the teacher will become
overwhelmed, suffer a sense of failure, provide insufficient support to other
staff members, and feel out of touch with the children involved. Teachers
must have an understanding of the job, as well as appropriate job experience,
in order to become an integral part of the teaching team.

In addition to qualified teaching staff, integrated classes require teaching
assistants who are willing to make a commitment to the program. They also
often require additional adults in order to ensure quality programming for
all children. Locating available adults can be very difficult. Whether the

adults are undergraduate students, graduate students, parents, foster grand-parents, or volunteers, they can make the difference in creating a smoothly functioning classroom and program.

The team of people working with special children is not limited to class-room staff. Other adults involved might include the principal, the social worker, the psychologist, the nurse, and bus drivers. Most frequently a special child will work with other teachers in art, music, gym, and library. It must be remembered that these special area teachers have most likely never received training in special education, and yet they are expected to work with children having special needs. Again, relating as members of an extended team may involve personality conflicts, authority struggles, ego problems, philosophical difference, communication breakdowns, differing needs for space, and personal needs for clarity and definition. In this last case, other dif-ficulties for the special area teacher may occur: (i) uncertainty regarding the needs of the child; (ii) uncertainty regarding appropriate lessons for a child and appropriate means of evaluating a child's performance; (iii) unwilling-ness or uncertainty with respect to supporting disabled children through ac-tivities, especially when teaching assistants are assigned; (iv) difficulty com-municating to teachers and assistants the amount of support desired; (v) disagreement on implementation of specific behavior management pro-grams. Certainly through professional approaches, such as communication, brainstorming, planning, and programming, these problems can be ad-dressed.

### Scheduling

Regardless of which model is chosen, scheduling is a major variable to be addressed. In an integrated situation, set up to benefit both typical and spe-cial children, a complex schedule is required. Typical children must receive quality instruction in all curriculum areas, as do their peers in other classes at the same level, and they must also receive the preparation required for work-ing at the next grade level. Children with special needs must receive quality instruction with their peers in curriculum areas in which they can keep pace and on skills in other curriculum areas which will serve them in their daily living. Children with additional needs—as assessed by SRA scores for typical children and by local or district Committees on the Handicapped for children with special needs—must receive certain special services. For typical children, this may come in the form of resource time, a reading lab, math lab, gifted and talented program, or a psychologist. For special children, this may come in the form of occupational therapy, physical therapy, adaptive physical education, or speech therapy. All children attend all special area subjects (i.e., art, music, gym, and library) as a group.

Creating such a complex schedule can be difficult, even overwhelming, for many teachers. After all, once the schedule is determined for the group as a whole, but with a stress on the needs of typical youngsters, a schedule addressing the needs of disabled children must be superimposed. Each disabled child has many individual needs, some of which can be addressed during a group activity in a particular curriculum area. Others will need to be addressed while the child with special needs sits with the typical children during a group activity but works (with the support of an assistant) at different individualized tasks, although in the same area. Sometimes a child must leave the room for one-to-one instruction, planned for by a teacher but carried out by an assistant. (All times scheduled for assistants must be planned by teachers, as planning is not included in the job descriptions for assistants.) Decisions need to be made as to which goals are addressed when, how they are addressed, what kind of a situation will be maximally beneficial, whether the behavior management the child needs can be provided by an assistant, and whether a child needs one-to-one instruction. A sample schedule segment is shown below:

9:30 to 10:00 : All typical children are involved with reading instruction or independent seatwork. Adult assignments appear below.

- Reading instruction for children at 2A reading level with Bob (regular education teacher)
- Reading instruction for children using DISTAR with Valerie (regular education/special education teacher)
- Cognitive/signing time for Randy with Ginny (teacher assistant)
- Speech time for Dan with Becky (speech/language pathologist)
- Reading comprehension time for Mary with Liz (teacher assistant)
- Concepts time for Stevie with Jean (graduate student in special education)

Moreover, particularly given the complexity of the schedule, transitions must be planned and each member of the teaching team must be on time. Schedule delays, like falling dominoes, impact on every member of the teaching team. Changes in schedule must be communicated to all team members.

Equally overwhelming for any teacher can be the task of planning for and supervising several other adults. In a class of 26 total children, 5 of whom are children with special needs, 2 to 4 of these children will probably require one-to-one assistance throughout the day. Once the scheduling is completed, the two teachers need to create plans to be carried out by the assistants, giving suggestions as to behavior management strategies, providing backup during instruction if such is needed (e.g., if a child loses control or persists in challenging), and providing feedback and encouragement. An assistant could have as many as nine or ten different assignments during the course of one day, these assignments staying constant across five days. A teacher's role would also include overseeing assignments for some portion of the special needs children and ensuring that education is taking place.

Overseeing assignments is more difficult if children are pulled out of a classroom in order to receive special services, such as adaptive physical education, occupational therapy, physical therapy, or speech and language therapy. Pull-out programs of this type can be a barrier to integration. If a child receives two or three of these services on a yearly basis, as many do, then these children work independently on their goals during specified times and without modeling or encouragement from typical peers. In addition, typical peers have no way of understanding how these services relate to their special friends or their time in the classroom. Moreover, and perhaps most important, if a disabled child receives two or three of these services on a regular basis, less time is then available to be in the classroom learning with, next to, and from nondisabled children. For any particular child, this could mean as much as four to five hours out of the classroom, or approximately 16% of a child's week.

Another disadvantage of specialized instruction outside the classroom is the possible lag in carryover to the classroom. Excellent instruction may take place, but this is conveyed to classroom staff mostly verbally at weekly team meetings. Alternative systems could be found to facilitate such carryover for effective programming.

### Child Ratios

A potential barrier for integrated programs is the assignment of too many special children to an integrated classroom—or the assignment of too many difficult special children, that is, those needing one-to-one assistance, strong behavior management, strong intrusion, or an alternative communication program. This is a potential barrier for several reasons: (i) the assignment of too many difficult children could mean too much energy is directed toward these children, and less energy is available for teaching the typical children or other mildly or moderately disabled children. (ii) Grouping too many children with similar needs and behavior can affect the amount of interaction which takes place with typical peers. If too much energy is focused on managing the behavior of several children or on reaching several special children, then less is available to stimulate and facilitate interaction between special and typical children. (iii) Similarly, children needing one-to-one assistance throughout the day are often children who cannot be grouped with typical peers during curriculum instruction and who have alternative needs to be addressed. If these children receive one-to-one instruction within the classroom, working next to typical peers, then typical children are exposed to children with special needs, to what they are working on, and to their means of expressing themselves. But if the child with special needs has many individual needs that can only be met one-to-one outside the classroom, or that would require instruction disruptive to a given lesson, then the chances for stimulating and facilitating interaction are reduced. (iv) If a group of children within a classroom have the same disability, characterized by similar levels of functioning and similar physical and behavioral needs, then this sends a certain message to the typical children of the classroom, who perhaps are being exposed to special children for the first time. If four out of five special children are nonverbal, for instance, then this could say to their typical peers that all children requiring assistance are nonverbal, that this is something to be expected. If three out of six special children in a classroom are aggressive, then typical children might think that disabled children are usually aggressive. If many of the disabled children in a classroom are limited in what tasks they can accomplish, then special children may be viewed by their typical peers as generally much less capable. Having special children with a variety of disabilities presents to typical children a picture closer to reality. Children with handicapping conditions are as much individuals as children considered to be normal or typical.

## Curriculum Content

One of the questions most often asked by those encountering an integrated class, or even the entire continuum for the first time, is "How do these classes compare with regular classes?" Prospective parents of typical children have asked, "Will my child benefit from such a program?" These classes might be very much like the classes that parents have known before, or very different.

In addition to presenting academic instruction in all curriculum areas— including reading, language arts, spelling, writing, mathematics, social studies, science, and health—teachers in integrated classes also include in their daily schedules meeting and choice times. While integrated classes emphasize skill development, mastery, and independence and enjoyment in application, as other typical classes do, and while they participate in all activities that classes at the same grade level participate in, teachers set aside approximately thirty minutes a day for a class meeting time and another thirty minutes each day for an individual choice-making time. Before discussing additional factors emphasized that link the classes within this continuum, it is important to discuss these two times, their importance to students, and their practical translations.

While meeting times may happen at different times in different integrated classrooms, many happen first thing in the morning. After the children come in, briefly socialize, say the pledge of allegiance, and listen to morning announcements, they assemble as a class to focus on some topic. Topics vary from teacher to teacher, class to class, grade level to grade level and year to year, but the importance of meeting is to assemble as a family group with all members present, thereby providing a forum for personal sharing, exploring of values, discussion, and problem solving. Some meetings focus on show-and-tell or news-of-the-weekend, particularly in lower grades, where each member's contribution is accepted and enjoyed for its uniqueness. Other meetings focus on topics for thought or topics for discussion. These encourage children to focus on issues and to discover their own feelings and values in a range of situations. Still others present real-life events and problems, challenging the students to create acceptable and workable solutions. At times, these meetings are forums for experiencing and discussing individual differences, with the goal that differences among individuals be acknowledged, accepted, better understood, respected, and valued.

The choice-making time usually happens later in the morning or during the afternoon. At this time, activities selected by teachers or students are presented, and each child is given the choice of what to do for those thirty minutes that day. Often at the beginning of a year, teachers will organize the activities for the choice-making times. Once the class becomes settled, children will provide input on activities they would like to participate in and topics of interest that they would like to learn about. This is an exciting means of allowing children some input into their own education and also of providing teachers with a format for presenting hands-on projects suitable for small groups that complement the curriculum areas. Children enjoy the time, look forward to it, and are more motivated to complete earlier assignments well so as to participate.

Choice time is a small group social time in which children can relax, get to know each other, converse, and become friends. This is true for the children with special needs as well; while each child might be supported by an adult in a small group, choice time provides an opportunity for the child to learn new skills or play behaviors, to generalize already learned ones, to relax, to interact, get to know peers, become friends, and demonstrate independence. Children also learn much about choices themselves. They learn to evaluate alternatives, to carefully select on the basis of their own wishes, to stay with an activity of choice for thirty minutes even if interest wanes, to see a project through to completion, to accept disappointment if a particular project of choice has already been chosen by the number of students who can participate for that day, and to experience independence and success in completing projects or in interacting with peers. Choice time becomes a popular time of the day.

Within these integrated classes, additional factors exist that reflect particular educational philosophies. The classrooms are set up as safe environments, relaxed yet structured settings where children have freedom to move about and gather their own materials while following a set schedule. Classes are taught by teams of teachers and assistants, sometimes including university students. Members of the team evaluate the performance of and set goals for students, utilizing a developmental approach to learning. A great deal of individualization takes place in planning and implementation as children are encouraged to learn at their own pace, meeting ever-present challenges and being guided to success. Teachers strive to make learning interesting, experiential, exciting, and fun. Self-evaluation, rather than judgment of others, is fostered. Competition is present, but de-emphasized. Within integrated classrooms, children are not singled out for being different. Differences may be noticed and discussed, as students come to understand their own strengths and weaknesses, but they are also accepted. People are valued.

Classroom environments are carefully created to highlight function. Sections are organized by theme, e.g., a *reading* corner, a *science* counter, and a changing *sensory* table. Charts or equipment relevant to alternative communication systems are set up to invite involvement. Daily classroom schedules might be posted so that children can anticipate events. Self-control and independence are encouraged in a setting where teachers call attention to positive behavior and role-modeling. Positive reinforcement is given in many forms: stickers, stars, charts, hugs, and praise. Even desks are strategically placed for maximum integration among classmates; particular children are grouped with clear intentions. Integration is structured in other ways as well—by scheduling social times, by pairing children often, by setting up peer-tutoring situations, by structuring interactions throughout the day. Facilitating the acquisition of positive self-esteem is a major goal of the integrated program.

At each point along the integrated continuum there is a focus on the whole child. Relationships, adult-child and child-child, take on special significance. Emotional well-being is carefully nurtured. Children are encouraged to express their feelings, desires, and ideas; and guidance is provided for affective and emotional growth. Teachers communicate regularly with parents and invite participation by families in classroom activities and school functions. Socialization is encouraged; interaction in pairs, small groups, and large groups is facilitated, with personal and group problem solving addressed. Children are encouraged to observe, think, make choices, and reach out to others. They are frequently asked to put themselves in the positions of others and to care about the thoughts and feelings of those they encounter.

## Parent Involvement

Parents have had a tremendously important role in creating the integrated program and in supporting it. Still, there have been times when these same parents have needed assistance and reassurance.

Parents of typical children, when faced with the prospect that their children will be educated in an atypical setting, sometimes balk at first, unwilling to take what they consider a risk. After asking many questions and talking with other parents, most proceed with little hesitation; a few proceed guardedly, asking questions all along the way. Eventually the integrated classes are better understood, and fewer parents express anxiety. Many instead request the programs in years following and continue to offer support.

Parents of children with special needs sometimes have a similar hesitation, which can be interpreted as protectiveness. While this is less common, it does happen that some parents are fearful that their children can't handle it, that they aren't ready, that they won't fit in, that they'll be teased by typical peers, or that they won't receive the specialized services that they need. Again, after asking many questions, talking with other parents, or visiting the program, these parents may cautiously try it out, only to find that their worries were unwarranted. It is a rare occasion when the parent of a disabled child expresses reservations after placement in an integrated class and an appropriate trial period for assessment.

The following section describes barriers to integration that the Edward Smith School currently encounters and strategies for overcoming those barriers. It is interesting to note that several of these were noted during the first year of the program. For example, staff turnover was an issue during the first few years. The special education teacher did not last the first year, claiming a variety of pressures, including demands to focus on the scholastic achievement of nondisabled students. Today, that concern is still present for all of the teachers at Edward Smith School and for teachers of integrated programs everywhere. The success of a mainstreamed program rests, at least in part, upon the quality of the instructional program for nondisabled students. While the regular education teacher was familiar with those academic concerns for typical students, she was not prepared for the individualized planning required for the special needs students. We learned then how important it is for the building principal to take the stand that in a team teaching situation in a mainstreamed classroom both teachers must share all the students. Regular education teachers must involve themselves with disabled students just as special education teachers will need to learn the curriculum for typical children in order to interact with them. The need to individualize instruction requires many skilled adults in a classroom to teach small and large groups and to work with individual children when appropriate.

## STRATEGIES TO OVERCOME BARRIERS TO INTEGRATION

### Administrative Issues and Solutions

In looking back at the evolution of this continuum of integrated services, one can identify certain barriers or obstacles to integration that arose or presently exist. Similarly, there are certain strategies that have been effective in overcoming these obstacles, as well as ideas generated by interested participants that might lend support to the program and facilitate mainstreaming. Ongoing assessment and problem solving are essential to improvement.

At the present time, there is at the state level no accepted model for integrating special and typical children. The state only recognizes programs for typical children that function alongside programs for children with disabilities. This necessitates that an integrated program be presented on paper differently from the way it actually functions in reality. Consequently, programs tending toward integration risk being refused funding unless they can creatively present themselves as the state requires. By recognizing integration as a viable model, the state could develop a corresponding funding formula, which would allow programs to apply for monies directly while describing the interaction of children as it actually takes place on a daily basis.

Although PL 94-142 exists and states that children should be mainstreamed in the least restrictive environment, the state does not distinguish programs which excel in this regard. If recognition of such programs occurred, consultation could be provided more easily to help develop other integrated programs around the state.

During the summer of 1984, the same children who were educated in classes with typical children during the year had to receive services in segregated programs. This came about because state policy would not allow typical peers to attend the program without additional staff assigned specifically to them, and hiring staff, as well as collecting tuition from families of typical children, brought with it even greater complexity. While the summer program of 1985 was set up to include typical children as well, this was only possible due to creative solutions put forth by administrators, parents, and teaching staff already involved with the integrated program.

At the district level, there has been considerable support to date. The district has (with a state directive and after many parent requests) set up an integrated continuum that in its present form exists at one site. A few isolated integrated classes exist at other locations. It has provided speech/language, occupational, and physical therapy, adaptive physical education, psychological consultation, social work services, and additional bus rides. In addition, teaching assistants have been provided in greater numbers than required by state regulations, substitutes have recently been assigned when assistants are absent, and materials have been generously provided to new integrated classes. An individual in the school itself has been allowed to spend considerable time acting as "coordinator" of the program. The district has worked with Syracuse University to provide financial support to some students in exchange for substitute teaching time. Financial support has also been provided for developing a community-based curriculum.

Still, several challenges clearly exist: (i) hiring new team members early enough to allow adequate time for team planning; (ii) attracting qualified assistants with relevant experience given salaries and benefits offered; (iii) inservice training—related to state regulations, district curricula, behavior management, and appropriate expectations—for new personnel; (iv) maintaining within each school an appropriate balance of typical children and children with special needs; (v) providing adequate and ongoing support to a quickly growing and complex continuum; and (vi) providing adequate and ongoing support for alternative efforts at mainstreaming. Already some of these challenges are being addressed through the innovative efforts of administrators, parents and teaching staff involved with the integrated program.

Actually, the labeling process itself can be seen as an obstacle to integration within this continuum, even though it might facilitate mainstreaming in other classes. Children labeled *blind* or *orthopedically handicapped*, for instance, can now be considered typical children and placed in an integrated program as members of the typical population, even though they still need additional services. This could leave the class unbalanced in terms of children with special needs. On the other hand, such an approach can enhance the possibilities for the same child to be educated in a less restrictive environment than was previously the case, particularly if that environment is a regular class.

It would seem that the present integrated program could be threatened by its own growth. Growing quickly, without additional support in staffing, could result in teachers being overwhelmed and unable to deliver the high quality of service that they have in the past. Allowing the present program to stabilize, without additional immediate expansion, might be optimal, as might putting a freeze on the number of students admitted and the number of students enrolled from other districts. Admitting students with handicapping conditions other than autism is a question that needs philosophical as well as practical resolution, even though what is practical may be at odds with what is philosophically justifiable.

Certainly a barrier to integrated education exists when additional sites for similar programs cannot be found. If other schools were willing to pilot or adopt such classes, this would speak to the tremendous number of students who could benefit. This is true of many other districts also that rather than begin a program of their own either send children to a more restrictive environment or petition individually for specific children to be accepted in an already existing integrated program. Neither alternative seems acceptable given the special needs of the child and also the need of the already existing mainstreamed program to stabilize and maintain itself.

One recent attempt to highlight integration, demonstrate its results, and underscore its feasibility took the form of a leadership seminar. The brainstorm of a Syracuse University professor with extensive experience in special education, the seminar involved having area building principals and district administrators visit existing programs, discuss possibilities, assess individual situations, ask questions, share experiences, and work together to create least restrictive environments for children with special needs. Certainly such endeavors offer hope for the future.

## Classroom and Building Issues

The administrative issues discussed above have had a definite impact at the building and classroom levels. Efforts have been made to develop creative solutions for resultant problems. Yet at the building and classroom levels, still other problems have required examination. Some of these were addressed earlier; positive directions are set forth below.

Clearly the model which maximizes integration for typical children and those with special needs is Model One, wherein two teachers divide responsibilities and formulate a schedule having teachers and children alternate between two rooms. Drawbacks of the other two models have been discussed. Still, within this model, decisions must be jointly made, assignments clear, communication ongoing, planning sound, the schedule flexible, and teamwork emphasized. Children must be supported where they need assistance and encouraged toward independence at all times. Where appropriate, programming for children with disabilities should take place with or near typical children, and activities should match the content area of instruction as closely as possible. Where this is not possible, one-to-one instruction outside the classroom might be called for. Yet even instruction taking place outside the classroom can be integrated through the inclusion or one or several typical classmates.

Similarly, it is Model One that will present autistic children to their typical peers in the most positive light, although similar results are possible utilizing Model Two, as has already been stated. It is very important that the climate in the classroom be one of acceptance, understanding, and respect. Questions related to differences can still be answered as they come up. Interventions initiated by adults should convey the same acceptance, understanding, and respect. A child who acts inappropriately can be firmly told that his actions affect others without the implication that the child is bad. Whenever possible, adults can set up situations to foster interaction and encourage the development of friendships. By and large, children are curious, open, and positive when provided with a safe, supportive, and stimulating environment. One is reminded time after time that negative attitudes are much more common in adults and that children, when given the room and the opportunity, generally respond positively to and enjoy each other. An interesting case in point comes to mind. Several years ago in the Salem Hyde classroom, a typical child new to the program, whose parents had diligently prepared her for anything she might encounter, approached the teacher and stated that she was sure there would be children in the classroom who looked very different and acted differently as well. She then sheepishly looked around and asked, "Are they here yet?" Since all children were present and accounted for, the three-headed monsters whom she had anticipated clearly looked very similar to the other children in the class.

It must also be remembered that special area teachers and adult assistants have most likely never received training in special education; yet they are expected to work with children having very special needs. Inservice education might appropriately be extended to these individuals.

At the present time, since inservice in special education is lacking, team meetings can be utilized for this purpose. Designing a system in which assistants may cut short their workday by 25-30 minutes, pooling time so that an afterschool team meeting can happen once each week, is invaluable. These meetings allow for sharing, discussion, instruction, problem solving, and coordination of all efforts. Also helpful for disseminating information, demonstrating approaches, and introducing techniques are role playing and modeling. The latter often happens on the spot with children. In addition, it might be helpful for classroom teachers to set up a one-to-one conference time with each special area teacher to discuss (i) specific needs of a child or children; (ii) possible means of evaluating a child's performance, particularly if the child is significantly below age level; (iii) assignments of teaching assistants and ways in which the special area teacher could support a particular child, even if only for part of a period; (iv) how classroom staff can best support the special area teacher; and (v) behavior problems that could be disruptive and ways these problems could be dealt with. At times, such discussion might necessitate the formation of short-term goals, a trial period of assessment, and a re-evaluation when appropriate. Such give-and-take can foster a climate of positive exchange and cooperation, thereby best serving the children involved. Such discussions could also examine the needs of typical children, the overall needs of the class, and ways to work together so that the subject area can be an exciting experience for participating students.

With respect to child ratios, integrated programs function best when the number of special children assigned to the program, and in turn to each class, is kept constant. It seems that too many special children in one classroom creates an out-of-balance situation that not only is difficult to manage, but offers limited possibilities for fostering interaction and true integration. The classrooms seem to work well if a typical:special ration of 3:1 is maintained; it is possible that a 4:1 ratio works even better. A key element to be considered here is the range of autistic children within a classroom, with attention paid to (i) a child's physical disability; (ii) whether a child is high functioning and demonstrating many skills, or low functioning and demonstrating limited skills; (iii) how verbal or nonverbal a child is; (iv) how difficult a child is in terms of behavior management. In order for the program to benefit all children involved and achieve the goal of integration, special children should be placed together who differ with respect to these critical variables. Perhaps of six children in a classroom, two might be quite low functioning, one or two difficult to manage, no more than two nonverbal, only one physically disabled, and several mildly to moderately disabled (and therefore high functioning to some degree). If five out of six children are aggressive, low-functioning, nonverbal, non-toilet-trained, or in need of constant one-to-one supervision, simply assigning more and more assistants to the class may not help, for managing the class then becomes more complex. Placing a range of special children within each classroom makes for manageability and broadens the educational experience of the typical children.

In order to make such placements possible within a public school setting, it might be necessary to think differently about some traditional policies for typical children. For instance, perhaps some children with special needs, following an ungraded program as they do, would need to stay in the same grade and classroom for an additional year. Similarly, perhaps some children with special needs should be allowed to skip a grade level and advance to a higher one, depending upon age and size. Certainly other possibilities for innovation exist.

Specialized services, such as speech/language, physical, and occupational therapy are definitely necessary in meeting the needs of special children. However, the question arises, Do children really need to receive such services on a one-to-one basis outside of the classroom? For some children and for some services the answer may be yes. But it is important to consider other possibilities for "therapy." For instance, could any of this specialized instruction take place in the classroom, where peers could observe or even participate? Could such instruction outside the classroom include a typical peer, who might form a relationship with a particular child, give encouragement, and him- or herself receive additional attention? Could assistants participate at these times so that effective carryover to the classroom would take place? Could such instruction, which is focused on agreed-upon goals, provide modeling for other adults and children within the classroom, thus extending the effects of therapy and making progress more pervasive? Obvious advantages exist when sessions are videotaped and replayed for classroom staff. Similarly, information gained from classroom observations can be useful in planning therapeutic interventions and in setting up a free exchange among team members so as to optimally benefit the child.

As mentioned earlier, the integrated classes often require additional adult help to ensure quality programming for all children. Each classroom of approximately 28 children (including 5 or 6 children with special needs) is taught by two teachers and several assistants. An additional assistant might be provided if a particular child has a strong need for management or physical assistance. Often the teachers agree to request a graduate or undergraduate student in special education (in order to facilitate teacher training). The number of adults in a class must be sufficient to meet the needs of children, but not be so many that there is a confusion of responsibilities and a problem with classroom management.

Another very important variable is the degree of independence of children in the classroom. Children must be encouraged to act independently, without leaning on adults who might be available. Adults can facilitate this by pulling back and by encouraging personal mastery. Many typical children placed in an integrated class one year will move on to a regular class the next. These children must be prepared to handle a regular class environment, where there might be only one teacher for twenty-eight students. Similarly, all children can learn self-reliance as it relates to personal choices, achievements, pride, and self esteem.

Teachers of integrated classes must always think beyond their own classrooms. A classroom does not exist in isolation; rather it exists side-by-side with other classrooms in the school, each of which demonstrates some personalized form of education. It also exists within the overall school environment, in this case the Edward Smith School. The beliefs and attitudes of other teachers, professionals, and adults within the school environment can support the goals of the integrated program or act as barriers to these goals. Of course, beliefs and attitudes are for the most part person-specific, and they must therefore be addressed on a person-by-person basis as much as is possible.

For instance, if there is an individual or individuals who believe that a particular child cannot learn, that autism is contagious, that behaviors manifested should be treated differently, that self-stimulatory behaviors will be imitated by typical children, that the typical children will not be served given integrated education with disabled peers, or that autistic children do not belong in public schools, then it is possible that the children themselves will be touched by these attitudes. It is possible that certain professionals may be critical of the program, may talk to others about their feelings, may express similar attitudes to children, may influence public opinion about the program, or could even become overtly negative on building issues. Obviously, this must be considered a barrier for integrated education, because it impacts on how accepted autistic children are within the school, on how others feel, on how the community feels, and on other building issues that may be unrelated. Most important, it can impact on how accepted integrated education is as an education of choice.

Certainly situations come up in any school building when a particular child is difficult and a teacher needs assistance and support, when two teachers disagree, or when a plan must be made and ideas vary as to what it should be. At these times it seems beneficial if teachers talk to each other directly and honestly—and listen and work toward a common goal. However, it often seems evident that no real problem solving process exists. Similarly, when colleagues or other staff have commented upon the integrated program or had questions related to it, such a dialogue has seldom taken place, either teacher-to-teacher or within a small or large group. When concerns go unacknowledged or unanswered, it often happens that they grow bigger and such a dialogue becomes more difficult. Among the concerns related to the integrated program voiced by other adults at Edward Smith are the following: (i) the many assistants who work in integrated classrooms, (ii) the need for assistants in regular classrooms as well as self-contained special education classrooms, (iii) the extra responsibilities often taken on by program assistants, (iv) the number of materials allocated to integrated classrooms, and (v) the amount of publicity focused on this unique program. Certainly these concerns need addressing.

Education and information might be helpful in the face of concerns, because when people understand a situation they are usually less fearful, threatened, or uncomfortable. Talking about the issues involved can also be beneficial, because misunderstandings and questions can be dealt with directly. Working with children might lend itself to learning by example. Asking willing individuals for assistance can give a newcomer direct experience with the needs of a special child, and carefully making this experience a positive one can result in a more accepting attitude. At times the children somehow teach the doubting adults just by being themselves.

Of utmost importance is for integrated classroom teachers to be a part of the school in addition to being a part of the integrated continuum. Sharing school concerns and getting to know other adults brings people together. Finding ways to assist other teachers and asking for needed assistance can create long-term bonds, as well as trust. Serving on school committees as an interested teacher, and not just as a representative of a grade level or continuum can allow for discussion of critical questions and foster a spirit of teamwork. Also important—for building respect—is following adopted procedures and offering suggestions for change in appropriate ways. Keeping the needs of children as the highest priority can facilitate clarity on the part of adults.

A hard-earned lesson for the integrated continuum at Edward Smith is that some criticism of what others have comes from not having enough personally. Some criticism directed at the integrated classes for what they have seems to stem from what teachers of regular classes feel they lack. It is important that these feelings be listened to and that a concerted effort be made to provide support for obtaining what is truly necessary. Teachers in regular classes often feel a need for additional assistance in dealing with difficult children and consequently might feel that a teaching assistant should be provided. Efforts could be made to secure additional adult personnel, including student and parent volunteers. Some teachers in regular classes might feel a need for additional materials. Sharing might be possible, even pooling certain resources school wide or by grade level, perhaps through the instructional specialist. And teachers could join forces in fundraising campaigns. In negotiations that take place on behalf of teachers, say by a teachers' union, it is essential that members of integrated classes be sensitive to the processes involved so as to be supportive and not in conflict. With respect to publicity, there are many exciting and noteworthy activities and projects that take place in regular classrooms. Somehow these must be focused on—through administrative channels, instructional specialists, school publications, and teamwork. If all teachers in a building could receive adequate support, attention, and appreciation, then criticism of others might well decline.

Beyond individual classrooms and beyond the school environment itself, parents have consistently demonstrated support of the integrated program through action. At times, however, in situations involving their own children, parents have also needed support, which one would expect. For parents of typical children notified that their child will be educated in an integrated classroom, many questions immediately arise. In years past, letters were sent explaining the program and meetings were held with parents of typical children *prior* to the beginning of school. The meetings served as a forum for questions and answers. As the integrated continuum has become a long-term part of Edward Smith School, different means of information sharing have evolved. At the kindergarten level, letters are still sent and meetings arranged. However, the Integrated Parent Group has generally taken on the function of introducing parents to the program. This group invites parents involved with the integrated program to regular monthly meetings and sets agendas that include questions about the program and discussions of classroom structure, autism, integration, social interactions, and other topics suggested by interested participants. In addition, parents talk informally to other parents, such as those with previous experience. Parents are invited to visit the classrooms to observe a typical day. A videotaped presentation is being made which will highlight important aspects of the integrated continuum for parents and other interested observers, including administrators and teachers from other districts, who often make appointments to visit and walk through the classrooms.

## PERSONAL PERSPECTIVES

Following are some personal observations about integrated education. They are based on my years of experience with integrated classes, both in a private and a public school.

First of all, many children, unhampered by adult experiences, accept even the most behaviorally difficult peers. Others, sensing a climate of safety, caring and acceptance on the part of adults, learn to value differences, even their own. There are always certain children in a class who are immediately active with their disabled peers—or with one in particular. Other students become active and comfortable over time, still others are helpful when asked to be, and some never show very much interest. Some who may be initially fearful of "differentness" ask questions and with understanding and experience become more accepting. In a climate where each person's individuality is valued, self-acceptance and acceptance of others evolve. One measure of the latter is a type of sociogram done yearly for several years. Each time this was done, children with special needs, even children considered severely involved, were chosen as best friends or close friends by some nondisabled peers, good friends by others, and not such good friends by still others. Similarly, during one recent Valentine's Day vote, when all children were asked to vote for one girl and one boy whom they considered to be "very caring," the girl chosen was a typical child considered by the district to be "gifted" and the boy chosen was a nonverbal and nonambulatory child with average or near average cognitive ability. Interestingly, what these sociograms often point out is that the high-functioning child with special needs is often chosen as a friend less frequently, probably because he or she is seen as a "strange" typical child and judged by "typical" standards.

It is this writer's experience that within these integrated classes special friendships eventually develop. Children call each other at home, sometimes visit after school, and invite each other to birthday parties. One mother of a child with special needs reported that her daughter had never received any phone calls prior to her experience in second grade, and another parent of an older boy said that she was thrilled when her son was finally invited to the birthday celebration of a peer. Certainly less teasing takes place as children come to know, accept, and respect each other. In fact, as children continue through school together, typical children sometimes become "advocates" for their disabled friends with other typical children. Recently, one parent of a disabled adult commented on her day's experiences while substitute teaching in an integrated class. She said that watching the children's acceptance of each other was a very moving experience, that she was surprised to see so little teasing, and that she and her husband had some time ago purchased a portable radio with earphones for her daughter—to help her block out the taunts of her peers.

Some of the special friendships which develop in these classes involve typical children who have had a difficult time in school themselves. Sometimes a child who has struggled with one or more academic subjects feels good in helping someone else. Perhaps when children are asked to look at themselves as individuals with their own strengths and weaknesses, they can better understand that self-esteem involves more than academic excellence.

The integrated continuum at Edward Smith School, despite the challenges it has faced, has been in existence for many years—in one form or another. In the early years, one class stood alone. Today six classes form an elementary school continuum, with still another at the junior high level. If one examines its history for the consistently positive variables that spurred growth, one would have to begin with the people of vision who set up a small alternative school called Jowonio. One would then need to mention parents who were willing to go against the grain in order to attain what they considered the best education for their children and then mention still other parents who lent support on a regular basis and continued to request what at times might have seemed like the impossible if in the best interest of their child's education. One would certainly need to mention a once small but growing group of committed teachers, administrators, and university profesors who have the notion that the integrated continuum represents the way the world should be. Most of the Edward Smith teachers involved in the continuum met on the average of every two weeks this past year in an effort to lend support to each other, discuss potential problems, and generate solutions. Several teachers then met regularly with building administrators for additional sharing and problem solving. Finally, perhaps most importantly, one would need to mention the children, whose attitudes and actions are often examples to the adults. Observations of the special and typical children together have said to all involved, "You're doing something right."

Below are two excerpts from personal letters, the first written by a child and the second by a parent. A fifth grade student wrote to her teacher about a child with special needs:

> I love to work with Brenda. But I want to help her learn too. My mother says it's important not to treat her like a new toy but to treat her as a person. I try to treat her as one of my friends. Do you think I treat her like a new toy? Be truthful! . . .
>
> When I grow up, if I ever do, I want to be a special education teacher. I know that no one could be as wonderful a special education teacher as you, but I hope I can come moderately close.

A parent of a typical fourth-grade child wrote to the principal about her daughter:

> I felt I needed to crow a bit about Diane's year in the integrated class, and to tell you about the impact that it has had on her. My husband and I were, of course, a little cautious about the idea. Diane seemed enthusiastic about the class from the beginning. She spent the early weeks trying to understand the behavior of the special kids, a process that has continued to deepen throughout the year. At the present time, she interprets her special classmates' and her own behavior in light of very sophisticated historical and environmental events. Recently, she related a tantrum of one of her classmates to a schedule change which prevented the child from going to a favorite activity. Several days later, she likened a tantrum of her own to the same factors and went on to express her sense that the "special kids" perhaps aren't "special" but (her words) "they're just more sensitive to stuff." We think that's a pretty spectacular insight for a nine-year-old!

While these reflect just a few of the many moving experiences that happen regularly in an integrated classroom, they convey the essence and spirit of the program as a whole. In reading these excerpts, it is easy to feel good about the program day-to-day and about the vision as it continues to take form.

## SUMMARY

This chapter has described the evolution of a complete mainstreaming program for students with autism. The program at Edward Smith Elementary School is part of an integrated continuum of school programs in Syracuse, New York. Students can begin at Jowonio School, an integrated preschool program, then move into integrated kindergarten classrooms at Edward Smith School and later into integrated classes through sixth grade. At that point they are transitioned into a community-referenced middle school program that combines integration in school with experience at community work sites.

The planning and implementation of this program began in 1979 (even earlier if one considers the evolutionary nature of the change process). Parents, working closely with educators, created the political climate for integration to take place.

Once a program is in place, the groupings and the instructional program should be re-examined on a regular basis. The original groupings at Edward Smith School were designed to include several students with autism in a classroom at each grade level. A model being considered for use and evaluation in the near future entails dividing the number of special needs students going to one grade level among four classes at that grade level; one or several teachers dually certified would assume responsibility for consultations and programming related to these students. While this model would have obvious advantages and perhaps some disadvantages, it is exciting for the degree of normalization it would achieve. But still critical to the workability of this structure is a team willing to attempt such a challenge.

The dynamic nature of a mainstreamed program is seen in the discussions of barriers and strategies employed to overcome those barriers. There are no easy ways to avoid problems. A willingness to engage in ongoing problem solving for the purpose of program fine-tuning is crucial for program effectiveness.

---

REFERENCES

Knoblock, P., & Lehr, R. (1986). A model for mainstreaming autistic children: The Jowonio School Program. In E. Schopler & G.B. Mesibov (Eds.), *Social behavior in autism* (pp. 285-303). New York: Plenum.

Chapter 14

# Lessons from
# Integrated Education

*Michael S. Berres* and *Peter Knoblock*

While this book has addressed both the theory and practice of providing integrated education to elementary students with moderate and severe disabilities, it has leaned heavily toward the practical side of the question. The philosophies of integration, mainstreaming, and least restrictive education which underlie this book's described practices have been a source of intense debate among educators since the passage of PL 94-142 in 1975. At times, it has appeared that the intensity of this public debate—played out in a wide variety of media, academic, and popular literature forums—has made us lose sight of the fact that increasing numbers of children with disabilities are actually being provided quality education in the most appropriate, least restrictive settings possible.

In the midst of this public debate, there have been many excellent changes made by groups of parents and educators in all parts of this country. In some parts, the changes have resulted in new types of programming for large numbers of children. In some parts, funding and legislative changes have resulted from these efforts. In other parts, the changes have affected only small numbers of children and may have gone unnoticed by the media and even other local educators.

Regardless of the size and scope of the new practices, the change to integration has always resulted from an initial small group of committed individuals with great patience and a shared vision of integrated, normalized education. This book is a tribute to the painstaking work of those people who have believed in the value of providing an integrated experience for children.

Most of the program descriptions have been written by people with the actual responsibility for implementation of the change process within their school, district, or region. It has been our strong bias as editors to provide the reader with a series of credible case studies detailing the change process.

We hope to have conveyed through this presentation of both the positive and negative sides of implementing integrated education that change is in fact possible—and not only possible but ultimately worthwhile.


## THE SPIRIT OF CHANGE

The evolution of a school system toward an integrated model of education can take many paths. These paths are clearly dependent upon a multitude of factors which are idiosyncratic to each school district. These factors include such things as a local district's philosophy toward serving children with disabilities, local and state funding practices, and the status of parent organizations in the particular region.

Some of the nine programs in the book were initiated through a very deliberate planning process of the nature described by Nancy Lamb-Zodrow. The programs in Madison, Wisconsin and Fountain Valley, California show this type of deliberateness. Other programs, such as the one in Santa Barbara, California, show the necessity of program advocates being able to utilize unplanned events to the advantage of their integration efforts. We have also provided accounts of programs such as the Albuquerque, New Mexico Side-by-Side program, which involved large numbers of students, and Olympia, Washington's Project MERGE, which utilized changes in traditional special education funding patterns. These larger change models can be compared with programs such as the one in Medford, Oregon, which was initiated to serve a single student, or the program initiated in upstate New York to serve five children with hearing impairments.

We have also included programs that involve a variety of degrees of integrated experience. The programs in Louisville, Kentucky and Syracuse, New York, for example, show how integration has been structured so that it is a full-day experience for both typical and special needs children. Other programs have developed schedules that provide integrated education for a part of the day or provide options in the amount of integrated time based upon the particular needs of the students.

A constant throughout the program descriptions has been the twin elements of time and patience. The movement towards quality integrated education has evolved slowly in every one of the nine districts. It doesn't matter whether one attempted to change the program for a small number of students or for an entire system. Change agents in Medford, Oregon, for example, experienced three years of initial frustration in their efforts to provide Eric with an appropriate integrated education. While the number of students is different in the Madison Metropolitan School District, the elements of time and patience are remarkably similar. The change process takes a great amount of both.

It is also evident that change does not appear to go forward in a single positive direction. The change process is composed of both positive and negative events. Some of the events are predictable. Other events cannot be predicted, but still often have a major impact on the progress and direction of change. All nine programs are excellent examples of "two steps forward and one step back." Despite the occasional setbacks, though, program planners appeared to always have maintained their commitment to the original vision of an integrated service delivery system. Dr. Stillman Wood, special services director in Olympia, Washington, has frequently noted that Project MERGE—as it is described in this book—is really only the latest stage of a change process that he has been directing for the last eighteen years.

## DEFINITIONS OF THE QUALITY OF INTEGRATED EDUCATION

This book presents nine studies of how districts have chosen to define and practice such concepts as least restrictive and integrated education. With the definitions provided by the editors in chapter 1, ten versions of the definition are provided to the reader. Rather than there being a single standard for what constitutes the "correct" definition and practice, it is evident that there are multiple ways of defining the concepts. For most school districts—even including those in the book that were eventually able to obtain technical assistance or special monies for their change efforts—there is very little help in trying to define these terms. It is uncharted territory.

Each of the described change efforts has placed a heavy reliance upon program advocates being able to continually ask and refine the question, "What is quality integrated education?" In each district, they are only answered on a temporary basis. This is because as soon as a program reaches a certain level of integrated experience (e.g., partial day integration of students in a district that has previously only had self-contained or segregated options), program advocates then tend to ask, "What's next?" That is, success in reaching one plateau of integration allows the program advocate to see that there are even higher plateaus which can be reached in the future.

The program for children with autistic needs in Syracuse, New York provides a vivid illustration of this process. As detailed by Valerie Fenwick, the program in the Syracuse City School District emerged from the experience of parents, educators, and students at a remarkable publicly-funded private school called Jowonio. The creation and maintenance of Jowonio itself involved a continual series of plateaus, each one a little more sophisticated than the last in helping children with autistic needs. At a certain point, it became evident to Jowonio staff that the next logical plateau was the exporting of the Jowonio model to the surrounding public school district's elementary program. While this process was rocky at times, it did eventually succeed. When this plateau of an elementary public school program was reached, planners quickly saw the need to expand the service option to secondary students. It is now evident that once the secondary option is fully stabilized, planners will begin looking at the higher plateau of community integration for young adults.

While it is hard for program planners to continually rise to new challenges, the benefits to students with moderate and severe disabilities are striking. Despite a lack of assistance in defining the philosophical terms, school districts are creating and providing high quality education to children in a myriad of new formats.

These new formats have resulted in a variety of new normalized educational experiences for children. In some of the districts, integration has proceeded to a point where children with disabilities and typical children are taught in adjoining classrooms for part of their day and then brought together for a part of the day. The preschool program in Santa Barbara is an example of a program that has currently reached this level of interaction. An obvious question that will soon be asked is how to increase that interaction from part-time to full-time. Other programs, such as those in Louisville and Syracuse, have already reached a level of full-time integration for their students. The questions that their staff will have to ask will concern the quality of integration as opposed to the quantity.

In essence, the nine programs have all embarked upon a kind of journey with no defined outcome. There is only a general direction. Program planners talk about their innovations and changes in guarded or qualified terms. While they feel good about what their students are now experiencing, they have no illusions about having created the perfect integrated experience. They view their programs as being in a continual state of evolutionary change and refinement.

This has required that the planners are secure in their values and beliefs. They are willing to continually hold their educational achievements up to scrutiny and systems change processes. This ongoing change process is clearly stressful to the participants. They continually look for ways to improve their programs by expanding the local operational definitions of integration and least restrictive environment. They are willing to risk the short-term discomfort caused to themselves and their districts because of the long-term benefits they know will accrue to the district and its students. They stand in stark contrast to educators who stand by outdated or ineffectual service models out of a fear of the difficulties attending change.

One of the lessons of change, then, is that it is continual. A program evolves to a certain point, and then its managers evaluate its status and begin to look for other ways they can further integrate their students. It means that not only are districts continually subjected to examination, but also that their program proponents need to be open to a continual re-examination of their own values and beliefs. It is a rigorous process, but one that is highly beneficial.

It is also clear that program planners learned to view these change processes as a positive problem-solving experience. Rather than abandoning the change process at obstacles or roadblocks, they adopted the belief that issues can be resolved. All of the programs to one degree or another institutionalized a formal planning and problem-solving process. Even those programs that recognize the importance of accidents or events over which they exert little control discuss their efforts to build as much of a proactive planning orientation as possible into their efforts.

In part, one must attribute this problem-solving orientation to the types of planners involved in the various change efforts. They possess a tenacity that allows them to always remain focused upon the long-range goal of integrated education. While they are accustomed to making small pragmatic course corrections, they never lose sight of the ultimate destination. It can even be said that these planners tend to use obstacles and negative events as ways to understand and implement even more rigorous system change models. The flexibility to choose among a variety of change strategies—depending upon the current trends of district politics—proved to be a very valuable survival skill in all of the described programs.

It was also evident that planners attempted to work collaboratively as much as possible. They learned to seek assistance from other regional sources of expertise about the most effective ways to change their systems. They learned to use people both inside and outside of their educational systems for technical assistance and support. But while they did use resources outside the organization, they made sure that prime decision making was conducted by those within the system, believing that the final decisions needed to be made by those who clearly understood the local district's conditions.

Finally, there were some planners who pursued change democratically. Rather than seeking to start a change process by administrative personnel that would then be implemented by direct service staff, these planners worked to include all impacted constituency groups in both the planning and the implementation stages. There was a strong belief that all participants—especially direct service staff—had to be involved in some aspects of the planning so as to feel a sense of ownership and have a personal investment in the changes. And by working in this collaborative fashion, it happened in almost all situations that people who were initially hesitant about integrating children with moderate and severe disabilities came to advocate the program goals.

## MAJOR LESSONS OF CHANGE

There are a number of valuable lessons that emerge from the nine case studies. The lessons should help program planners or managers begin to analyze their current change strategies with respect to variables that had a clear impact in other school districts. The following lessons mainly concern the need to work with or change staff attitudes and the equally important need to provide effective inservice and consultation to parents, staff, and administrators.

### Staff Attitudes

An important lesson of the case studies is that the most significant factor accelerating or hindering integration efforts is the attitude of staff (teachers, support staff, administrators) about students rather than the abilities of the students. Those programs that experience success in the integration of children with moderate and severe disabilities are those that pay attention to both the pedagogical and attitudinal needs of the receiving settings. Integration efforts that address only the pedagogical needs will run into major attitudinal resistance.

This is hardly a surprising finding, for we know that the integration of special needs children—especially those with severe needs—is typically viewed as threatening by receiving teachers and administrators. Receiving teachers often cite such factors as inadequate training, minimal support from administrators, insufficient time, and overcrowded classrooms as reasons for their hesitancy in serving more-involved students. Compounded with their often realistic observations, though, is mystification about children with different types of behavior. Teachers come to "fear the worst" and administrators grow concerned about their pending responsibilities for special needs children.

Planners successful in integrating children are those who directly confront the mystification surrounding special needs children. Planners utilized a variety of strategies to work with teachers and administrators and to break through attitudinal resistance. They provided great amounts of information to the impacted staff through written materials, interprogram observations, and staff development. They allocated major portions of or entire staff meetings to addressing the pending integration changes. They provided opportunities for staff to vent their fears and frustrations. And in some cases, they even provided opportunities for staff who they believed would never change their attitudes to teach elsewhere. And once the integration process was operational, they continued to provide their direct service staff with on-going sources of technical assistance so that they never felt alone or abandoned in serving the special needs children. That is, program planners committed themselves to doing whatever was reasonable to help staff move beyond the prejudice.

The main idea was to allow staff to get to know and understand the special needs students for what they are, that is, more similar to than different from regular education and mildly disabled students already being served in district buildings. It was also evident from the studies that planners tried to impress upon their staff that most of the teacher interaction with special needs students would revolve around normal teacher techniques rather than on exotic or unusual special education interventions. Most planners attempted to emphasize teaching techniques for special needs students that were likely to be already in use by the receiving teachers and staff.

In summarizing a massive study of 25 integrated programs, Robert Bogdan (1983) reached a similar conclusion about the critical importance of educator attitudes. If the teaching procedures for successful integration have been clearly articulated for the past decade, why then, asks Bogdan, do some efforts at integration not succeed?

> The question we should be asking is not, Does mainstreaming work? It clearly does. We have seen students with severe disabilities learning and prospering in integrated settings, while enriching the lives of their classmates and their teachers. . . . But we have also seen less encouraging situations. And we have come to understand them not as indications that disabled children are inherently incapable of success in mainstreamed classrooms. Rather, these supposed failures of mainstreaming are problems of organizational arrangements, internecine politics, and a lack of will and skill of school personnel. (p. 428)

As stated by Bogdan, those programs successful in implementing integrated service delivery systems dealt with the attitudinal biases and fears of staff. Rather than assuming that educators were bad teachers or bad administrators for being initially hesitant, these program planners assumed that attitudinal resistance was natural. And they assumed that it could be altered to the point that those initially hesitant would eventually come to be proponents and supporters of integrated models.

## Administrative Support

Program planners put great effort into obtaining support from all impacted administrators. When such support was more difficult to obtain, it was evidently more difficult to create an integrated program. Planners paid particular attention to seeking support from building administrators whenever possible. Building administrators are truly the people who can make or break integrated change efforts. They set the day-to-day tone for all activities that occur within a building. They can create an atmosphere in which building staff look at integration as a positive problem-solving situation requiring collective action or an atmosphere in which integration is viewed as a burden that the staff must endure.

Planners worked to involve building administrators in the actually program planning and implementation so as to increase the number of proponents supporting the integrated change efforts. In doing so, integrated models came to be supported not only by the initial proponents—who were often people working outside of the impacted buildings—but also by respected people who were willing to have part of their day-to-day lives altered to better serve children with disabilities.

Planners also required the support of building administrators because of their ready access to direct service staff. Knoblock and Goldstein (1971) have written that teaching is a "lonely" profession—and this is especially true for teachers who are placed in a classroom with children whose needs are severe and challenging. Being in classrooms for the entire day, teachers have little contact with other adults and often tend to feel unsupported in trying to meet these challenges. A building administrator, with the ability to move through a building, is one of the very few individuals who is able to provide support and consultation to teachers when they need it.

## Direct Service Staff Support

The nine program descriptions have stressed the importance of program planners working to foster the support of those staff who will be directly charged with implementing the integrated service models. Nancy Lamb-Zodrow discussed the advantages of using a change model that had a participatory basis in program planning and development. Without the inclusion of teachers, aides, and support service staff, much in the way of planned change will remain precisely that—only planned.

The participation of direct service staff in program planning and development leads to a widening of the base of support for integration. This widening of support, especially among the teacher ranks, will be important, since opposition to integration is often based on the additional stress placed upon building teachers. The programs described in this book made great effort to have teachers and other staff directly involved in major, if not all, parts of the planning. Some programs, such as Olympia's, sought the active participation of all teachers but were understanding when a particular teacher said that he or she could not make the type of changes that would be necessitated by the changed program.

The methods used in dealing with teachers always involved respect. Program planners appeared cognizant that teachers frequently feel decisions are made by people who have little understanding of what actually takes place in their classrooms. Planners attempted to involve teachers and other direct service staff in a way that would allow them to feel the change was partly influenced by their views. Efforts were made in most programs to avoid teachers feeling that the change was based purely on an administrative decision.

Another advantage of participatory program development is that it brings those people into the ongoing review and course correction process who have the most immediate sense of the program's strong and weak areas. As feelings of ownership for the well-being of the program are spread among teaching staff, they are likely to raise any concerns which might pose a threat to the overall operation of an integration effort.

It would be hard to conceive of any complex educational change such as integrating children with severe disabilities taking place effectively without the ongoing support and assistance of those staff most directly involved in the change. To not attempt to fully involve the impacted staff is clearly to risk hurting a program through the passive-aggressive behavior of those staff. To attempt the involvement—as demonstrated in the program descriptions—will lead not only to better programming for children but also to greater definitions of competence by teachers who have succeeded in making a new model of education work.

## Technical Assistance, Consultation, and Staff Development

The move to an integrated service model places burdens on staff that may be entirely new to them. The complexity of the children's needs will create a variety of needs for assistance. It is critical that teachers and other staff have access to others who can provide them with feedback, observation, and other forms of assistance, thereby minimizing or eliminating feelings of frustration, abandonment, or helplessness.

The nine programs all developed sources of assistance to direct service staff. Some programs utilized consultation through a teacher-to-teacher system. Others used relationships with regional service districts or agencies. Some developed technical assistance relationships with university programs.

And some utilized a combination of all three approaches. The most profitable type of technical assistance was that provided on an ongoing basis rather than irregularly or infrequently. Staff had more faith in models where the consultant was available to them as needed so that they could continually address current issues. It also makes direct service staff confident that the consultants have a working knowledge of the conditions of particular classrooms.

It was evident that many programs preferred to use training that would work with the entire multi- or interdisciplinary team that served a classroom or group of children. Rather than attempting to provide assistance to a single teacher or a single principal, technical assistance was given to all professionals; they could then use the assistance in developing collaborative responses for working with children. This practice facilitated generalizing change across all impacted settings.

Most of the consultation described in the nine programs was characterized by an effort to help the direct service staff develop the necessary skills to be able to work with children on their own in the future. Consultation generally helped program staff develop self-sufficiency and expertise in ever-widening areas of concern. Consultants spent time helping program staff with questions in particular curriculum content areas and with developing ways that building staff could serve as resources for one another.

Program planners placed a great emphasis on high quality staff development activities. Effort was expended to make sure that the chosen inservice activities grew out of needs identified by direct service staff rather than solely out of needs identified by planners, administrators, or others without a direct in-class set of responsibilities. Program planners also attempted to utilize inservice presenters who the staff viewed as having credibility in the field, which usually depended on their having direct experience with the types of problems faced by staff rather than merely theoretical knowledge.

Finally, planners provided a balance of one-to-one consultation opportunities, small group problem-solving sessions, and larger staff inservice experiences. These staff development activities were open to regular and special education teachers, support staff, and administrators—and in some cases, parents. Every effort was made to use these activities to bring together staff from programs which too frequently received separate inservice training.

### Student Preparation

Planners developed training programs aimed at both the typical and special needs students with the same deliberateness used in developing training programs for teachers, support staff, and administrators. They realized the importance of training both sets of students to cope with the challenges of an integrated learning environment.

Students with special needs were increasingly provided with the skills needed to cope with the academic curriculum and the skills needed for approaching and interacting with their regular education peers. In several programs, this meant the direct teaching of social and interactional skills. It meant, for example, teaching special needs students in Syracuse how to make eye contact and initiate interaction with typical peers. It has meant doing task analyses of social skills with the same precision used in many traditional academic task analyses for students with mild disabilities. The end result has been to heighten the chances for successful integration due to the proper preparation of special needs students.

It is also noteworthy that programs placed significant emphasis on the preparation and training of typical students so that they could learn to appropriately interact with their special needs peers. Special education integration efforts have faced major problems when they overlooked the importance of preparing the receiving set of peers to work with and reach out to special needs students. Because typical children are exposed to the same cultural biases that are possessed by adults, it is important to teach the process for interacting with special needs students. Planners did this through a variety of activities, including awareness sessions, peer-tutoring models, and the teaching of social skills through direct instruction formats.

When children are provided this type of assistance in learning about one another, they quickly—or at least more quickly than their adult counterparts—learn to approach their peers with lesser degrees of bias. For many program planners, this impact on typical children was an unanticipated gain. The planners generally believed in the importance of providing their special needs children with typical peer role models. What they did not anticipate was the extremely favorable reaction generated among the typical peers. At times, the reaction was reported by the students themselves. And at other times, the reaction was made evident through parental reports. Rather than experiencing special needs children as unusual, typical students in these programs came to see integration as normal.

### Parent Participation

A final lesson from the programs concerns the importance that staff placed on parent participation in the education of their children. While all too many special education programs restrict that participation to the yearly meeting with parents for discussing a child's IEP, these planners viewed participation as including much more. Parent involvement meant open invitations to the classroom; serving on advisory committees to the district; functioning as district-sanctioned peer counselors and advocates for other parents; lobbying with local, regional, and state educational and social service agencies for funding support; and active participation in the development of effective teaching strategies that could be generalized from the home to the school and back.

Utilizing parents in these types of activities did not always come easily to professional educators who had been trained to think of themselves as the sole definers of curricular direction. It meant giving up some initial feelings of territoriality in the hopes that the advantages created from the collective product of home and school would outweigh the disadvantages of a more open process. This does not mean—as Nancy Lamb-Zodrow indicated in her section on the value of participatory planning—allowing all parents access to vital decision making. But it does mean an honest reappraisal and reaching out by special educators on those questions where they might develop true working relationships with parents.

## FINAL CONCERNS

This book is about more than just an educational issue. It is about more than just the changing educational rights of students with moderate and severe disabilities. It is about how we, as a society, view issues of citizenship and participation. The way we respond to students with disabilities has ramifications for the way the larger society will be structured. Perhaps this is why it is so difficult to change educational structures—or at least why it takes so long to change them.

One thing that emerges from the evolution to integrated education is the realization that educators cannot return to past practice very easily. Once an educator says, for example, that separate educational programs no longer make sense or fit their notions of how educational and larger communities should be structured, they can never again accept the existence of such programming with comfort.

This same phenomenon also occurs with the parents or caregivers of students who have been served in integrated models. Once they have seen their children participate in integrated programs, it is very difficult, if not impossible, for them to imagine service being provided in a separate system. While parents are often initially hesitant to have their children educated in integrated settings (which they view as less safe and more challenging), they frequently become strong advocates for integrated programs after witnessing their children in such settings.

The same may be said for each of the groups affected by this change. As the group—whether educators, parents, regular education students, or in many cases the special needs students—experiences the potential of integrated education, the hesitance or resistance changes to support and advocacy. It is as though the educational process is seen in an entirely new light. The old logic simply doesn't fit anymore. The philosophical assumptions supporting separateness cannot be maintained against direct experience.

This book profiles the experiences of educators in nine school systems from different parts of the country. They are certainly not the only educators involved in promoting integration. We could have chosen others, perhaps even other programs in which the integration has been implemented in more sophisticated ways than those described in this book. In fact, as editors, we run the risk of having readers necessarily equate the nine programs as being state-of-the-art simply by their placement in this type of volume. The issue of integrated services is too complex to utilize any single simplistic definition of state-of-the-art practice. Any such definition would be short-lived amid the constant changes in both the theory and practice of the issue. Although we believe that each of the programs currently contains essential strengths, and that the collective volume represents a progressive direction for special education, we also know that each program must resolve its own set of problems, limitations, and unanswered questions. But our intent was to show more a process than a final product. It was to show that commitment to an ideal (the right of all children to participate together in learning) and to a process (a participatory, problem-solving process) can lead to a continually improving model of service for students with moderate and severe disabilities. The chapters describe a group of educators who always assumed that integration was possible. They never questioned their basic convictions. Their only questioning was about the particular change strategies necessary to procure integrated educational experiences for their students.

## Creating One System and One Future

Writing about the schools of tomorrow, John and Evelyn Dewey (1915) made the following prophetic statement:

> A truly scientific education can never develop so long as children are treated in the lump, merely as a class. Each child has a strong individuality, and any science must take stock of all the facts in its material. Every pupil must have a chance to show what he truly is, so that the teacher can find out what he needs to make him a complete human being. (p. 101)

Today, becoming a complete person means having a future. And special educators and parents are combining efforts to guarantee that for all children individual needs are met, strengths are recognized, and futures are envisioned.

Visions of children's futures may differ, but all parents share the desire to have their children reach their potential. This typically involves learning to make friends, acquiring skills to facilitate independent functioning in schools and communities, learning to make choices and decisions, and learning to live as independently as possible within communities.

The trend toward mainstreaming and integration coincides with the effective school movement initiated by regular educators to identify organizational factors that positively influence classroom learning. Both of these developments emphasize diversity and the importance of a quality education for students. Most importantly, they recognize the value of creating learning environments that maximize the opportunity for all children to learn.

Creating effective schools requires the realization that the structure and climate of a school can make a difference to successful student functioning. Educators have identified a number of variables contributing to school effectiveness, including, but are not limited to, recognition of the importance of the principal as a school leader; setting clear goals and objectives for the attainment of academic achievement; monitoring of student progress; and creating a predictable and orderly learning environment in which high expectations are set (Bickel and Bickel, 1986).

This fortuitous coming together of two movements—one within special education and the other within regular education—bodes well for children's development. When we identify the factors that create an effective school, we can improve the instruction for all students. And when we emphasize the importance of individualizing instruction and the value of diversity, as mainstreaming and integration do, we can apply these principles to all students, disabled and nondisabled.

The maintenance of a dual system—regular education and special education—no longer appears desirable, particularly in light of the commonalities inherent in the two systems discussed above. It is conceivable that the maintenance of systems that separate students and teachers perpetuates the ideological and economic barriers described in chapter 1.

In recent years, there has been intense criticism by professionals of the existence of separate educational programs for lower-functioning regular education students and those special education students with mild deficits. Current research trends strongly suggest that the main differences between these two groups are the artificially contrived labels necessary for school districts to receive funding rather than actual differences in the types of academic or affective behaviors exhibited by these students. The result of this questioning has been the growth of a basic education system that is more flexible and skilled in serving students with diverse needs. This book has provided a series of working models in which the same questions are being posed about separating children with moderate and severe special needs from their typical peers. We make no claim that such an integration of students with more severe special needs is an easy process. We do, however, provide examples of educators who have committed themselves to ending a barrier between children in the same way that the barrier between regular education students and those with mild deficits has increasingly been called into question.

There were those who said that the integration of regular education and mildly disabled students could never—and *should* never—happen; yet it is happening in large numbers of school districts all around the country. In the same way, many lay and professional people have said that it is not desirable to bring together children with moderate and severe disabilities with their nondisabled peers; yet this form of integration is also happening and succeeding. We know, in fact, that some of the program managers described in this book initially held negative beliefs about the efficacy and desirability of such integration.

By creating one system, we can explode the myth that regular classrooms should exist in which the students function on more or less the same level, with other students excluded on the basis of their special needs. And by moving away from this myth, we can move toward a world in which all children grow to live a life of quality and dignity.

---

**REFERENCES**

Bickel, W., & Bickel, D. (1986). Effective schools, classrooms, and instruction: Implications for special education. *Exceptional Children, 52,* 489–500.

Bogdan, R. (1983). "Does mainstreaming work?" is a silly question. *Phi Delta Kappan, 64,* 427–428.

Dewey, J., & Dewey, E. (1915). *Schools of tomorrow.* New York: E.P. Dutton.

Knoblock, P., & Goldstein, A. (1971). *The lonely teacher.* Boston: Allyn and Bacon.

# Index

# Contributors

DOUGLAS BIKLEN, PHD
Professor and Director of the Division of Special Education
  and Rehabilitation
  Syracuse University
  Syracuse, New York

KRISTINE E. DAVIS, MA
Itinerent Teacher for Visually Impaired Students
  Jackson Educational Service District
  Medford, Oregon

VALERIE FENWICK, MS
Special Education Teacher
  Syracuse City School District
  Syracuse, New York

CHRISTY L. GROUND, BA
Special Education Preschool Teacher
  Santa Barbara County Schools
  Santa Barbara, California

MARIANNE K. HESSELTINE, PHD
Assistant Professor of Special Education
  Syracuse University
  Syracuse, New York

ELLEN J. KNIGHT, MA
First Grade Teacher
    Medford School District
    Medford, Oregon

JAMES A. KNOLL, MS
Doctoral Candidate in Special Education
    Syracuse University
    Syracuse, New York

NANCY LAMB-ZODROW, MS
Technical Assistance Coordinator
    Inservice Training and Program Development Systems
    University of Washington
    Seattle, Washington

MICHAEL MACDONALD, MED
Project Coordinator for Categorical Programs
    Olympia School District
    Olympia, Washington

EILEEN F. MCCARTHY, PHD
Assistant Professor of Educational Administration
    University of Wisconsin at Madison
    Madison, Wisconsin

LUANNA H. MEYER, PHD
Associate Professor of Special Education
    Syracuse University
    Syracuse, New York

SANDRA MLINARCIK, MS
Developmental Specialist
    Seven Counties Services, Inc.
    Louisville, Kentucky

JUDY K. MONTGOMERY, PHD
Director, Program/Student Services
    Fountain Valley School District
    Fountain Valley, California

MARILYN PATTERSON, BS
Parent and Advocate
  Medford, Oregon

MICHAEL SHOULTZ, MS
Doctoral Student in Educational Administration
  University of Wisconsin at Madison
  Madison, Wisconsin

LINDA SIEGELMAN, PHD
Supervisor of Special Needs Programs
  Olympia School District
  Olympia, Washington

JO THOMASON, EDD
Private Consultant
Former Assistant Director, Special Education
  Albuquerque Public Schools
  Albuquerque, New Mexico

STILLMAN WOOD, EDD
Director, Special Services
  Olympia School District
  Olympia, Washington

BETH YEAGER, MA
Head Preschool Teacher
  Santa Barbara City School District
  Santa Barbara, California

# About the Editors

MICHAEL S. BERRES is the Special Education Program Supervisor for the Bellingham School District in Washington state. In this capacity, he coordinates special education services for approximately 700 children with a variety of special needs. He has previously worked providing technical assistance to the special education programs of 25 school districts in the central part of Washington State; as an administrator in a fully integrated primary school in Syracuse, New York serving children with autistic needs; and as a teacher in mental health and school settings in Philadelphia, Washington, DC, and Santa Barbara, California. His educational background consists of degrees from Syracuse University (PhD), American University (MEd), and the University of California at Santa Barbara (California Standard Teaching Credential in Early Childhood Education; BA).

PETER KNOBLOCK is Professor of Special Education and Area Coordinator in Emotional Disturbance in the Division of Special Education and Rehabilitation at Syracuse University. In addition to teaching a variety of university courses, he is the founder of the nationally known Jowonío School—a fully integrated school serving children with autistic needs along with their typical peers. Prior to his work in Syracuse, Dr. Knoblock worked as a clinical psychologist, school psychologist, teacher, and counselor in various settings in Michigan and California. He is the author or editor of several books, including *Teaching Exceptional Children, Teaching and Mainstreaming Autistic Children, Teaching Emotionally Disturbed Children,* and *The Lonely Teacher.* His degrees (PhD, MS, and BA) are from the University of Michigan.